Kickstart Your Relationship NOW!

Move On or Move Out!

BY

Dr. Margot E. Brown

Table of Contents

Family   227

PART VII   237

Couple   239

ACKNOWLEDGMENTS

MY STATEMENT OF GRATITUDE

I want to first acknowledge my husband, Troy, for his positive energy and commitment to creativity. Also, to the days when we were both writing two separate books! That was amazing. I am so grateful for your determination to live our lives together with full support for each other's healthy choices in life as partners and as best friends. I would not be who I am today without your love for all of these years. Troy, I want to especially acknowledge your cookbook, *Portabella Mushroom Party*. I never get tired of portabella mushrooms! Thank you for being you, my love, and thanks for cooking while I was busy writing.

I also want to acknowledge our family, friends, and colleagues for their continued love, friendship, and professional guidance.

I thank Bookmasters, Inc., especially Shelley, for their support for my goal. I also thank you, Tim, for your excellent communication and critical eye on both the creative side as well as the mandated deadlines needed to push the project through on time.

I am very grateful to Brian Feinblum at Media Connect (Finn Partners), New York, for choosing this book and for holding my hand at every stage of the process. I appreciate all that you have done for me, and I am very excited about our future path together, toward success!

The most important person I wish to acknowledge is you, the reader, for taking a chance and choosing to read this book because YOU are worth it! I acknowledge your desire for healing and determination to positively change. I thank you for your support and wish you well.

The journey in writing a book is still a mystery to me. However, it is very much like life. You start out with one intention and, as you write, the final result becomes something very different. I appreciate the process and remain in awe of its powerful journey.

DEDICATION

I dedicate this book to my beautiful husband, Troy. I appreciate the days and nights you listened patiently as I read pages and pages to you, awaiting your input and feedback. As always, you are a natural sounding board, resonating with love, support, and an often-needed critical eye for those areas needing improvement or fine-tuning. Thank you, sweetheart, for all the years and all the wonderful moments we have shared together. You are my best friend and the love of my life. I thank you for being my husband and my soul connection forever and forever. My heart is yours!

Introduction

WHY AM I WRITING THIS BOOK?

I am here to help you help yourself. My commitment to you is exactly that. If you picked up this book because you don't believe in therapy—it is all good. As you continue to read the following chapters, remember the ultimate goal is to gather facts so that you are more enriched and can integrate that information into your own being. By understanding what you believe and who you really are—today—right now—is very important! If you start seeing negative patterns in most of your relationships (love, family, work) or need something that you are not getting from them, and you want things to be different—then this is the book for you!

This book is about you. This book will give you tools so that if you want to CHANGE YOUR BELIEFS AND THEN CHANGE YOUR BEHAVIOR—you can! I've always said, whether it is a workshop, a semester class, a book, the Internet, a lecture, or whatever—the payoff is that you are open to receiving more information. The golden nugget is the knowledge you get. Even if you only learn one thing, you are more enriched. My hope is to guide you toward that pot of gold within you. You hold the treasure. You are the precious one who is capable beyond your own limited vision. Your capacity to turn your life and your relationships around in a positive direction is within your reach because all you have to do is desire it with passion, believe in your self-worth, and know that you deserve what you are striving toward. Right now you are in a state of readiness as you continue to read this book. I promise to give you my best. The rest is up to you.

It was probably ten years ago when I said suddenly to one of my couple clients, "Ya' know, one of these days I'm going to write a book called, "*The 72-Hour Rule*." Then, I would ask them if they knew what that was. Of course, they did not, because I had just thought of it. I knew at that time, the key to their problem was being stuck—and not knowing what to do about it. They were locked in a cycle and I needed to get their attention. So they listened while I told them the plan.

You have taken a HUGE step just by reading this far. First and foremost, congratulations on picking up this book and wanting to do things differently—maybe, for the first time! And, if you have tried and not succeeded in the past, then perhaps this time could be different.

YOU ARE THE KEY IN ALL RELATIONSHIPS

When you look at it from its basic concept, it makes sense . . . doesn't it? The common denominator in all of your relationships is YOU! You may want to have power to change others, but we know that is not reality. The only person you have power over to change is you! That is why when you are taking care of yourself and loving yourself and hugging yourself (virtually) and making yourself a priority . . . that is not selfishness. Selfishness is a label that most come up with to feel guilty for taking care of themselves. No! It is NOT selfish to take care of yourself. Going to the doctor, exercising regularly, watching what you eat, being more assertive, and asking for what you need . . . is NOT selfish. Practice saying "No" to others once in a while. It is appropriate and very healthy. WHY?

You are the master of your life, and only you can know what you need and want now and ten minutes from now. Ultimately, it is *your* head that hits the pillow every night. You are the one who lives inside your own skin. You listen to your own thoughts before you even verbalize them to others. You are number ONE! You know when you are hungry, you know when you are thirsty, you know when you are sleepy and tired, and so forth. If you are not paying attention to any of those things, my question would be, "Why not? Why are you putting something or someone ahead of your own needs?" Remember it is NOT selfish, but rather a requirement to take care of yourself. The more you take care of yourself the better partner you will be, the better employee you will be, and the better parent you will be. Note: In this commentary, I am referring mostly to those who ignore their own needs and tend to be outwardly focused on everyone else's needs instead of their own. Of course the balance is to give and to take!

ARE YOU WAITING FOR SOMEONE ELSE TO CHANGE FIRST?

So what are we talking about exactly? If you are dissatisfied with your life, or unhappy about how it has all turned out, and you are willing to take a deeper look at what that means, then perhaps you are ready for change. If you want your life to be different, then you hold the power to make those changes. If you keep hoping your partner will take the first step toward positive change, more often than not . . . you will be disappointed! If you want a new career, a different way of living, more money, or new neighbors, then you have to look at what is it that got you to where you are now. What have your choices been in life? What decisions have you made that resulted in where you are now? How did you arrive at this strategic moment? Why are you reading this book now? I think the answer is because you are ready for change. Good for you!

FEAR VS. AVOIDANCE

We cling to the old way of behaving and thinking because we are consistently drawn to the familiar even when we know that it is unhealthy for us. Let me repeat myself. You are reading this book right now, and it is most likely an indicator of your need for something else in your life (change).

If the thought of change makes you anxious, or excited, or apprehensive, that is natural. However, people often wait. They wait until the very last moment, or the last day, or they wait years later until they are absolutely desperate for change. So, instead of being desperately afraid of change, they become desperate to change. What does that mean? It means the fear of change fed their avoidance of change, but over a period of time it shifted to where the pain of not changing became stronger. In desperation, they broke through their fear and avoidance to go for it and make the change! They could not stand the pain of staying stuck in fear and avoidance. Ultimately, when they took the first step towards change, it was a relief! It certainly felt different but a "better different" than the previous stuck/trapped feeling they had experienced for possibly years.

YOU HOLD THE POWER WITHIN YOU FOR CHANGE

When I say that you are the key to change, it is because "you have all the answers available to you . . . within you." Your inner Wisdom and your Core Self contain a wealth of information guiding you through life, but first you have to listen. So, if you are nonspiritual that is fine. If you don't believe in something outside your self or a Higher Self, that is fine. I will say, however, that your core energy, your intuition (which we all have), is present and available to you whether you believe it or not. So accessing that "self" is key to understanding your own needs and wants. Your first priority and challenge is to have a relationship within yourself. THEN, you will be more prepared in a healthier positive and unique way to relate to another person! This connecting to self will hopefully bring you closer to fulfilling that core part of you that yearns to be understood, acknowledged, accepted, and valued in an intimate and loving way. Even if we were talking about a job instead of an intimate partnership, it is still your challenge to become intimate within yourself first and foremost. If you were to begin taking steps toward positive change in your life right now, how do you know where to begin? You could choose to do the complete opposite of what you have been doing. However, I am not certain that is the answer. Oftentimes, in life, people swing from one extreme to another and neither extreme is the complete answer, because each choice is reactive to an event, a person, or a place.

The first step toward change is for you to simply pay attention to YOU, right now in this moment. HOW? Simply by identifying what it feels like when your needs are being met and when they are not. Do you know the difference? Let's do a quick check-in as an example of how to connect within yourself.

#1—STEP ONE: Identify how you feel (right NOW).

EXAMPLE (emotional question): "How do I feel emotionally NOW?"

EXAMPLE (physical question): "How do I feel physically NOW?"

EXAMPLE (answer): "I feel anxious; my chest feels tight."

#2—STEP TWO: Acknowledge that emotional or physical feeling without judgment.

EXAMPLE (Do not say): "That is so stupid! There I go again, over and over, worrying when I know it won't change anything."

EXAMPLE (Say this): "Oh, I'm anxious. That's interesting. I wonder what that is about?" (Be curious without putting yourself down).

In PART II, of this book, you will learn how to manage those negative thoughts.

Even though this is a book about couples, the underlying theme here is YOU. Each of you contributes to the dynamic or dance between you. As you read this book, I encourage you to continually be mindful of Self. In other words, pay attention to you! First, you must be aware of what you bring to the table in your marriage. "The Dance" that I refer to within this book is really about the interactive step-by-step journey that a couple takes in getting closer to each other—or in keeping their distance.

RECOMMENDATIONS

I can only say, if possible, try to read this book together as a couple. In doing so, it might open up the lines of communication between the two of you. NOW THAT IS WHAT I CALL COUPLE'S THERAPY—the do-it-yourself kind—even if you take 15 or 20 minutes a day after the kids are in bed, or before your favorite TV program. Just read a couple of pages, or one chapter at a time and then discuss it! You could talk about how you disagree with me, or how you've thought of that idea yourself, or you could listen to your partner share her or his ideas on the topic. You never know, it could be a time of connection—a way to share some third-party information together with each other or just have a regular time set aside for the two of you.

If you are reading this book alone, please share it with your mate. I qualify this by stating that now is one of those times when you have to decide if that is appropriate for both of you. There are many more chapters to follow and if you have a toxic relationship that has power dynamics not suited to sharing at this time, then you have to make certain that you take care of yourself first. However, if that is NOT the case and you simply feel awkward in asking your spouse or partner, then I ask you to take a step forward for yourself and the marriage or partnership, and take it to the next level. You are obviously reading this book because you are curious and you want more out of the marriage or partnership or more from your partner. Or, perhaps your relationship is fine and you just want a "tune up." Maybe, your spouse is thinking and feeling the same feelings that you are but doesn't know what to do about it. Or perhaps, your partner does not even know that you need or want something more. The question is this, "What are YOU going to do about it?" It could be as simple as reading this book by yourself, reading it alone and then sharing with your spouse, or it might mean you read it separately silently and then come together to talk about it. Finally, you could read it out loud together as a couple's exercise—your choice.

MY STYLE

Have you ever gone fishing? Have you ever seen someone fish? Well then, you know that you can have a rod and reel and fishing line. Fishing is fishing isn't it? However, you can go to the river and fish, you can go to the ocean and fish, you can go to the creek and fish, or you can go to the lake and fish. Yet, these different settings require adjustments in exactly how you fish. You might need a different length of rod or a different test line (strength of fishing line).

Different approaches or styles of working with people in relationships exist. I consider myself to be a short-term, results-oriented couples counselor who seeks a deliverable outcome. That means, I want you to experience a positive change and I want to see you change in a positive way. The deliverable outcome is you changing your beliefs and your way of behaving and coping in your relationship with your partner. This approach is grounded in thoughts, feelings, and behaviors. My approach is to have a limited amount of counseling sessions with each couple. My style is collaborative, meaning that I included each partner in the decision-making process of how to move forward. It is all based on agreement for change.

Part of my style in helping both couples and individuals take the first step toward change is to either normalize what they are doing correctly or to dramatize what needs to be done differently. The extreme of that is to STOP doing the negative right now. My storytelling is a culmination of both my therapy experience and my life experience (something they don't teach you in graduate school). I rely on stories as a way to help my clients see themselves more clearly. Couples either see themselves in the story or, more frequently, see the differences between the story and themselves as a couple. It's just a way of enhancing their ability to be less emotionally attached to their individual position within their own relationship. In keeping with my own style of couple's counseling, I have numerous stories to tell throughout this book. All are based on some element of truth but, of course, modified to eliminate identifying factors. In other words, my stories are meant only to clarify and provide insights into behavior—individually and as a partner.

COLLABORATIVE VS. MEDICAL MODEL

According to Wikipedia, "pathogen" is a Greek-derived word with two parts. The first part, "pathos" means "suffering" and "passion." The second part, "gen" means "I give birth to." So no wonder I tell my clients that the problem I have with psychotherapy is that it is based upon a pathogenic medically based model. The basis is that you are sick; I am the doctor; I have the power to heal you. Medicine investigates and "rules out" or "factors in" certain criteria needed to make a diagnosis and treat the patient. However, over the years, I have found myself steering away from this premise.

My approach lends itself to a more collaborative and interactive model—one that empowers the client couples to be healthy participants in their own treatment. In other words, we talk, problem-solve together, and slowly my interaction becomes less intrusive as they use the tools to negotiate their own outcomes. I am there as a facilitator and educator in the beginning, but toward the end of my short-term approach, the goal for the couple is to interact, explore, and work through to the deeper issues blocking them from intimacy and happiness. They do all of the work. I often say, if you come here for me to "fix" you, then you have the wrong therapist. My intent is to empower the couple as a unit to do the work and be successful, regardless of the outcome.

"Being successful" means that they might do the work and re-engineer their love for each other—become closer than they were prior to drifting apart. Or, "being successful" might mean that they both decide that their relationship is over and they want to civilly or even lovingly separate and divorce. My only agenda is to help them with their agenda, as long as their agenda includes healthy functional communication and respect for each other.

HOW TO USE THIS BOOK

This book is not comprehensive by any means! Any one of the topics that I have touched on could easily be a book by itself. In one way, this was frustrating for me because I wanted to deliver as much valid information as possible, but if I covered each topic in depth it would go well beyond a short paragraph or chapter. Therefore, my goal for you—the reader—is to inform you and, hopefully, inspire you.

I hope to provide you with enough information for you to either validate what you know, add to what you know, or inspire you to seek out more in-depth information from other resources. Either way, it is a Win-Win. I tell my clients that whatever you decide, make an informed decision, rather than an uninformed one! You can always take the information and decide to do nothing immediately. That is OK too. Some of the information that you get may spur you on to take steps that needed to be taken a long time ago. Perhaps, the information contained within this book will guide you to uncover, rediscover, or expand upon your knowledge of Self. That is critical because you are very important. You and your partner can also expand your knowledge of each other and your relationship—together. You are the starting point. You will always be the starting point in any relationship. WHY? <u>Because the first and primary relationship you have is the relationship you have with yourself</u>—that is what YOU bring to your marriage, relationship, partnership, domestic partnership, significant other, or soul-mate. I wrote this book to help you find your way toward more fulfilling relationships, filled with joy and appreciation.

DISCLAIMER

Rather than delineate all of the various types of couples by sexual orientation (heterosexual, gay, lesbian, transgender); by culture, race, religion; or by societal norms (married vs. living together or monogamous vs. multiple partners), for simplicity, I treat marriage or partnership, or spouse/partner/mate as interchangeable. I also refer to the other partner as her or him or perhaps him/her or her/him but it could also mean him/him or her/her. Please understand that personally I am open to all possibilities. I appreciate your understanding.

This is an INCLUSIVE book. In other words, I include all types of couples and do not judge what determines a couple by any standard. So even if I use the term "marriage," "partner," or "spouse," depending upon your ideology or what state you live in, I am referring to your relationship, which for some of you might be a same-sex partnership and for many others, a heterosexual relationship. I encourage you not to get hung up if I use same-sex pronouns and you are in a heterosexual relationship. The important point is that you find what works for you in this book. My hope is that you are open to the possibilities of what the story means to you as a partner in a relationship. Please do not dismiss the message because I did not use the pronoun that refers to your specific situation.

SO WHAT IS MY GIFT TO YOU?

I am certain only you can decide that after reading this book. However, in these first few pages allow me to say that I have always been "results-oriented." As a cognitive (thoughts) therapist, the goal is to be short-term and have a desirable and measurable outcome. This is a fancy way of stating that I hope to bring you many little golden nuggets of information in each chapter. At the end though, the big wish on my part is that you are able to gain a deeper understanding of yourself and your partner. In doing so, you will be able to communicate more effectively and get more of your needs met. Wouldn't that be a good thing?

PART I

It All Begins With You
Thoughts, Beliefs, Behaviors

THE WINDOW BLIND

I used to stand in front of my plate-glass window in my high-rise office and point to the venetian blinds. I would tell my clients that each shaft of the window blind was a cognitive choice and a decision-making point in our lives—quit our job, go back to school, go to Europe, have a baby, get married, get divorced, take the promotion with more pressure, or move to another state. Whatever our decision is, it eventually adds up to one venetian blind slat after another and that leads to a window covering in an office. The window covering in front of the plate-glass window winds up being our entire life—a decision to turn left for 350 feet followed by another to turn right for 5 ½ miles—after all of the twists and turns—we wind up where we are today. This gives pause for thought because we see how our decisions have led us to this point in time. Our choices, our decisions, and our thoughts dictate the life we lead. It all adds up in the end.

You don't have to become frozen in fear or overanalyze every strategy. Balance would include some analysis, a little fear, a good strategy and then some reflection to gain insight into what you are thinking now and understand the ramifications of your choice to move forward. Your thoughts, feelings, and behaviors lead to events, people, and life. So if you want a glimpse into your future then just pay attention to what you are thinking and feeling right now. At this very moment, what are your thoughts, feelings, decisions and values? In which direction are you headed? In which direction do you want to be headed?

WE ARE WHAT WE THINK

I've been telling my clients for years that we are what we think. Pay attention! Easier said than done, for sure! Yet, your challenge is to stop texting; take out your ear buds; turn off the TV; go outside on the deck or in the backyard, and sit quietly in a chair. Listen. What do you hear? Notice what you are thinking (what is that inner dialogue . . . the chatter inside your head?).

We chatter all the time between our ears, and as a society with technological advances, we are consistently bombarded with noise, visible stimuli, and information. When you are in a car at a stoplight, look around you; everywhere people have their heads down, staring at their smartphones. The technology is amazing, but it is pulling us further apart from ourselves. But we can't blame it on smartphones. It is not technology that separates us from our inner selves: It is us.

We are the ones who choose to look externally for answers. We strive for external visibility or proof of our worth or of our acceptance by others. We look everywhere but within. Or perhaps I might say we look everywhere and oftentimes the last place we look is within ourselves.

HOW DO YOU BEGIN TO CHANGE?

I believe in change. Change begins with awareness, gathering information, making an informed choice and then acting on that choice. You picked up this book for a reason. You are still reading this book for a reason. The reason is that your relationship is suffering and you don't know how to make it better. Because you are lost as to where to begin and don't know what to do, I am telling you now. **This book is based on one thought and one feeling and one behavior at a time. It is about having acute awareness of how you are feeling in the moment, identifying your thoughts in the moment and observing Self—how you are behaving in the moment—and based on** that information, coming to a different conclusion as to what to think and feel about the situation and then DOING IT DIFFERENTLY. Now do you get it? I hope so, because putting your partner down, is not the answer. Using someone close to you (your spouse) or someone at work to your advantage by putting them down to feel better about yourself is really dysfunctional, unhealthy, and negative. I am asking you to get your head out of the sand and to really check yourself out. Stop making excuses for your behavior and start today to commit to doing one thing different that is positive. In other words, take one step forward toward your marriage. Provided that each of you is not abusing each other verbally, you might even begin by asking your partner what he or she would like YOU to do differently instead of consistently choosing the behavior you have been doing (like verbal put downs). That would be a great start. Good for you!

VALUES

I used to say that values are like telephone poles (sorry, I am dating myself—I do realize now there are underground fiber optic cables), and that beliefs are like the wires running between the poles.

Exercise: Take a pad of paper and draw a circle representing the sun with lines extending from it like the rays of the sun. Or if you prefer, you can think of it as a wheel and the extending lines from the wheel are its spokes. Now this exercise is for you to identify your core values (the sun or wheel); the rays of the sun are your beliefs that sustain you in acting on those values.

First, it is important to identify your top 5-to-10 values. Write a separate value as a sun/wheel on a page. As the spokes to each wheel, start listing those beliefs that you have pertaining to each respective value. If your partner is willing, have her fill it out for herself and then you can discuss and share and match, or not match each other's core values and beliefs.

If you choose not to do the sun/wheel exercise, you could still numerically list out your values and put statements of belief next to them. Then, you could exchange lists to see how similar or common your shared values are. The goal of this exercise is not to get you bogged down in semantics; there are many words that closely describe the same thing. Also, if one partner places a value in 5th place and the other partner listed it in 1st place—it really does not matter. What matters is that you both wrote down the same value as one of your top 5 or top 10 values! Believe me, this is what matters.

What are those big-ticket items you call values? Is it education, money, sex, socializing, family, traveling, religion, work/career, or owning your own house (there are no wrong or right answers)?

VALUE: Education

BELIEF: "I think having a college degree is important for my self-worth and for my ability to give back to society in my field of interest."

VALUE: Traveling

BELIEF: "I have wanted to see the world ever since I was a child." "I believe that traveling expands one's horizons and is very educational." "I want a partner who loves to travel like I do."

This can be a very telling exercise. I have seen couples get excited to see what their partner wrote down. This really opens up a dialogue about what is important to each of them and what is important to them as a couple. Actually, any good premarital counselor will have couples do marital assessments targeted to help couples identify shared values and possible disconnects—areas of future conflicts or breakdowns caused by different values.

As far as couples and the dynamic between them is concerned, my experience has taught me that they can cope more effectively with the irritations of personality differences or differences in taste, like, and dislike for the smaller things in life THE MORE SIMILAR THEY ARE IN BIGGER TICKET ITEMS SUCH AS VALUES! So, the couple who has big dreams together and shared common goals is more likely to make it together because their values hold them together. When you share similar values in money, education and children, who cares if one person likes a different toothpaste? That is nothing compared to the joy of finding someone in your life who shares your dream so that you can walk down the path of life together, believing and trusting in each other for the long haul.

If you are married to someone and you share VALUES plus a few likes and dislikes—then, you have a LOT going on for you!

I counseled one young couple years ago—it was very telling early on that they did not share a lot. He was creative and had a job that kept him working the swing shift; she worked a corporate gig that kept her working the day shift. They hardly saw each other and they were drifting apart when I saw them—two separate lives with two separate sets of friends. Unfortunately, I was not successful in helping them. I spoke about VALUES and said unless they worked extra hard to start including each other in activities and finding activities that they both loved, I didn't see it getting any easier for them. They were young, without children, and they were living as individuals instead of as a couple. Even now, with children, I see couples who are living as individuals. Usually, it is easier to live as a couple when you don't have children. So this particular couple had already steered away from each other and neither was putting a lot of effort into making a turnaround for the better. There is much more I could say about this situation. There are so many ways to analyze this or that, however, my efforts mostly focus on WHAT ARE YOU GOING TO DO ABOUT IT? AND HOW DO YOU BEGIN? I leave the "Why" to other therapists.

What has struck me over the years, both as a person and as a psychotherapist, is that values change and shift over time—directly correlated to growth and evolution of Self. Exposure to life, people, careers, places, and trials and tribulations can result in change. My thinking is that if we are going through life with our eyes wide open, then we can't help but be empowered and enhanced by growing, learning, and understanding who we are, what we want, and where we go (or where we think we want to go).

I am certain you have met others in your life with whom you've lost contact and then rediscovered, only to realize that they're stuck in the past. They have not grown. Their values have remained rigidly constant over the years. It is a weird feeling when you see who they are and how they used to be (not too much different) and then you see today how much you have moved on to other things of importance. This is growth. Look at the couple who decides to have a child. Once the child is born, they can't imagine what life would be like without their beautiful child. They have made a choice, they have made plans, they have had a child, and then they have adjusted in creating a new life together (all three of them). This is growth—one step at a time—one day at a time.

You've heard the story or have probably known some couple who wanted children very much. After they had children, what happened? For some, it does not turn out positive. Could it be as simple as they could not make the needed adjustments to accommodate the newest member of their family? Could it be that simple? Maybe. Maybe it is that one or both could not make the adjustments to include the newest member of their family in a new healthy dynamic. Because of their lack of adjustment, they suffered, their mate suffered, and their family suffered. How sad. In the *Diagnostic and Statistical Manual of Mental Disorders* (DSM-5), there is a code that describes "adjustment disorder." You see, we are constantly challenged in life to make adjustments. We get a new boss, we graduate from school, we have a baby, we get married, we get divorced, we move, we get laid off, our parents die—we have to make adjustments or we get stuck. Being stuck is NOT living. Values are a mirror of what fuels us to keep on moving and get out of bed every morning. Think about it, talk about it, share it, and then think about it some more. Do you think you have shifted in values over time, how so? What were you both like together when you met? Do you feel that your shared values are different now, or the same? How is that?

Can you describe that to each other? Remember when you used to think prawns and scallops was fancy food at the all-you-can-eat buffet? Now, is it a fancy dinner in the big city with lobster or veal? One way of kick-starting this path of self-discovery is for both of you to pull out the early photos from your marriage. How many years have passed? Look at the photos and what you were wearing and how your hair was styled. How old were you then? Do you remember what your thinking process was back then? What was important to you then? What is important to you now? Talk about it.

MONEY

Along with religion, sex, and politics, money is definitely one of those sensitive topics in a relationship that can lead to an argument. Money is tied to our values. Individually, it can go as far back as whether or not you got an allowance as a kid and how you were taught to use money. What did you learn—save all of it; spend all of it; get in debt behind it; argue about it; save part and spend part? If allowed, money can cause some of the most potent problems in a relationship or marriage, leading to divorce or separation.

Spending Habits—How to Find a Solution

Do you and your mate have similar spending habits? Do you spend while your partner screams at you for spending? Or, do you both try to outspend each other? Is money an issue that always causes stress in your relationship? If so, perhaps you need to re-evaluate the focus of the arguments around money to compromise, collaborate, and work together more effectively. Personally, I don't like compromise. I see it as a lose-lose scenario. Each person has to give up something. Collaboration, on the other hand, means that each of you works together to problem-solve. Problem-solving could involve compromise, but it does not have to. Together you can find a creative outside-the-box solution that satisfies you both rather than each of you give up something.

Hoarding vs. Overspending

Are you both savers to the extreme? Do you save a lot, never go on a vacation, and make personal sacrifices, but inside you would prefer the money belt to be a little looser? It is fine if it works for both of you to save, however, if there is any hidden frustration or internal uptightness in one of you because you resent saving as much as you do, then you need to talk to each other openly and communicate your needs and feelings. The same holds true for the partner who wants to save but has a partner who spends and spends.

Such polarity can only result in frustration and possible secrecy until both of you start on a plan together. There are so many factors to consider—Are you both working?; Is only one of you work-ing?; Do you have shared checking and savings with no personal account? Remember there is no right or wrong. What is good is that you have a plan, and that you stick to the plan until further notice, and then you make needed adjustments and then stick to the revised plan.

There are so many ways to curb spending. The first approach is to talk about it; the second approach is to find tangible solutions that really limit the spender—to help that partner comply with the bigger game plan (paying off bills or saving more than you have in the past). I believe anything is possible once you put your mind to it.

If both of you agree that saving is great but you need to treat yourself a little bit—then do it! Treat yourself! Have fun without guilt! If one of you keeps trying and the other partner derails your ef-forts with one expenditure after another, then you need a new game plan—perhaps, a separate account with an ATM debit card attached to that account for allowance purposes only. That way, credit cards and access to bigger savings accounts are avoided. If bigger purchases need to be made, then one partner has to save 1 or 2 months for the big-ticket item. It CAN be done! You have to work together. First talk about it and then decide.

Money Is a Value

Because money is a HUGE issue and is tightly tied to your value system, it is possible that over time your values about money might evolve and change slightly or dramatically. Either way, when individually or as a team, you make those value shifts around money, communicating to each other about what is happening is important.

As your children grow up and their needs change, you might need to make adjustments for yourself and the family. If mom, for example, has not worked in years and the kids are teenagers and money is tight, mom could choose to return to work part-time to show that she wishes to participate financially. In this case, her efforts to return to paid employment are symbolic of her shift in values (gender role—mother). The money earned is symbolic of her contribution to the family's monetary needs. Her spouse makes the gender role-shift, allowing someone else to contribute as the breadwinner; the children are acknowledged as needing different things from their mother as they age. The adjustment is made full circle; mom has increased freedom, increased self-esteem, and a little more disposable income for herself. Her partner has less pressure and more connection to the marriage, and the kids feel entrusted with more freedom but also more pride to see their mother growing and contributing to the family in a way they have never seen.

Kids Need to Work

You have tremendous power over your young children as they observe both of you and how you spend or don't spend money. You are instilling important values in them. Your teenagers need to do some type of work to develop independent skills, to help give them financial freedom, and to help you out financially (at least with their personal expenses).

Some of the biggest disappointments in life have been parents who loved their kids so much that they showered them with gifts and money. These kids grow up with "entitlement" issues. As young adults, they emerge into the world with a handicap. Figuratively speaking, one hand is tied behind their backs. Internally, they are not really certain that they can make it on their own without their parents' help (because the subconscious message they have received is that they can't do it by themselves). Externally, they exhibit ego and entitlement. This facade is to cover up their inner lack of security.

As therapists, we tell our clients that they do a disservice to their children when they spoil them. These children grow up confused and uncertain of themselves. In their personal relationships, spoiled children grow up to be unhappy adults. So, teach them the value of money. Educate them about investments. Help them get more education. Let them emerge into the world with tools and self-support, not inner conflicts about their abilities to make it on their own. Let them find out through their own efforts the meaning of money, hard work, education, and achievement.

Have a Plan

In today's economic environment, the scene could look very different from this example. It's possible that one or both caregivers is unemployed or has had bouts of unemployment. This stressor tied to the family or couple's revenue stream is critical to everything else we have talked about in this book. Think about it, no money or less money = stress = fear/anxiety and uncertainty of the future = prolonged unemployment = low self-esteem or lack of goal-directed career = depression = a string of other negative, maladaptive coping mechanisms (I don't want to list them because they are so negative). Please note that just because I started down that path does not mean it automatically happens. I am only pointing out the possible negative ramifications.

Without delineating blow-by-blow, problem-solving techniques for money-saving alternatives with a reduced income flow, I would encourage you to use your mind and time wisely. You can look up all kinds of self-help money-saving ideas on the Internet (e.g., Google and Yahoo Finance). If you are lucky to have a financial advisor, I encourage you to go for some objective help—solutions that would be customized to your specific situation today. Whatever you decide—to make compromises; to cut back; to stop charging; to cut up credit cards and pay them off; to openly discuss the bills together as a couple; to refinance; to get two part-time jobs instead of one; or to talk to your financial advisor—whatever you decide—please do it together.

Once you think about a plan—a short-term, 4-month plan connected to a long-term plan of 3-to-5 years—make the plan, agree on the plan, have a voice in the plan, get excited about the plan, and then execute the plan TOGETHER as a team!

Money and Gender Role in the Family

For the sake of example, let's assume the breadwinner in the couple or family is male. For single-income families—when one partner works and the other stays at home—the breadwinner has a high level of control over the money in the family. When there is shared participation in revenue (money coming into the family from both partners working), then more often than not, this results in shared management of the monies within the family.

As a counselor, I have seen many examples of how couples deal with money in their lives, and I have heard all kinds of intimate details about checking accounts and savings—investments to wills. Regardless of whether couples are married or living together, when they make money decisions separately, they are less happy and more dissatisfied than when they make decisions collaboratively. This also includes couples in which one partner works. When money decisions are made together, there is more satisfaction. In addition, I have found that when both partners have viable careers with strong income streams, and both contribute to the family money, the women who create a separate money reserve for personal spending are happier than those who consistently had joint monies. I don't know if this is a gender-specific outcome (women like nonessentials and don't want to have to explain the significance of a purchase to their mates).

Perhaps as my professor once told me, he found "liberated couples" who professed to be well rounded and free from gender-specific role identification. However, upon further examination, he found that while both worked and earned competitive salaries, it was the woman who also did the housework and grocery shopping, picked up the kids from daycare, prepared dinner, helped with homework, and did the kids' baths and bedtime reading. So actually, the recently emancipated couple free from gender roles was actually NOT SO FREE FROM STEREO-TYPICAL ROLES! She just worked and took care of the house and he just worked. Just adding career/job/work to the female's already full set of responsibilities is skewed when you label it as a liberated (balanced) relationship.

I must also say that my statement is unfair to many men I have met over the years who are just as liberated but also serve as the primary caregivers of their children. When the roles are reversed—the female has the career that keeps her at the office late—it is the man who works in the home all day—picking up kids, cooking dinner, and so on. The problem is, there are not enough of these men to call a majority.

Common Complaints for Couples

"YOU DON'T MAKE ME A PRIORITY!"
MAKE YOURSELF A PRIORITY!

I have listened to hours of high-functioning couples who just needed a sounding board to provide feedback on logistics, balance, support, and personal freedom—for each of them! Today's society allows us to pack in a lot more activity across the board because of technology and our ability to supposedly communicate faster. In the 21st century— look at the possibilities.

People are texting while they drive, they go to work and answer 150 e-mails every day, and they listen to book audiotapes while on the way to work—it is massive communication, ongoing and non-stop. Partners participate in a world of stimuli, activities, responsibilities, and communication with their own feelings and thoughts in addition to their primary relationships (partners and children). No wonder every-one feels as if there are not enough hours in the day. On top of all this, couple's therapists advise couples to spend 20-to-30 minutes at the end of the evening on communication! It is a lot, but not impos-sible. It is a matter of priority.

I have heard that a lot, "I feel like I'm not a priority." That is indeed a terrible feeling. Remember part of ownership is owning your partner's intention. I can hurt you and I am very sorry that I hurt you but at the same time I need you to hear me when I tell you that my intention was NOT to hurt you. Are you still hurt, YES! Of course, you're still hurt. My having a different intention does NOT EXCUSE what I did that hurt you. Bottom line, I have to OWN that I am responsible for hurting you and you have to OWN that my intentions were not to hurt you. So if we both OWN it, then we can move forward.

My sense of couples and being part of a couple myself is that intention is powerful and gives our relationship a lot of flavor. There is no way that I'm going to stay in a relationship with someone who has bad intentions toward me! Heck NO! I need to be a priority in his life and he needs to be a priority in my life. We need to be each other's best friends and everything else that flavors that positively, like TRUST AND LOVE AND RESPECT! Why would I choose any-thing less than that? If I did, then that is a total reflection of what I think about myself. If that is the ONLY thing you ever remember by reading this book, just think of me standing on top of a mountain say-ing it loud and clear. You deserve to be a priority in your partner's life as does (s)he. The thing about relationships is that they don't work on automatic pilot. You have to nourish them, or they do not grow. I have heard many couples complain that neither one of them shows the other kindness. Well? When are you going to start being kind to each other? Are you kind to yourself? If you are kind to yourself—great—if not, why not? Start today to make some positive changes.

PLEASE DON'T SETTLE

Isn't it fascinating how and why we come together in relationships? It is true, that years ago you may have chosen to come together as a couple for specific reasons and are together today for very different reasons. That is OK. Actually, I perceive that is good because it means that your relationship is evolving, rotating, and changing. The glue that brought you together is still holding you together. If you said that nothing had changed, I would think that you might be referring to that glue that has held steady. When you look at photos from 25 years ago and look in the mirror, you can see lots of changes (external), but what fascinates me the most is the stuff on the inside. Can you both talk to each other right now and reminisce as to what it was like when you first met? What was it like between you during your early years and what if anything is the same or different now? Sometimes a walk down memory lane can be very healing.

The saddest thing to me is to hear couples say that they have drifted apart and that they both have been unhappy for about 2-to-5 years. WHAT TOOK YOU SO LONG TO SIT DOWN AND TALK ABOUT IT? Oh my goodness, not only is it a loss of precious time of your life and both of your lives, but the unhappy part of that scenario is that you both settled. Please don't settle in your partnership.

I had one beautiful woman come to me with a 1-year long affair and told me that she was not "in love" with her husband; she was not "sexually attracted" to him. Although she cared for him, she wasn't sure that she really "loved" him. Actually, she didn't think she had ever felt love when she married him 25 years ago! So I asked her why on earth did she marry him? She said that her girlfriends and everyone told her that he was a nice guy and that she was a fool if she did not marry him. So, she married this "nice" man and never really loved or desired him.

I asked her how she handled that after all of these years. She replied that she just faked it; she faked everything. Please, all I can do is tell you that you are worth so much more than a fake relationship. I say this with a sad heart and heavy spirit, but your partner is worth more than what you have dished out all of these years, even if you have faked it. He deserves better and you deserve better.

There are no words to describe what I feel even as I write these words. Be true to yourself and truth will find you. I would be curious if we were sitting in a room right now together, what you would think of that story? Is that you? Do you know someone similar? Does that story rock you like it rocked me? None of us is perfect (perfection is only an idea—it is not real), but the important part of not being perfect is being real. Please be you. Please be real to yourself and to others, especially to your partner. This is the key. **This is a major key to the entire journey of love.**

LOSS OF SEXUAL DESIRE

First, you must go to your doctor (or find one) and get a complete physical exam (blood test, urinalysis) and discuss your health. This is nonnegotiable. How can you even begin to address this important issue without having a reference point or baseline to gauge your overall health? Pick a doctor with whom you feel comfortable and talk to him or her. You'd be amazed at the number of clients I have who said they had the same doctor for decades but they didn't really feel comfortable with him or her. Wow! There are so many doctors to choose from. Talk to friends. Ask them what their doctors are like and if they would refer you. Make it happen!

A complete physical exam is vital, so that you can rule out anything biophysical that might be contributing to your low libido. As I am not a physician, I can only name so many symptoms that can possibly contribute to low libido.

What I see in my private practice is a pervasive diagnosis of 34-year-old men who exhibit Erectile Disorder (ED) and women even younger who cannot get pregnant. I almost feel like our society is crumbling—men who cannot perform sexually with their partners and women who desire children but cannot become pregnant. What is happening? Are we becoming robots who eat and speak but nothing else? As the stress levels of society have increased over the past 15 years, especially since 9/11, anxiety and overall fear have depleted our resources—literally. Of course, this is only my opinion. I'm just reflecting back to you what I see and listen to day after day.

Overall, it is only a matter of commonsense to know that physical problems (diabetes, cardiovascular disease, hypertension) can contribute or result in ED in men. Add to that obesity, cigarette smoking, and excessive alcohol—you have a recipe for poor success in beating ED. Now add some psychological factors (low self-esteem, depression, anger, anxiety, guilt, negative feelings and marital stress) and you have increased incidence in ED symptoms. More than 30 million men in the United States alone have erectile disorder. For females, the data are comprehensive—ovarian problems, hormone imbalances, thyroid, endometriosis, obesity, male partner performance (low sperm count), and many more physical/psychological problems—all result in low fertility.

In therapy, I hear stress, stress, and more stress. We already know that stress contributes to a range of physical problems—from the common cold to cancer. In my office, I hear about working 85+ hours per week, eating dinner with the family, and then answering another 200 e-mails after dinner. I listen to couples who sleep in separate bedrooms, or don't sleep, or have busy schedules (work, kids, soccer, homework, overtime, no date nights, etc.). No one talks to each other; no one eats dinner together; everyone leads separate lives under the same roof.

I get that it is easy to race on the freeway from one exit to the other but you have to start carving out time for Self and time for your partner, otherwise nothing else will change. Please do not wait until it is too late for your body, your psyche, your marriage, and your family. You can make a difference. Begin now to set some personal goals for yourself for 1 week and stick to it for the next month and then the next 3 months. Then, set more goals for the next 6 months. Then, set more or similar goals for 1 year until you have rhythmically incorporated some wonderfully new and healthy habits into your lifestyle. Eventually it becomes effortless and natural to take a walk around the block with your spouse before dinner and to sleep in the same bed, and to date each other on Friday nights—one step at a time.

JEALOUSY

My mother told me when I was about 8 years old that jealousy was a big green-eyed monster and that it eats you up and spits you out! I never forgot those words and I am grateful to her ever since for telling me that. I have tried to live a life with relationships that excluded jealousy. Have I had a couple of twinges of jealousy? Absolutely, but I quickly identified it and stopped my train of thoughts that led me to that green-eyed monster's cave. I remember what my mother told me and I have worked very hard not to succumb to that evil monster. If you let jealousy rule you—it will.

You won't find happiness that way. It erects a huge 350-foot wall made out of cement and rebar that climbs to the heavens. This wall of jealousy comes between you and your partner and it does not allow for intimacy, trust, or genuineness. Check yourself out, stop minimizing your jealousy, and do something about it. STOP!

WHAT HAPPENS WHEN ONE OF YOU OUTGROWS THE OTHER OR MOVES IN A DIFFERENT DIRECTION?

This is a very important topic. We all grow at different paces. We are each unique. There is no mechanical handle that all couples can hold on to and take the ride together forever at the same time. We each have our thoughts, dreams, and goals. Plus, we each process our own conscious level of awareness at our own pace. What does this mean? It means that at the end of the day, it is our own head that hits the pillow. We are our own person first before we are a couple. Knowing that, we are responsible for ourselves first—the best we can be. Growth is a natural process of evolution. We evolve as we receive stimuli. As humans, we are propelled by activity and productivity—to create, to initiate, to perform, and to produce. It is a natural drive within all of us. Human beings have a highly developed brain capable of abstract reasoning and problem-solving; this is what sets us apart from other species.

Considering the complexity of our development, there is much to factor in when we meet our chosen partner, and there is even more to consider while we remain together for extended periods of time. It comes down to the balancing act of remaining true to Self (not losing yourself in the process of bonding with another person); while simultaneously giving to the partnership and spouse love, attention, and energy. This brings up the next balancing act. To give, love, share, and support without smothering your partner. It is very important that he or she has the freedom to be his/her own person, just as you have been. The gift of giving is allowing your partner to do his or her part in giving back to you in this marriage! If you block the flow of energy between you, then individually you can prevent and artificially alter the natural progression of Self in your marriage. What does this mean? It means that if your wife likes to ride bicycles on the weekend for 100 miles, then your job is to support her in her own interests. Her job is to support you in your desire to play in golf tournaments or take up ice hockey. The balance is to be each other's main support, allowing your mate to grow and create and perform. Believe me, you wouldn't want it any other way.

I have met nice couples over the past decades in many relationships. As babies were born and their responsibilities grew, the demands on their time resulted in one or other of the partners saying to themselves:

"Am I happy?"

"I don't do any of the things I used to love."

(surfing, tennis, snow skiing, golf, etc.)

"I used to play the piano and I haven't for years."

"I started to take oil-painting classes but then I stopped, and I don't know what happened."

Whatever the reason, or no matter how long it has been, the key is for each of you to maintain your togetherness without sacrificing your personal growth. Just because you are a couple or a parent, does not mean that you put your own needs and interests on the back burner!

On the other hand, I also had the privilege to meet many nice couples who were at the other extreme of achievement and creativity. They were high-level executives and had traveled the world—spoke multiple languages, made money, closed business deals, or held fellowships as medical practitioners all over the planet (usually in different continents at the same time); they all faced the challenges of being physically separated while pursuing their individual careers. What is the balance? How do you maintain that personal boundary of giving to Self, partner, family, career, and education? It is more time than any single day allows. However, if you are paying attention to Self (thoughts, feelings, behavior) then your internal focus will allow you to share that intimate information with your partner (no matter how far away) and in that instant—you are connected and intimate and nurturing your relationship. If you don't, it could be that tiny step that steers you in different directions over time. No conversation is too little to share. Keep the connection flowing between you!

So, to answer the question at the beginning of this section, "What do you DO when you feel that you're shifting and changing and growing beyond your partner? What do you DO when you are integrating all kinds of exciting changes in your own life and you feel that you are processing information at a faster rate than your partner? What happens when you see yourself aspiring to different ideals when it seems your partner is as slow as molasses and falling behind in the growth dimension? What happens when your partner continues to refer to the same old conversations that you've always had? What DO you do?"

One thing is for certain, we all grow at different paces. Your partner can tell you something wise today and you won't hear it, get it, or understand it until your best friend whispers the same exact thing in your ear and you tell your husband what you've just learned. His response? "I told you that myself multiple times!"

We all learn and move along the path of growth differently. From my perspective, this is the most challenging and precarious point in the relationship. Why? Because you might get frustrated and convince yourself that you do not need to bide your time and wait for your partner to hurry up to get his or her act together. You might talk yourself into a divorce, conclude that you are bored, or start to believe that it will always be like this.

What's the answer? Do I know the answer? No, but my take is that you could be right, wrong, or partially right. The dilemma is in deciding if you can be patient enough to wait for your spouse to "hurry up and grow" or to decide it's over—patiently support or not support him during his time of hibernation when a few years ago he had done exactly that for you. The decision is yours, for sure. Remember, however, that you need to step outside of the box inside your head and really evaluate what is the best step.

#1—Talk to your spouse about what you are thinking.

#2—Make it clear, do not sugar coat, and always deliver the message with love and concern.

#3—Find out where your partner is coming from.

#4—I deter you from giving it a time limit. Artificial deadlines never work, except to put undue pressure on yourself and your partner. Then, if you put an arbitrary deadline on how you think your partner should behave or think by a certain time and you do not share that timeline with them, how fair is that?

#5—Communicate with your partner about what you are learning so that your partner can grow along with you. Just think about it—if you are receiving new information that helps to shape new thought patterns within yourself, don't you think it is important to share that with your mate? I do. Most definitely! If you don't, that is the beginning of the end. When you start to experience something new that stimulates you and causes changes and growth within you, talk out loud with your partner. For example, you take a class and excitedly talk about it to your classmates. Your husband says: "How was the class?" You respond: "Fine." That's it? NO! That will not work. I challenge you to rethink that approach. That is a sure-fire way of widening the gap between you!

I once counseled a couple who came from two very different family backgrounds. She came from a wealthy family from the city and he led a simple life in the country. It was quite evident that she grew to appreciate country-living—hunting, fishing, and so on. However, the exchange was not even. She did not reciprocate her love and appreciation for city life (museums, art, opera, etc.) with her husband. She chose to exclude him from those activities and continued to attend events with her mother or adult brothers. Over the decades, her husband had remained very much the same simple man who enjoyed nature and the country life (where they lived). She complained that he didn't get this or that and that he was stuck. Granted, the dynamic between them might have been his lack of interest in those activities. From what I heard, she had even excluded him from even having a voice in becoming more interested in those activities. She regularly excluded him from participating in most of her city-oriented activities. She did not verbally abuse him, but there was a slight edge of superiority in her having the knowledge and him not. Talk about a gross imbalance!

#6—If the gap is wide and the path between you is currently headed in different directions, then perhaps going to counseling might help clarify what is happening between the two of you.

I've always been a "doer" and a "shaker" and a "mover" so do NOT listen to me as I project my own series of frustrations upon you. In other words, it might feel like you are both stuck. Perhaps, it is just a pause. However, if your partner is NOT doing his or her fair share of paying attention and speaking up for what he or she wants—acting very disinterested—then, you really need to help him or her functionally interact with you. Your partner needs to talk, engage, and dialogue with you about why they choose to stay in that one spot. Do not nag, but please do not ignore your partner either!

Have you outgrown your partner? Have you changed ideals and values? Do you no longer share the same values as when you first met? The only way to find out is to begin talking to each other.

Example: You agreed not to have children and now you want them very much but your husband will not budge, and he reminds you that you promised him prior to marriage that you did not want children either.

Example: You really want to go to graduate school but your partner is not enthusiastic; it won't cost a lot of money and you don't understand his or her reaction to your own goals.

Example: You just got a job during this terrible economy and your job is the primary income at this point; unfortunately, you have to move out of state to stay with this very solid but profitable company, but your husband doesn't want to do it, even though it would not be forever.

Do you understand what is happening? Are you aware of your thoughts and feelings? Do you know how your mate thinks or feels about the situation? If not, now is the time to explore and share.

Of course, if we are talking about a major problem, or issue, or diagnosis of some kind that is blocking your partner's progression to the next step, then, you owe it to him or her to help them get the resources they need to feel better or stronger. Some of my private practice clients, however, had been this way for years and nothing has changed. This is a clear and definite "Red Flag." You need to get help—individually and as a couple.

It may be easy to read this book, and get all fired-up and filled with new ideas and then want to do something about it TODAY! Please know that I WANT you to WANT TO DO SOMETHING about it. It is important that your partner is in a state of readiness to move along the path of growth with you. That is why talking to each other like best friends and inquiring is your duty as a good friend and as an intimate partner.

As I've said before, if you feel that you've tried to no avail, then you need to communicate that to your partner before you leap to the next step—out of frustration. You need to give your partner a real "HEADS UP." Tell your mate that this is important and you are committed to making a change—a deal breaker for you (but not as a verbal threat—only if it **really** is a deal breaker). Is it a deal breaker for you?

Only you can decide. Just remember to treat your life partner the way you would want your partner to treat you. It sounds hokey but, seriously, no matter how frightened you might be, or impatient you might feel right now, or that you're more frustrated than you have been for months and years—you owe it to yourself and your partner to take the high road and treat him or her with respect as you begin to uncover what is happening between you.

Can you think of something that you might have done to contribute to this slump that you are both in? When was the last time the two of you had a real conversation about what the next steps were going to look like? Do you know what you want in the short-term and long-term? Does your spouse have the same long-term view? Whatever you decide, the more balanced and even your mood is now, as you begin to inquire into your spouse's thoughts and feelings, the better it will be. Just because you read this book today does not mean you need to have a huge conversation tonight—unless, you are reading this book together and have been reading it together from the beginning. If you both have talked about each chapter after you read it together, only then, would I say that you are probably both in a state of readiness to move forward with a conversation. Talk about how you feel now that you have both been in different spaces. Take care of yourself and take care of each other.

HOW IMPORTANT IS SPIRITUALITY TO YOU AS A COUPLE?

There is a difference between spirituality and religion. Religion is a formal, dogmatic highly structured institution that gathers individuals who follow a set of beliefs, attitudes, and practices regarding the expression of faith. Religion is a commitment to the service and worship of God or a supernatural deity. Spirituality is the connection to Spirit and is a more personal relationship as it pertains to the individual. A religious person can be very spiritual (not automatically). However, a spiritual person does not have to be connected to an organized institution of faith and often chooses to pursue the more individual aspects of faith-based expression, maybe privately and quietly.

Why talk about spirituality in this book of couples and relationships? I think it is an important aspect of any relationship—especially given today's evolving and growing society. More people are being exposed to alternative ways of demonstrating faith in something outside of themselves as well as identifying an inner core Higher Self. If a couple is to grow and evolve as a couple, I would be remiss in not mentioning this very personal aspect. In a later chapter, I provide an example about a silver-haired, elderly couple who have a major conflict regarding spiritual values. In this example, you can see how powerful the link to a shared common set of beliefs can be in a marriage.

Does it mean that you both need to think and believe the same way? No. That is the point. When you meet the love of your life, everything is up for grabs. The beauty of a couple being able to share their personal spiritual or religious beliefs together is a very powerful bond. It means you aren't just negotiating as partners in finances, lifestyle, education, family, and love. You also have the benefit of incorporating your spiritual beliefs into your togetherness. It integrates more opportunity for moral guidelines and ethics to connect your values as a couple as you move through life stages together. Can you make it as a couple if you don't have that shared view? Yes, although you might have to work at it a little bit harder.

I think the answer lies within each person as to how important one value is over another. Remember, each of us is growing and evolving as individuals constantly being challenged to adjust to life's stimuli. It is important to evaluate our scale of values to determine where our personal faith or belief system is. Then, you have to decide if your chosen partner is not of the same belief, is that acceptable to you? Are you more passionate about spirituality? What does it mean to you? If you are religious, do you participate actively in your church- or synagogue-related activities and expect your partner to do the same? Or, does your religion expect your partner to do the same?

As a spiritual person, who was once very religious, I saw my own personal transformation take place, and it consciously signaled a turning point in my relationship. I had to decide if it was OK if my husband never saw things the way they were unfolding for me spiritually. More than OK, I had to assess whether this could be a deal breaker for him. What then? How do I figure out what is important to me, if I feel internal pressure by my own choices, knowing that it might result in a feeling of separateness from my partner? The questions are limitless.

In the end, I had the best of both worlds. I got to figure it out for myself and I was blessed with a husband who supported my choices. Eventually, through that acceptance, we grew even closer because of our mutually beneficial spiritual growth. So a value that was very important to me evolved within my own core scale of values and also flowed naturally into my relationship with my spouse.

In therapy, I have seen couples from all different cultures, religious and spiritual beliefs—often sticking points between them. If not an issue for them, it usually was for their parents and in-laws. Or, it was an issue in how to raise their children in America where there are so many other choices. Remember, those hot button topics for couples? Yes, religion can be HUGE, but is hopefully not a deal breaker.

POOR COPING LEADS TO POOR OUTCOMES

It All Comes Down to Making the Adjustment

Not to oversimplify something so important, but it seems that all the rules of healthy collaborative nonjudgmental communication go a long way toward figuring out who needs what and why in your marriage. In reality, as long as you have the tools to talk, listen, and reflect on with your partner, then you can communicate, negotiate, and collaborate functionally. Given all of these tools, I would summarize by saying that so much depends on your values and the weighted importance or the intensity of your values.

Continuing with the previous example, let's examine a situation in which your mate either doesn't understand the importance of your spiritual principles or adheres to something more formal and religiously strict. You've concluded that it doesn't seem to fit between your two different religious/spiritual styles. In this case, adjustments in the marriage must come from both sides. You each have to reclaim your marriage as a priority without sacrificing your own faith or belief system. What I have just said is probably at odds with most religions that require the "other" partner to convert to the same faith.

I get it. My thinking is that personal integrity and alignment with values have to come first. As very different partners with differing values, you must figure out together how to integrate what you need from each partner's value system to bring you closer together—not further apart.

Is it a requirement for a couple to connect spiritually or religiously together? No. Rather, think of this spiritual sharing as an opportunity for both of you to connect at a deeper, faith-based level. So, if you miss out on this connection point (spiritual togetherness), then the next question is, how strong are you as a couple in other shared connection points in your marriage? Do these connection points allow you to share, talk, and participate on common ground? These are key questions.

Example: Faith can be like the operating system in your computer. If you both have different platforms then you can each still operate your computer, send e-mails to each other, look up topics on the Internet, and conduct business. It could very well be a seamless difference. The mutual respect you each have for personal choice can enrich your marriage, primarily because you choose other commonly shared areas to be strongly tied. It's like your differences in some areas make you stronger in the areas in which you find common ground. If that is true, then it really does boil down to the couple's ability to make the necessary adjustments within their relationship to adapt to changing needs, values, and interests. Thus, couples who constantly face redefining their marriage every time there is a new information input or shift in values or beliefs continue to grow stronger together. I am not talking about re-engineering your marriage, but re-assimilating your marriage by integrating new stuff.

THAT IS WHY HEALTHY COMMUNICATION IS IMPORTANT! Healthy communication in all of its components is not just talking together; rather, it is HOW you talk together. Remember it is all about the inclusion of the other person and their perspective. So if one partner likes a Mac and the other likes a PC, it doesn't have to be an issue, unless you want to make it an issue.

WHAT IF YOU'VE JUST MET? DO YOUR HOMEWORK!

Before you conclude something about the other person such as: "She's the one. I'm in love!" or, "He's wonderful, I can't live without him," or, "I am nothing without…," I strongly encourage you to interview that person. If you've got this far in this book, you probably have some excellent ideas on what to talk about—values—what's important to that person? You can talk about dreams and goals. Is there a plan attached to the goal or dream? Is it practical? Talk about sex, religion, money, and kids. Talk, talk, and talk some more.

Talk about career and career goals. Listen carefully with a fine-tuned ear to discern what makes this person get out of bed in the morning. What drives them? The next topic of discussion is for you to identify and talk about what drives you. What are your goals?

When you listen to the other person talk, try to distance yourself just slightly by listening objectively (without emotion). If your own family (mother, father, siblings) is close, can you imagine this person sitting at the dinner table with them? What would they say about your choice of partner?

Is this the most important answer—what your family thinks? For many, it is another important piece of the puzzle in terms of gathering evidence, hard facts, and objective information about this person. It is a way of you slowing yourself down.

Look at it this way, it avoids harsh wake-up calls or surprises a few months or years down the road, when you realize that the two of you are not well-matched in important areas that help make a long-term relationship survive. I realize this is really easy for me to say and probably much more challenging for you to implement, especially if you are just feeling so wonderful that you just dove into this new relationship without much thought. I caution you. When the infatuation starts to fade and reality sets in, it will be those common values, goals, and practical strategies that will sustain the marriage after the kids are in diapers and college tuition fees come due. Let's face it. Life is full of challenges and stressors. Why invest emotionally without caution, when you can always invest emotionally tomorrow with more investigative information at your fingertips—WHO is this person? You deserve to find out.

Finally, how do you really feel when you are in front of this person? I'm not talking about the "I'm in love feeling." I am talking about YOU. Can you be yourself in front of this person? Are you relaxed with the silences between you? Do you feel heard? Do you think this person is interested in you as a person? Does his or her behavior match the words expressed to you (in other words, do they show you in small ways that they genuinely care about you)?

Do you both argue? Arguing can be a good thing and not so good, it depends on how often, where you argue, and how the two of you argue. Pay attention to HOW the two of you argue. Is this someone who will have your back in good times and in bad times? Are you up for supporting this person emotionally, financially, and physically—in good times and bad? Is the giving reciprocal between you? Or, is one person doing all the giving and the other all of the taking? Pay attention!

Bottom line, you do not want to wind up in some therapist's office considering divorce because you were too busy listening to all of your friends who told you he was a great guy. Or, because you were too afraid to be honest with yourself to admit that there was something not quite right, but he was so cute, and you both looked great together, and he had a great job. NO! If you ignore that inner voice that speaks to you when your head hits the pillow at night, then you are ignoring your inner Self and your HIGHER SELF. You are ignoring the part of you that knows. Please stop and listen to yourself as well as to the other person. Take just a little more time and if this is really the right person, you will be validated with more information coming to you that justifies that conclusion. You have nothing to lose. I always say, it's better to find out before you have a mortgage and babies. Do your homework and you will be much happier down the road of life together.

DON'T MARRY HIM TO CHANGE HIM (OR HER)

Big Mistake! That's when, after years of being married, the wife tells her girlfriend that, when she married her husband, she thought he would change (to her liking). Why would anyone think that? My motto has always been: WHAT YOU SEE IS WHAT YOU GET! That sums it up from both my personal and professional experience.

Let's look at the metaphor: The river can rise and its banks can swell. The silt can build on the bottom of the river. The alder trees can grow and create shade where there was once sun. The surrounding hills can erode and cause rocks to fall into the river bottoms creating large shadowy pools for the fish to spawn and congregate. The shady areas with boulders can cause algae and moss to build. Yet, the river remains the river regardless of those internal changes (some visible and some invisible).

At the end of the day, you are still you. Have you changed over time? Maybe, more on the outside than on the inside—or just the opposite—more on the inside than the outside. Perhaps your values have shifted, you are more educated, you make more money (or less), and you look older. However, some basic premises remain the same. At the core, we are who we are.

Does it mean we can't change? If that were true I would not have become a therapist. I totally believe in change! If you want to change, then you will change! If you want to shift your value system, then you will. You want it—you got it! I'm talking about you honestly identifying what is your true heart's desire. This is not about what you profess out loud to others. This is about your core desires. No matter what you really want (deep down inside)—positive or negative—then it will happen!

What about marrying him to change him? We can only change from within ourselves. **We cannot demand change in others**. If you are still thinking that, then I encourage you to re-read the **"SHOULD"** section in the cognitive chapter of this book. You **ONLY** have control over yourself, **NOT OTHERS**! You **will** be disappointed if you pursue that belief. You deserve to be happy, to have riches, to be healthy, and to be loved. First however, you have to believe in yourself and love yourself and do it for yourself, first. The rest will figure itself out.

What is a major theme of this book? Look within and when you discover how beautiful you really are, then embrace yourself and acknowledge YOU. It means you simply give yourself a mental hug and believe in taking positive steps. Start by saying kind things to your-self. As soon as you start mentally supporting yourself and being kind to yourself mentally, you **will** receive miracles on your doorstep. As soon as you are good to yourself and you start doing for yourself because you believe that you can do it, then **EVERYTHING CHANGES**! You **will attract** the healthy partner you have been wanting for years. You **will manifest** a healthier and more loving re-lationship than you ever thought would happen in your current marriage. You **will be happier** and the people around you will be happy for you (and they themselves will be happier around you)! How cool is that?

The more you keep looking to others to make it right, or to make you happy, or to give you what you want, or to do it differ-ently, then the more you will be disappointed in life and in love. It might work for a while or it might seem like it is working even for a lifetime. However, I am not referring to external looks (house, car, money, etc.). I am talking about a deeper understanding of SELF and of YOUR PARTNER. I am talking about a deep connection (inti-macy, love, friendship, and respect), that is reciprocated. It just flows. The good news is that it gets better because you both give and you both take (receive), in the marriage. That is the best part! **You can make it happen. It all begins with YOU.**

HELLO AND GOODBYE

It is imperative that you greet each other every morning and every night! Sorry, but I've heard every excuse in the book—the reason it is important is because for those of you who have children, it might be the only 4 minutes of intimacy for the entire night! Eye contact, big smile, and "Hello!" with a kiss on the cheek or lips. Why don't you try being a couple's therapist for about one day? I wonder what percentage of all the couples have some kind of argument or mis-understanding about something so small that can be traced back to how the morning or evening started. Well guess what? The evening starts with you coming home from work and greeting your spouse and your kids! It is not OK to just greet the kids and the dog and not your spouse! People tell me that it really isn't that big of a deal. I believe that drifting apart and the "no big deal" part of not greeting each other is just another bad habit. If you have children, don't even get me started! Why on earth would you want to teach your children to **not** greet each other? You are demonstrating to your children how men treat women and how women treat men. Show them the best way possible to keep that connection going. It literally takes about 3 seconds to say hello—"Hey honey, I'm home! Oh it's good to see you! I almost called you after lunch to hear your voice, but my boss came in and grabbed me for a short meeting that lasted 2 hours! How are you doing?"

You get the idea. I get all excited when I think about the possibilities when you start trying this "old-fashioned" technique out. It's called, MEET AND GREET. Amazing, how it brings a smile to someone's face! Even if you don't have kids, it could still be the key to setting the tone for the rest of the evening or day. Don't we all want someone in our life who walks through the front door and tells us that they missed us? We are so important to them that the sound of our voice makes everything "right" for them the rest of the day! Wow! How wonderful for you to be able to do the same for your partner!

EVERYTHING IS A CONNECTION POINT!

That is if you want it to be. The thing that bugs me about most psychology books and psychotherapy sessions is that we (counselors) are trained in theory. In graduate school, I always wondered how theory helps a couple. What I want to know is how do you break down the theory step-by-step so that your client (the couple) can take the skills home, use them, and practice them? Wouldn't it be wonderful to get to the point where these techniques become such an easy part of your life that you feel better and more engaged with your lover or spouse and things are pretty good? This is not about programming you to do certain behaviors at 3:00 P.M. or 6:00 P.M. or at midnight. This is about remembering how easy it was to pay attention to your mate back when you first met. What happened? You tell me! It was probably a promotion at work with more responsibility, add in a couple of kids in diapers, the stress of paying bills, aging parents, graduate school at night and the little things that made it click so easily at the beginning of your marriage are lost and forgotten. I am challenging you to remember! I am asking you to go buy a greeting card and sign it and put it in his sock drawer. I am asking you to go buy her most favorite pastry at the bakers or buy some roses at the grocery store and bring them home. Go on to your computer and make a homemade card in Microsoft Word. Add a little color around the borders and give it to her. Have it say in the middle, this is a certificate to go out to a movie and hamburger this Friday. Just take 5 minutes and think about your relationship. MAKE IT A PRIORITY. Infuse your partnership with love, attention, and positive energy. The results will blow your mind!

I would adamantly prescribe to all of my couples that they say "hello" at night and "goodbye" in the morning as they leave for work. I have only met a handful of couples who have said to me, "Oh we're really good at that! We always greet each other as soon as we walk in and when we walk out to the driveway in the morning. We hug and kiss—no matter how late we are running." They smile as they say it. Do you also know that when I politely ask my couples who are not doing this to please do so (I insist), they return proudly with huge smiles on their faces. It FEELS GOOD! Of course it does!

PART II

Your Thoughts Are Important!

PAUSE FOR THOUGHT

What Are You Thinking?

Whether or not you agree with me, it will still happen anyway. So listen up! Thoughts drive emotions and then we act on those feelings. There is a huge connection between what you believe and say to yourself and how your life, relationships, career and money turn out! Isn't it time for you to pay attention to your thoughts? Everything we do is thoughts manifesting into behavior. If you lean toward the New Age premise, it easily translates from thoughts-feelings-behavior to thoughts-feelings-vibrations-manifestations. So whether you believe that your thoughts are manifesting your current relationship or not, it does give pause for thought.

So what are you saying to yourself right now? What is your mind-set? If you cannot identify your thoughts, then I ask you to take 5 or 45 minutes and just sit there. Instead of texting, watching TV, or talking to someone, focus on the moment, your heartbeat, your breathing, and your emotions. Focus on your thoughts. Then, once you have identified that, keep practicing. The key is to identify what you are feeding your psyche (mind/soul) with and if it isn't positive stuff, then it's no wonder you're not feeling positive.

I tell my couples, it is really easy to start saying negative things about your partner. First, you focus on how different he or she is, then you start picking away at what bugs you. Then, you start getting irritated and more frustrated as you continue your inner dialogue on how this marriage is never going to work! I say, "Well, keep thinking that and you most certainly will talk yourself into a divorce—quite easily."

What Is My Role? I Have to Pay Attention to My Thoughts Too

The tricky thing about being a therapist is that I have to consistently keep check of myself to make certain I am not forcing my value systems onto my clients. A simple example would be if I had an argument with my spouse—what am I going to do? Am I going to negatively focus on everyone's male partner and pick at him? NO!

That is a HUGE NO-NO in the world of psychotherapy. So, the challenge as a facilitator, arbitrator, mediator, collaborator, and psychotherapist (all different roles by the way), is to be centered and grounded in observing one's own thoughts and feelings. This is imperative to assess or evaluate what is going on in the room with the client. Is that my feeling? Or, am I picking up her feelings? This is a long topic, but needless to say, I just want to point out that the third person in the room (i.e., the therapist) is challenged to be in tune with Self and others.

Your challenge, however, is to be in touch with your own thoughts and feelings and also be mindful of your partner's messages and feelings. This interactive cycle is powerful. Once in synchronization, you both will fluidly and rhythmically find that you can ebb and flow through thick and thin. You can find trust, love, and respect and communicate your way through all of it. **The essence of your love for each other begins with your love for yourself. It begins with YOU! It begins with your trust, love, and respect for Self!**

When I start talking like this, it reminds me of how something sounds easy enough but without sounding negative, I would emphasize that you will need to apply effort within that simplistic framework. What am I saying? For example, if you decide to cut out salt from your diet, it sounds like one item. It is one condiment. It is one ingredient. "OK, I can do that. I can cut out salt from my diet." You can, but imagine your dismay when every box, can, and prepackaged item you pick up at the grocery store tells you that salt is in it! WOW! Now what? Well, you need to start by rethinking your premise. For example, you stop buying the items you have been buying. It is time for you to think outside the box! Ha! That means, you buy fresh produce, you cook from scratch at home, you use alternate salt-free spices to give your food "umph" without the salt. Pretty simple— right? Well, yes and no. You are determined to quit salt, you've kept saying to yourself, "I'll find a way to make it work and love my new way of cooking and eating." And you do!

Congratulations! You have found the key to change. So with respect to thoughts and feelings, I would say in this example, you did not give up on yourself. After all, you were fighting for your own well-being. At the end of the day, you have to decide if you're willing to do your part in making the needed changes to help your marriage. It takes two, right? You can't just wait for the other person to make the changes first! You each have to participate and be accountable for your part in the dance.

WANT TO CHANGE YOUR BEHAVIORS?

The most direct and effective way to modify negative behaviors and emotions is to change the cognitive patterns that elicit them. In other words, THOUGHTS, FEELINGS AND BEHAVIORS. Have I said this before? Yes. I totally believe in it. I hope I can explain it in such a way that you can use it in your day-to-day life. Let me give you some tools for life right now!

Thought Stopping is a simple and effective tool. The reason I am sharing this tool is because everything begins with Self. At its very core, the couple essence begins with you first! YOU! In the section called "Time-outs," I guide you through a series of questions about physical symptoms, emotions, and thoughts. Well, that is how your thoughts are connected to emotions and to your body. I'm certain you've heard of the mind-body connection? Well, I lead you backward from your physical body to your emotions to your thoughts (cognitions), in order to help you identify your thoughts. What are your negative thoughts? If you have negative thoughts about yourself, your marriage, or others— they are negative thoughts! It is amazing how familiar these negative thoughts can become. It took me a long time to identify my own. Fortunately, a lot of excellent literature exists out there—the Internet, books, and so on. Even New Age literature—it all speaks to the concept of mindfulness. This is what I teach my clients.

The goal of this exercise is to identify your negative thoughts sooner rather than later. Some people call it obsessing, brooding, or ruminating. Whatever you call it, the goal is to be aware of those thoughts and stop them rather than be overcome by them. First, allow me to briefly describe each segment of cognitive theory and then afterward, I will describe the theory in more detail.

Step #1—IDENTIFY THOUGHTS: See your thoughts like a movie reel or like a ticker tape of thoughts flowing through you. Identify your thoughts. Are they positive or negative? If positive, then let the thought go on its way; if negative, follow the steps. At the end of the steps, I will briefly explain the sequence.

Step #2—SAY "STOP, STOP": Say it out loud (if you are alone), "STOP." If you are not alone you will have to scream "STOP" silently. Otherwise, people might be concerned about your behavior. When you shout out, "STOP, STOP, STOP!" reach out with your entire arm and hand out in front of you at arm's length and say, "STOP, STOP, STOP!" Your hand should be bent at the wrist as you jerk your arm forward while shouting "stop" at the same time. This is very powerful. When you shout STOP, something biophysical happens. Your heart starts pounding, your lungs start expanding, and you feel strong.

Step #3—VISUALIZE THE RED STOP SIGN: Next, I would like you to visualize a stop sign. We see them every day. They are large red signs with white letters—STOP!

Step #4—PRACTICE BEHAVIORAL DISTRACTIONS: Getting out of a chair; walking into the next room; going into the kitchen to get a glass of water; walking across the office building to the restroom; going to a quiet room and saying a prayer; reading a book; calling a friend; going outside for a walk—these are all examples of behavioral distractions.

Step #5—VISUALIZE: Relax in a chair or on your bed, close your eyes, and imagine you are somewhere safe that is beautiful to you, perhaps a meadow with wild flowers, or the ocean. Choose a positive memory of a happy time in your life—when you received an award. Or just think of someone you love. Just visualize this safe and special scene or person (be sure it is positive). It can be a real memory or fantasy (imagination). See the colors, see what you are wearing, what does the sky look like? If you see yourself in the mountains or at the ocean, then smell the fresh air. Feel the positive feelings. Be there in your mind as if you are there now. Feel it.

Step #6—BREATHE: If you have taken yoga, be sure to breathe the way your yoga instructor taught you to breathe. Close your eyes, breathe slowly in through your nose and slowly out through your nose. Do it three times. Focus on your breath. Listen to your breath. Inhale and exhale. Can you hear your breath pass through your nasal cavities and out your mouth? Use your imagination. Imagine breathing in a cluster of sparkling glittery stars and then exhaling them into the room all around you. See the room light up as a result of your breathing.

Each of the above techniques is a different aspect of cognitive theory used at different times for different reasons. This is NOT a Step 1, 2, 3, 4, 5, 6 sequence. The only sequential process is Step 1, Step 2, and Step 3. In this theory, cognitions are both words and visuals/imagery/symbolism. Behaviors are behaviors—the link between thoughts that emanate in feelings and how we act on those feelings. That is the sequence. Once you identify the negative thoughts, STOP THEM, and visualize the stop sign—you have blocked the flow of negativity!

EXAMPLE OF STEP 1, 2, 3

I am sitting in a chair thinking, and after 15 minutes (instead of 3 hours and 15 minutes) I realize, WOW! That's a negative thought. I have been sitting here for a few minutes and now I'm worried about this or that. Do not chastise yourself for not noticing sooner. The point is to identify your negative thoughts as soon as you can and when you do, stop them by reaching out your arm and with your hand facing up say, "STOP! STOP!" (Shout loud if you are alone, or shout silently within your own mind.) Then pretend you are walking down the street to the corner and see a huge stop sign up on a pole. Imagine yourself reaching up to the sign and without a screwdriver you yank the sign off of the pole (because you are so powerful) and you bring the large red stop sign into your lap. EVERY TIME YOU SAY, "STOP" YOU SEE THE STOP SIGN RIGHT IN FRONT OF YOUR NOSE. And, if 15 minutes or a couple of hours later you find yourself thinking the same negative thought or another negative thought, just repeat the exercise as needed. In summary, identify the thought as negative, say "STOP!" bring the stop sign into your lap, and see the word "stop."

I once had a scientist as a client who said to me after I gave her this technique, "Well, that means if you are thinking negative thoughts 99 times a day you have to reach out and say STOP! STOP! STOP! 99 times!" I smiled and told her, "Yes." She did it and it worked. Studies show biochemical and electrical changes occur in the brain as the result of thinking positively vs. negatively. I have been doing this exercise for more than 20 years and it has helped me beyond anything. We are so programmed with negative thinking—the news, work, newspapers, billboards, and TV programs. The list goes on. My big concern is that negativity is all around us and we are mostly oblivious to it.

I often ask people what they are thinking and they reply, "I don't know." Then I ask them what are they feeling and the response is, "I don't know." The issue is we are running around like a chicken with no head; we are disconnected from our body, our psyche, and our Spirit. It is time for you to pay attention to yourself. Do you know how you are feeling right at this moment as you read this book? I encourage you to spend at least 10 or 15 minutes a day in quiet. Perhaps, before you put the keys in your car, you can sit behind the wheel of your car, breathe deeply, close your eyes and try to listen to your heartbeat. What is going on inside of you? Do you know what your last thought was? Was it a positive thought? Was it a negative thought?

EXAMPLE OF STEP 4 BEHAVIORAL DISTRACTIONS

Continuing along with the example just described. You are sitting in a chair for the last 40 minutes, thinking over some worry, some negative thought. You aren't even aware of it. Then, one negative thought leads to another and you feel sorry for yourself. You start to look at your life and realize how unhappy you are. Then, you suddenly realize that you are headed into a downward spiral and you realize that you have been sitting there beating yourself up mentally; you feel terrible. So you take the example of thought-stopping one extra step: You identify the negative thought, shout out loud if possible (or shout silently within) and reach your arm out in front of you, say, "STOP! STOP! STOP!" Then, you visualize a stop sign right in front of your nose. The next thing you can do is get up from the chair, walk into another room, and do something else to distract you from sitting in that chair and beat yourself up mentally! Behavioral distractions totally work; unfortunately, they just don't have sustainable effectiveness. They work immediately but only temporarily.

Let's say you are at your job, and you get up from your desk and walk across the building to the restroom. You pass other people's cubicles, you nod to people in the hallway, and you walk past the break room. Because of the influence of outside stimuli, after a few steps you have probably already forgotten the negative thought you'd been saying to yourself just minutes ago. Distractions are really effective for derailing you from the onslaught of negativity.

EXAMPLE OF STEP 5: VISUALIZATION

Actually, visualization is more powerful than words, thoughts, or cognitions. Visualization, imagery, and symbolism are very powerful. This aspect of cognitive theory can be used whenever it seems that it would be more appropriate to visualize something and see it with your mind's eye. By closing your eyes and seeing something peaceful (could be imaginary like a sunset), or something that actually happened but that was ONLY A POSITIVE HAPPY MEMORY—by seeing that in your mind's eye, the imprint of that image goes immediately to your subconscious! This is very powerful because as soon as it happens you are already emanating a positive emotion (or vibe) that starts signaling to others that it is positive. Others react positively to that sense they have about you, even though they have no idea you just imagined yourself in a meadow with wildflowers. If you were to ask them (please don't), they might respond that they felt comfortable around you.

I was a career coach during a stressful time of high unemployment in the high-tech sector in Silicon Valley, California, at the beginning of 2002. Unlike today's unemployment, it was more localized by in-dustry sector. I worked in a consulting firm and among the many job candidates that I interviewed, two men stood out. Neither had a col-lege degree in engineering. However, they had worked for a company for more than 20 years with titles of "Senior Engineer." They had the title; they did the work of Senior Engineers; they got paid the salary of a Senior Engineer; but once laid off by their company they were left to compete with hundreds and thousands of engineers who held Bachelor's degrees in engineering. This was tough.

Each candidate was desperate for work and rightfully worried that he might not find a job. One of my main concerns was that they both reeked of desperation during our mock job interviews. I thought to myself, the interviewer will sense their desperation immediately. So I offered a simple cognitive technique they could implement whenever they needed it.

I asked each candidate to see himself interviewing successfully with a company representative reaching out with a big, "Congratulations you got the job!" and a paycheck. They both did the exercise. It helped them a lot. Forgive my bluntness, but desperation is very evident in an interviewee. You can see it in their eyes and you can feel it in the room. It's not good. You probably want to know the outcome. Well, one can-didate did get a similar job, although at a lower salary than he had been paid previously. The other candidate took longer to find employment.

With my past health problems, I would close my eyes and visualize a beautiful white light flowing through my body from the top of my head to the bottom of my toes. For me, the white light represented a pure and healing light, a whole and healthy body at the molecular level. Once I had finished the exercise, I would open my eyes and realize that my subconscious had sent messages to every molecule in my body to make it whole and healthy. I would rely on this exercise faithfully as a way to well-being. I am a short-term therapist and see up to 32 people a week. I have long days of talking with clients, listening, empathically paying attention, analyzing, and focusing on outcomes best suited to the needs of my clients. I want my clients to walk away with a tool they can use to enhance the quality of their lives. Visualization is easy to do and you can implement it right on the spot (in your car—not while driving—at home, in the yard, at work, etc.). Very powerful!

EXAMPLE OF STEP 5: BREATHING

This is another portable exercise. You do not need a pillow, a chair, or anything to do it. All you need is a quiet space to close your eyes. Closing your mouth and breathing in through your nose and exhaling through your mouth can be very healing. Whatever manner you choose to breathe, breathing by itself is very grounding and centering. For example, when you are sitting in that chair I described earlier and you realize that you are thinking negatively, YOU IDENTIFY THE NEGATIVE THOUGHT, you shout out loud if possible, or shout inside silently: "STOP, STOP, STOP" by reaching out your arm and hand, then you VISUALIZE THE STOP SIGN right in front of your nose. Imagine you are at work; while sitting at your desk, you breathe slowly a few times. Open your eyes and you have a moment of cleared space. You are no longer thinking those negative thoughts and you feel better. Please note that the act of breathing can be a form of distraction. When you breathe, you are focused on the sound of your breath. You hear yourself breathe in through your nose and out through your mouth and you say to yourself, "Am I doing it right?"

"Breathe in and breathe out." Then, quietly you open your eyes and perhaps at that moment you are a little more grounded and centered.

All of these steps can be effective. I have built my private practice around those tools. I once said to a client, "Even if you walk out today and did not return to therapy, I would feel good (although you're not there to make me feel good), because I would know that I had given you the tools for life."

IRRATIONAL WORDS

Please allow me to give you my passionate feedback on some specific words. Some therapists call them TOXIC WORDS; other therapists call them, IRRATIONAL WORDS. Why? Because they make NO sense! If you said these words to me, I would get upset. If I said these words to you, you would get upset. If you said these words to yourself silently, you'd get upset. THEY MAKE NO SENSE! Here goes…the words are: CAN'T; NEVER; ALWAYS; and SHOULD.

CAN'T

You often hear this with kids. "I caaaan't. Mommy, I can't!"

Remember this little trick. Whether or not it is a child or an adult, when you hear someone say out loud, "I can't," I want you to replace that word with "WON'T." Actually, "can not" translates to, "I don't want to." If someone does not WANT TO, that's cool. I can take that a lot easier. If they choose not to because they have no desire, that is much more understandable in my book (excuse the pun) than if they keep repeating the word "can't." Can't makes no sense, because they CAN and are totally ABLE TO DO IT, whatever "it" may be. So if they are capable, able to, and can do it (if they want to)—then there is no such logic as can't. So when I hear, "can't," I just say to myself, "Oh, that's right, they don't want to." Whatever they are saying to me makes a lot more sense and I am a lot less frustrated.

NEVER/ALWAYS

This pairing of words is what we call "absolutes." This is an all-or-nothing scenario. Couples get hung up with this language a lot. I once instructed a couple about "Never and Always." I guess I did not make myself clear enough, because she immediately turned to him on the couch, raised her voice and said, "YOU NEVER TAKE THE GARBAGE OUT!" and he matched her intensity with, "YOU ALWAYS SAY THAT TO ME!"

Needless to say, they were off and running. I thought, how did this happen? This is an example of what NOT TO SAY! I could tell right away that these were their favorite words in an argument. These words make no sense. I had to stop them and as a typical therapist, probe and ask questions to ascertain exactly when was the last time he emptied the garbage (it was 8 months ago). The point is this, there are so many variations on that, isn't there? What if he empties the bathroom garbage into the kitchen garbage and thinks to himself, "I emptied the garbage"? Life is not that simplistic. It is not black and white. It is not 100 percent all-or-nothing. There is a lot of gray—a lot left open to perception and interpretation. So, these words ("never" and "always") are totally irrational and can quickly result in irritation, frustration, anger, and upset.

SHOULD

Of all the words mentioned, the word "should" is a tough one because it is a lot more slippery than the others. You can clearly hear "CAN'T." You can clearly hear "NEVER" and "ALWAYS." However, the challenge with "SHOULD," is that it can be spoken clearly and directly—or not. Let me give you an example.

I apologize, but the example I give you is absolute (just to make a point). It is an artificial example. The truth of the matter is that we all blend all three of the examples described next. No one purely uses just one type or style when using "should."

Example 1: Some people speak in paragraphs and they clearly use the word "should" out loud. They say things like, "The government should do…" or, "My landlady shouldn't do…" or, they might say, "You should…". You get the point? You can clearly hear them use the word "should."

Example 2: Other people speak in paragraphs and although you are listening, they don't use the word "should." They use words out loud that mean the same thing as should but they don't say "should" directly. They use words such as: MUST, OUGHT TO, HAVE TO, SUPPOSED TO. These words and phrases mean SHOULD, but if you are listening for the exact word, "should," you'll miss it. That's not to say, however, that these substitute words will not stir you up the same way that "should" does. Of course, they get you all riled up in the same way. So pay attention!

Example 3: Finally, other people speak in paragraphs and they do NOT say, "should, must, ought to, have to, or supposed to." These people speak clearly in full sentences, but the challenge is that you cannot hear any of the words we have been talking about. Unfortunately, they speak and when they make a point, there is silence when it comes to "should." They speak an "unspoken should." I guess if you were to analyze it, you might say that they use a back-door approach—"I'm really disappointed to hear that you decided to do A, B, and C." I call it the silent expectation. There is an inferred or an embedded "SHOULD" even though you cannot hear it directly. They're saying, "You shouldn't do A, B, C." This is the biggest challenge in "should." This word is irrational just like the others. Think about it: when someone says, "You should do this or that," don't you have some kind of a reaction? Even if you have no reaction, it is still a behavior. I've always been a rebel, so that kind of sentence would definitely get my hair standing on end. One of life's lessons is about learning to deal, right? You bet. How do we deal with a word like "should"?

SHOULD VS. POSITIVE SELF-TALK

You can't control others and how they will respond or act toward you. You can hope and ask for what you need but there are no guarantees as to the outcome. This is another of my favorite statements when I think about reacting to someone else's irrational statement to me. IT DOES NOT MATTER WHAT PEOPLE SAY OR DO,

WHAT MATTERS IS HOW I REACT AND WHAT I CHOOSE
TO BELIEVE ABOUT MYSELF (author unknown).

What does that mean? It basically means that I have no control
over anyone but myself. When some other person at work or my
neighbor or my lover, does or says something—the ONLY thing
I have control over—is HOW I COPE WITH THAT INFOR-
MATION, HOW I REACT OR BEHAVE AS A RESULT OF
THAT EVENT OR SITUATION, AND WHAT I CHOOSE TO
BELIEVE ABOUT ME RIGHT NOW. So in the end, people can
"should' on you all day long, but you have to decide how to deal.
You have to take care of yourself in your own head and in your own
thoughts. You have to manage your "Self-Talk" so that you can be
your own best friend.

Is it really worth it to flip out when your husband says for the 50th
time, "Where are my keys?" Do you really want to spend all of that
negative energy in getting worked up and angry? Take a breath and
deal—either that or come up with some other effective way of dealing
with it as a couple (like a bowl on a table in the foyer of the house—
put your house keys in the bowl as soon as you come in the door).

Let me clarify the last part. We all know that assumptions can kill
any chance of effective communication. Well, guess what? The same
holds true for our own inner dialogue (Self-Talk). What matters is
what I am feeding my own psyche! Do I choose to believe I am less
of a person because of how I perceived another person's viewpoint?
What if I got it wrong? What if I took it to be negative and they did
not mean it to be negative? What if…?; What if…?; What if…?

Example:
You say to me: ***"The color of your shoes don't match your outfit."***

I think: *"She doesn't like me, I bet other people don't like me. What made
me think I could be successful in my field? My mother never taught me how
to dress. I am such a loser."*

WHAT JUST HAPPENED!? First, you made a statement regarding
the color of my shoes not matching my outfit. Next, I misconstrued

that to confirm my own negative Self-Talk that basically said I was a loser.

Let's replay that differently:

You say to me: "*The color of your shoes don't match your outfit.*"

I think: "*Wow, my shoes don't match my outfit. That is good information.*"

I respond to you: "*Thank you for the feedback, I'll take it into consideration next time I wear this outfit.*"

Or maybe I say something a little less diplomatic, and I nod back toward you and I say, "*I hear ya,' but I like them anyway.*"

The point is this: I have choices as to how I want to cope in response to stimuli. I could go nuts, and make that one comment ruin my entire day, or go out at lunch to the shoe store and buy some other shoes, or I could just take it—like water off of a duck's back. I know who I am, I know why I wore those shoes with that outfit, and everyone is entitled to his opinion. Maybe I even realize that the shoes don't really match, but they are comfortable and I like wearing them anyway. Who knows? The power in that example is that—I, you, none of us—has power over others (except perhaps a parent over a young child). We don't control anything or anyone. We only have control over ourselves and our Self-Talk. I think you get the point.

Thoughts, Feelings and Behaviors

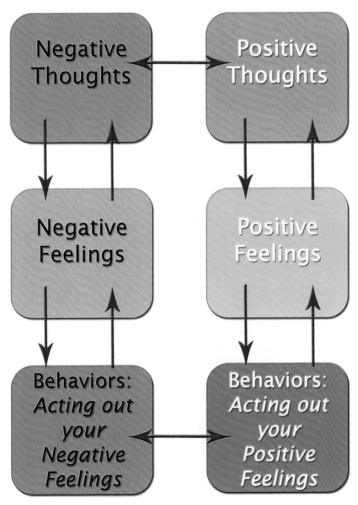

Thoughts, Feelings, and Behaviors

YOU ARE IN CONTROL OF THE REMOTE (Change Channels)

Years ago when I lived in California, there were months on end of nightly news headliners that showed individuals being hurt, mutilated, and killed by dogs. I remember naively asking my husband what he thought was happening? As a little girl, we had never heard of such a thing! He stated the obvious to me in very simple terms. He said that animals are just like people. They are stressed out! My husband said that people are moving fast and live in environments with sirens, people and traffic—daily urban living. He said that people are stressed out and dogs pick up that negative energy and then lash out violently.

Think about humans who have thoughts rambling around between our ears. We jump from thought to thought, we assume, and we partially hear because we are thinking of something else while half listening. Pick a reason. **We have multiple chances throughout the day to miscommunicate.** We have all of this negative mental chatter going back and forth in our heads about how terrible we are, how our boss is going to fire us, how we'll be alone forever, or about how our spouse is probably cheating on us. The list goes on. There is a strong chance we overreact emotionally to others when they speak to us and we jump to the wrong conclusions. It is an over-reactive cycle. Welcome to the human race. Your job is to IDENTIFY the thoughts, STOP the thoughts and CHANGE those thoughts. With respect to "Self-Talk" (mind chatter), please stop or skip over the negative and replace it with positive statements.

"CHECK-IN"

In couple's communication, your job is to check in with your partner to clarify what he or she is saying and verify to him/her that you understand his or her intentions correctly. Then, you can begin to check in with yourself and figure out how that process feels and what conclusions you have made. Can you imagine coming to a conclusion without all of the facts? I am certain you can, because we have all done it! This seems like a lot of hokey-pokey—not to mention a lot of work. To check in with your partner to make certain that you understand what you think you heard takes 4-to-11 seconds tops! In our heads, we think that one extra sentence to explain what we mean will take too long. Taking a few extra seconds to say a couple more words can really go a long way in smooth, interactive, flowing information between you—"Just to be sure I understand what you're saying, are you saying this or that?"

You can do it! And with repetition, you will become very proficient and effective in having even-tempered conversations with your partner. This can result in a lot less fighting, a lot less yelling, and an increased feeling of closeness and love. How does that sound? It might sound like a sales pitch but it is my sales pitch and I totally believe in it. Practice it and you'll be glad you did. Check-ins are very important.

BECAUSE—BUT—AND

Because: Further, I would add that to over-communicate, you need to explain a little more by adding a dependent clause starting with "because" to your independent statement. For example, I could say,

> *"When I told you I didn't want to, what I meant was, 'I don't want to because I am really tired.'"*
>
> *"When I said that a few minutes ago, and you looked at me and you told me that I looked angry and I grunted, 'you know what I'm talking about.' I guess I should have explained myself a little more."*
>
> *"What I meant to say was, I didn't want to disappoint you because I knew you had your heart set on going, and I didn't want to fight with you. I just wanted to have everything be mellow tonight—just the two of us, but not go out. Is that OK?"*

These are what explanations should sound like—examples of taking a thought and stretching it out just a little bit by adding a "because" statement. The more information you can provide, the easier it is to avoid heated arguments.

But—And

"But" is a straightforward discount of the previous statement.

Example: "Thank you for the directions, but I think it is left not right." (Thanks but I think you are wrong.) Or, "You did really well sweetheart, but you missed one part while cleaning the counter." (Thanks but you didn't really help me because you did not do it right.) Or, "Thanks for your help, but I think I've got it." (In other words, please do not help me, I don't need your help.) So, BUT completely discounts anything that was said just prior to it.

I listen to couples all day long, say "But—But—But." They completely discount their partner's efforts, thoughts, or beliefs by repeating this word. I imagine that one day I am going to get a T-shirt and have a huge sign on the front that says, "YES" in a large circle and on the back of the T-shirt have a sign that says "BUT" in a large circle, crossed out. Below that the T-shirt would read, "YES / BUT means NO!"

Next time you catch yourself saying "BUT," I encourage you to delete "BUT" and add "AND." It would sound like this:

"I want to run errands with you too, AND my hope is that you will not get frustrated or impatient."

"I want to run errands with you AND if you decide to come I need you to be calm and patient with me, is that OK?"

"Thanks so much for the directions, AND I'll see how that works."

In summary, BUT /AND are both conjunctions and they link ideas, however, the "BUT" DISCONNECTS two ideas and the "AND" joins or links the two ideas together.

CORE NEGATIVE BELIEFS

Although I am a firm believer in the cognitive STOP SIGN to help you feel better in the short term, there are plenty of ways to "slice the pie," as you well know. The cognitive tools presented to you earlier on in this book are just what you may need. I have used these tools for decades both in the therapy room and in my own life and they have helped me and many others. However, the big criticism with cognitive behavioral therapy is that it is a band-aid approach and does not look deeper. Actually, from my experience, this is not accurate. By examining negative thoughts as previously explained, you can delve further to help identify the core negative beliefs beneath those negative thoughts. The premise is that your core, deep-seated (subconscious) thoughts are driving your conscious negative thoughts—analogous to you sitting in the back seat of the car with your negativity and worries and self-recriminations, with the real driver in the front seat behind the wheel of the car with your subconscious belief schema or belief system. It is these negative core beliefs that impede your ability to move forward in life.

If you can recognize your false assumptions and negative beliefs about life, you have tapped into the "cognitive schema" or core belief system by which you operate. Going back to the car example, the car you choose to drive in is the operator of your belief system. Let me get more detailed. What are your assumptions about yourself? What do you think about life in general? What are your thoughts about relationships in general? What do you conclude about your own intimate partnership? What do you think about your spouse or partner? What have you concluded or assumed over the years about these things?

Some Examples of Core Beliefs

"You work hard and then you die. Life is hard."
Wow! Does that mean you work hard but you don't get anything? Is life rigged so that no matter how hard you work—you won't get anything?

"There's never enough. There's not enough to go around."
This is HUGE. When you are in business for yourself, do you go around thinking that you're never going to make it, or there are only so many customers in the world and your competitors took all of the available customers? Or, in your corporate job, that there are so many jobs at the top, but not enough for you?

"I'm afraid of my own power. I am not powerful."
So what does that mean? Are you a victim of life's circumstances?

Imagine having no power in your own life. Is it true?

Do you believe that forces outside of yourself control the outcome of your life (such as: economics, God, your boss, the government)?

What is it that you fear? We all have fears. That is natural, but it is very important for you to identify them. Do you fear success? Do you fear being alone and that no one will love you? Do you fear being laid off?

Exercise to Help Identify Core Negative Beliefs

You get the idea. These are powerful concepts. If you are not sure if any one of these ideas works for you, I would challenge you to take a blank sheet of paper and draw a line down the center of the paper lengthwise. Write down your negative statements that you say to yourself in your mind every day (the one's that you use the Stop Sign on). Write them on the left side of the paper. Then, on the right side, write down the opposite of that sentence.

Negative Self-Talk Example: On the left side of the page: "I am fat and stupid." (I heard this a lot as a cognitive therapist.) So opposite this statement, what could you write instead?

Positive Self-Talk Example: "I *accept* myself as I am today. I deserve to be *healthy* and *happy*. I have *value*. I am *creative* and *intelligent*. I give myself permission to start taking better care of myself physically and mentally right now."

Now, take a close look at the positive counter statements that are opposite to your negative sentence. You don't have to use mine; you can use your own. Look at the concepts: HEALTHY (physically and mentally), ACCEPTANCE, HAPPY, VALUE, CREATIVE, INTELLIGENCE. Now, if we were to write some core negative beliefs or schema stemming from these concepts we might accurately conclude some of your false assumptions about life. Let's examine the possibilities:

POSITIVE CONCEPT VS. NEGATIVE BELIEF

◊ **HEALTHY (physical and mentally) vs. UNHEALTHY**
"I am fat, I am stupid." The belief is that you are unhealthy both physically and mentally, which make you undesirable and unlovable. Perhaps you believe that you are inadequate and will be alone forever.

◊ **ACCEPTANCE vs. UNACCEPTANCE (rejection)**
This is an all-or-nothing scenario. By believing that you are fat, there is an inherent belief that you cannot change. If you are stuck being fat and you can't accept it, then, you feel even more stuck. The belief is that you are unacceptable and unworthy. You'll never be good enough or attractive.

◊ **HAPPY (emotional well-being) vs. UNHAPPY (misery)**
Feeling miserable. Feeling like you're emotionally unable to examine other choices to begin positive change toward the happiness that you deserve. The underlying belief is that you do not deserve to be happy or that happiness will always be out of reach.

◊ **HAVING VALUE vs. HAVING NO VALUE (worthless)**
So, you have decided that your presence does not add value. In other words, you are invisible, you are worthless, and your presence is in-significant. Some analytical therapists might say that you are fat, overweight, or obese because this is your mechanism for achieving significance or substance. The more physical space you take up, the more presence you have on this planet. It is your way of compensating for believing at a core level that you are invisible.

◊ **CREATIVITY vs. STAGNATION (slow or no growth)**
Being stuck—no movement, no growth, just being there, treading water. No feelings of inspiration to create, to desire, or to produce. Just sitting still but in a kind of deadness, not a quiet reflective way. It is just a waiting game, no movement. Is your belief that you will wait and something miraculous will happen to you? Is your belief based upon you thinking that it is safer to be still and wait? What are you waiting for? Is your belief that you need to be rescued from someone rather

than use your internal resources to rescue yourself from yourself? Is
your belief that you are not creative and that you don't know how to
be creative? Is your belief that if you are your true and real, creative
Self that you will be ridiculed by others and you will be shamed? Do
you fear shame? What is your core belief?

◊ INTELLIGENCE vs. STUPIDITY (lack of intelligence)

If intelligence is having the capability to use your mind for a variety
of functions from abstract thought to learning, problem-solving, and
communicating, then, if you lack all of these you must be empty.
You don't have what other people possess. You are different. You are
less than zero. Is your core belief system that you are less than zero?
Are you really not as smart as others? Do you really believe that all
of those beautiful people on TV and the Internet are smarter than
you? Does that mean you don't have a chance at reaching for the
shining star or grabbing the gold ring (whatever that means for you)?
Does this mean that you believe that you are the odd man out? That
is a lonely conclusion. Are you lonely? Do you believe that you will
always be alone because you are stupid?

In the end, you can see how they all interconnect: your low self-
esteem leads to self-medicating through possibly overeating or, to your
being really depressed; feeling kind of stuck; not having any current
goals in your life right now; feeling passive about life; or, being lax
about taking care of both your physical and mental needs. I encourage
you to make your own list. This list was an exercise that I conducted
with you in this book. It is not a format I use for: "I am fat; I am
stupid." Rather, the format is following the breadcrumbs that lead
to the BIGGER false assumptions that you have concluded about
yourself and others.

PART III

Pay Attention to You!

LANGUAGE IS IMPORTANT: COMMUNICATION WITH SELF

What a powerful concept! How do we communicate? Of course everything begins with Self. If you are not in touch with your own thoughts and feelings then how do you expect your partner to understand what you need or want? Are you in touch with your own wants and needs? Do you know what you are feeling right now? Can you identify your feelings? This is the beginning of communication. It might be difficult and the first step is the hardest. Only when you can identify where you are as an individual, can you begin the process of communicating to your mate and to those around you.

Often, one partner will say in response to, "What are you feeling right now?" "I don't know." Well, this might sound flippant, but if you don't know—no one else is going to know. It is important for each of us to take and make the time to get clear with Self first. How can you do that? One way is to have a "check-in" with yourself. It doesn't matter if it is 5 minutes or 25 minutes, just as long as you have some alone time to be with yourself. When you're alone ask yourself, "What am I feeling in my body right now?" Are you tired, hungry, or bored? Is your left knee twitching and your right ear itching? Second, ask yourself, "How am I feeling emotionally right now?" Are you upset (what does that mean?), are you sad, mad, glad, feeling bad? Is it a positive feeling or a negative feeling? Finally, "What are you thinking?" What are you saying to yourself right now? Identify the chatter in your head. Do you sabotage yourself with negative thoughts such as: "I'll never be good enough"; "I am fat and ugly"; "I will be alone forever"; "This marriage is not going to work"? Whatever negative messages you are saying to yourself, ask yourself this, "Is it helping me to say these negative things to myself?" I am certain the answer is "NO!"

So, continue reading and we can discuss this in more detail.

In order to have effective and healthy couple's communication, you have to have clarity within yourself. After that, it mushrooms to all aspects of your life: team meetings at work, family meetings, neighbors, recreational groups, and so on.

Emotions

THE ANGER CONTINUUM—THE ROPE OF ANGER

Exercise: Take a string/rope (real or fantasy) and stretch it diagonally across a room from one corner to the other. Make incremental marks on the rope every 2 feet so that you can identify each mark with a feeling. I call these increments, "The Anger Continuum." At one end of the rope in the first corner of the room, you have marked IRRITATION. Two feet more along the rope, you have marked FRUSTRATION. After 2 more feet, you mark RESENTMENT. Then, 2 feet further along the continuum, you mark ANGER. Finally, jump to the other corner of the room (even if it means going 6-to-20 feet further) and mark it with RAGE! I call this the "Rope of Anger." Anger is usually somewhere in the center of the room with the incremental emotions leading up to anger. However, from anger to rage is one big leap. I think of all of the other incremental emotions as "cousins to anger." In other words, they are all related. It is important for you to know that once you've hopped on board the Rope, even if you've only landed on IRRITATION, you need to know that once accelerated, you are on a tightrope that could lead to anger or something more. Of course, this transition of acceleration is different for all of us. The point is, that being irritable and frustrated are forms of anger because they are cousins. From this perspective, you might ask yourself, why am I dabbling in this negative emotion? I can tell you the answer(s).

#1—You are thinking anger-producing thoughts.

#2—It is a habit for you.

#3—It feels more energizing and empowering than feeling scared, fearful, anxious, hurt, or sad.

#4—Physiologically, your lungs are expanded, your heart is beating faster, your adrenal glands are fibrillating and you feel a rush of Cortisol in your system that is pumping you up. Cortisol is helpful in small doses but sustained or long-term levels of Cortisol are destructive to the body and can cause physical problems affecting weight, heart, aging, and the body's immune system.

Your job is to identify what's happening to you sooner rather than later.

HOW DO YOU KNOW WHEN YOU ARE ANGRY— SCARED—ANXIOUS?

This is the key to managing your own anger. Sometimes we know when we are angry and at other times we see OUR anger reflected in our partner. Sometimes we are in touch with our own anger and other times we are more reactive and in touch with our partner's emotions—we are so disconnected from ourselves that we just slide along, cut off at the head and neck. It is time to pay attention! What are the first cues of anger? What are your physical symptoms? What part of your body does anger begin in? Name them right now. What exactly does anger feel like? Does your anger have a color or does your anger have a physical sensation? Does your anger have a lesser emotion attached to it (like irritation, frustration, fear)? Next time you start to get angry, I want you to NOTICE the very first thing that you are aware of. What is that? Name it now. What is the second thing you notice about getting angry? What is the thought you have that is attached to that physical and emotional sensation? Please identify that thought now.

Communicate with Your Partner

If you are reading this book as a couple, this would be the time to share that information with each other. Just to be clear, this is a technique that each of you needs to do and then share with the other— "Hey, remember when I told you about that stomachache I get when I am upset? Well, I am starting to get that stomachache right now and I think I need a time-out."

This exercise will NOT work unless there is mutual respect and understanding. This is not about having the last word. This is about respecting your partner's expression of feeling in a language of body sensations that lets YOU KNOW that the ball is in your court and YOU HAVE THE POWER to stop the arguing now. That's right! Take a time-out, stop talking, or empathize and say, "I am sorry to hear about your stomachache. I guess I was getting heated and didn't realize it. What do you need from me right now? I don't want to argue with you sweetheart. Tell me what you need and I promise I'll do it." This completely unhooks you from the dynamic that is hooking you both in a cycle. This makes you invested in THE RELATIONSHIP, rather than being invested IN BEING RIGHT OR BEING HEARD, OR BEING THE WINNER.

So, basically, what you and I are talking about right at this moment in this chapter of the book is "Mindfulness." Are you starting to see the theme? Does it seem like almost every time I talk about both of you as a couple, I keep bringing the focus back to YOU? Why is that? You are in charge of you and your partner is in charge of him or herself.

So, the power to monitor your own feelings and then to manage your own feelings is the key. Everyone else in the equation can do what they have to do. That does not dismiss one person from being responsible. If you are committed as a couple or you are in couple's therapy, certainly, you are EACH RESPONSIBLE for your own behavior (thoughts and feelings). This is not where one person holds ALL OF THE RESPONSIBILITY for his or her partner. That does not work. It takes two to share the burden. It takes two to make the change. One person/partner/spouse cannot love enough, give enough, or change enough for both of you. That scenario will blow up in your face and in your partner's face!

If you don't address your own anger or release your own anger, then you allow it to hang around. This can only result in powerful anger. Call it want you want, stewing in your own stuff will just get more volatile (like pop goes the weasel).

Self Is Important

As an executive coach and career coach, I once interviewed a candidate and was very concerned about him. He was in a marriage that looked great from the outside but did not allow him to be his real Self in the relationship—a good man who took care of everyone else's needs but his own. He worked hard but was in a job he hated; he was a good father. Yet, because of his demanding wife, he never really had a voice in the marriage. My mentor at the consulting firm told me that he too was concerned about the candidate's well-being, based on his score on a survey. I realized that my candidate was a ticking time bomb, perhaps in anger, but also physiologically. He could have had a heart attack. As my mentor described it, my candidate needed to start taking better care of himself. Absolutely! It was so validating to hear someone else passionately say what I also strongly believed. Self is important. All other relationships stem from the core. Paying attention to Self is NOT SELFISH! It only feels like selfishness because you are out of balance. When you are out of balance it is harder for you to make the necessary adjustments as you are further away from your comfort zone. There are books written just on this topic alone. Stuffing anger, fear, anxiousness, sadness, you name it—any of these can possibly manifest into physical disorders, diseases, emotional irregularity, the common cold, and much more.

EGG METAPHOR

I would describe to my clients my "Egg Metaphor." The hard shell of the egg protects the yolk. If you think of it in terms of emotions, the shell is the defense mechanism of anger. Anger protects our psyche from some softer feeling or emotion that makes us feel more vulnerable. So the egg's hard shell protects the yolk. Even though the hard shell has a function, it is important to get in touch with the softer emotions too. Our hard shell of anger makes us feel strong! I feel more comfortable when I'm angry than when I am stuck in a downward spiral of fear, hurt, sadness, or anxiety. Who wants to stay stuck in sadness? When we say, "I am sick and tired of feeling sick and tired," we can pop out of that stuck place to become angry, which provides us with a sense of momentum and forward energy.

In the world of therapy it is often taught that if you can move a client from sadness to anger, you have made progress. The theory is that when the client can express anger they are more engaged, as opposed to being depressed and disengaged.

Feelings come in layers and what we often see is one emotion that covers or protects other deeper more vulnerable emotions.

IRRITATION over **ANXIETY**

FRUSTRATION over **SADNESS**

RESENTMENTS over **HURT.**

ANGER over **FEAR**

OR, it could look like this:

Eggshell _____ **anger**

Less visible feeling _____ **disappointment**

Deeper feeling _____ **hurt**

So if feelings come in layers, can you identify what are your own layers of feelings? Is it disappointment, hurt, or sadness? Is it anger, fear, and anxiety? Is it frustration, anger, or hurt? The surface feeling is the one the rest of the world sees and the softer more vulnerable feelings (feelings 2 and 3) are the less visible feelings. However, they are all interconnected. Identify your emotional layers and you have revealed a huge inner part of your own cycle of coping! Every day, if you could just take 5-to-15 minutes to sit in silence (no phone, no TV, no dogs, no kids) and listen to your heart beat. What are you feeling? Sit there until you can name that feeling! THIS IS SO IMPORTANT! Congratulations! Now share it with your partner next time you are aware of your feelings. Keep practicing this technique and it will become easier—just like lifting weights at the gym. The more you do it, the more automatic it will become and you will become more balanced in mind, body, spirit, and feeling. Take your first step toward self-awareness now.

A MAN WHO CHANGED

I remember talking to a couple who openly described how dad (the husband) was a yeller and a screamer. I clearly remember him telling me how beautiful his preteen daughter was and that she was such a good girl (and she was). However, my concern was about his anger and how it affected his wife (sitting right next to him) and his daughter. His wife candidly explained to him in the middle of the session how negative his yelling was and how it caused her much anxiety. He acted kind of surprised—like he had no idea. I gently brought up the topic of his daughter, wondering out loud how his behavior affected her. He defiantly snapped back with a statement indicating that his daughter was fine and there was nothing wrong! I backed off. Toward the end of the session I asked out loud once more about the negative ramifications of his anger and volatility on his beautiful daughter. He commented that he wasn't sure. His wife responded with, "Let me tell you about how your daughter feels about your anger. She is very anxious and walks on eggshells around you all of the time." She provided examples. He was genuinely shocked and sincerely saddened by this news. He expressed his concern for both his wife and his daughter and then looked at me and clearly stated his desire to change his behavior! Now that's what I mean by "owning it"—a beautiful man, loving father, and good husband.

That same man walked out of our couple's session with an entirely new outlook on life, himself, his career, and his family. He had opened his eyes. Do you know what we concluded in our collaborative therapy sessions? He described in detail how stressful his life was at work and that he was very anxious but did not want to admit it. You know, it's OK to use words like "stressed out," "upset," "tense," and so on. But goodness, don't ever say something like "anxious." Well, he was anxious and when I advocated for him to go to his doctor he surprised me with no resistance. His wife supported him in his efforts toward change (she did not blame him). He kept his doctor's appointment and with some prescribed low-dosage meds and about six couple's therapy sessions—life became pretty darn good. They both self-reported that even their daughter's behavior had changed when she started to bring friends over to the house! I was honored to be there and see it all unfold. Thank goodness each of them had the love and the courage to take the steps necessary to make it happen.

This is an example of a high-functioning individual who was able to be empathic in seeing how his mood and behavior affected others he loved. He owned both his anger and his angry behavior. In addition, he was able to acknowledge to himself and to his partner how his behavior was not working, and then he made the commitment to change. Finally, he changed his negative behavior! That is a good story.

MALADAPTIVE COPING MECHANISMS FOR ANXIETY

Amazingly, people still take the simple way out or believe in some myth that they heard would be a way of coping with anxiety. I call it, "treating the symptoms." I had one male client who was going to the doctor for "irritable bowel syndrome," "ulcers," and "sleeplessness." I realize just as you do that we live in a world where you have to be your own medical advocate at times. It is essential that the doctor get the complete picture. This guy probably went into the doctor's office and complained about this aliment and that ailment. They were real complaints and real disorders. Unfortunately, the helicopter view from 5,000 feet up would have clearly identified that many if not all of these somatic (physical) ailments, came from one major disorder—anxiety. The doctor treated everything appropriately, but the big picture remained elusive. Anxiety was the driver of the physical problems. I told the client to go back to his doctor and explain all of the other physical and emotional problems he was experiencing. "Tell him you are demonstrating clinical signs of anxiety," I said to him. He agreed and went to his doctor's office and got on a low dosage anti-anxiety medicine.

Obviously, these efforts can be clumped together in a group called, "Fix it now." Instead of self-medicating through excessive drugs, over-the-counter pills, or drinking alcohol to get a buzz and take the edge off, I recommend the following more effective and longer-lasting methods for coping with anxiety.

FUNCTIONAL HEALTHY WAYS TO COPE WITH ANXIETY

#1—Get a complete physical exam with blood work and urinalysis from your primary physician. Talk to your physician about your anxiety and how you don't sleep, how your thoughts are obsessive, how you feel unsettled and restless, how you worry or talk about your marital stress, and how you have physical symptoms of anxiety (stomachaches, headaches, backaches, rashes, etc.). Talk to your physician about the possibility of low-dose medication to alleviate the symptoms of anxiety.

#2—Seek a professional counselor, psychotherapist, or psychologist to talk intimately about how you feel, what you think, and how you have been behaving since you've been anxious. This is to allow you to have a personal advocate who is totally committed to your well-being (not couple's therapy). Or go to a group therapy that commits you to 5, 6, or 8 sessions. That would be a short-term commitment that helps you get started.

#3—Do positive Self-Talk. Say nice things to yourself. I've had many clients nod their heads in agreement and say something, "OK, BUT IT'S GOING TO BE HARD!" That is a negative statement. STOP!

Instead say, "Every day in some small way, I am taking care of myself more and more. Today, I am taking a big step toward healthier choices. I love myself, and today I love putting good, delicious, nutritious food in my body." Also say 40 times a day out loud, "I LOVE to exercise!" Say anything that you would want your best friend to say to you with lots of love. Try being your own best friend.

#4—Decrease your caffeine intake. Caffeine results in jitteriness. So re-evaluate your foods (sodas, coffees, teas, chocolates, etc.)—anything with caffeine can increase anxiety. I had one attorney who came to me with panic attacks. I started out asking about his caffeine intake; he was having 12 lattes a day. Right away we strategized on a way that he could have his coffee, but with a lot less caffeine and fewer cups (not after 3:00 P.M., with food, or one-half cup, etc.).

#5—Exercise regularly. Does that need more explanation? Exercise will increase Serotonin and Dopamine and help tremendously with anxiety. For example, dopamine gives us the feeling of bliss, pleasure, appetite control and positively impacts our ability to focus. Serotonin provides a calming effect on our brains and bodies. Low Serotonin in the brain results in the following symptoms (to name a few): insomnia, irritability, spontaneous tears, emotional irregularity, inability to sort out your feelings, and a lack in ability to discern between imminent danger or crisis (flight/fight).

Try walking around the block three times a day. Only join a gym if you intend to use it regularly. Perhaps the beauty of joining a gym is to get a personal trainer or to join their ongoing aerobic classes. Join a Zumba dance fitness program! Start jogging Monday through Friday. Get a treadmill and put it front of the TV and force yourself to do 15 minutes a day or more. You know what you need to do.

#6—Get adequate sleep. If you are highly anxious and not sleeping, the dilemma is that lack of sleep can complicate your anxiety and manifest and mimic other disorders. I used to hear many clients say, "I don't want to take anything to sleep. I get it." Guess what? The more you keep waking up at 3:15 A.M., the more your neurological pathways are paving the way for you to keep waking up at 3:15. Low-dose meds can help block that programming and help your body get back on track! It is not normal to wake up repeatedly or wake up and stay awake at night. This has a negative impact on your circadian rhythm and will cause an imbalance in your sleep/wake cycle (sleep deprivation is known to mimic depression).

#7—Eat healthy. Really take a look at your sugar intake. What do you keep saying to yourself about sugar? "I have to have sugar!"; "I love my sweets!"; "Don't ask me to give up sugar!" Well, then I won't. However, I will tell you to take a look at Step #3 and create some positive Self-Talk about your sugar intake. How about saying, "Starting now, I will consume less sugar and feel better, healthier, and more balanced."; "Starting now, I am cutting back on my sugar intake and I feel free, I feel good, I have more energy."; "I am no longer a slave to sugar; I am satisfied and satiated by the smaller amounts of sugar I am using now."; "Every time I use sugar in my coffee it tastes too sweet."

GENDER-BIASED ANXIETY

Certainly, I saw this in both sexes and I have no statistical data to support my point; however, after doing short-term therapy for many years, I can say that I have seen my share of men with complaints about life. They are all unhappy at work and in their relationships. I often tell them in front of their spouses that they display anger for the world to see. They are really anxious underneath and self-medicate their anxiety with anger. I am certain that I am NOT the first person on earth to notice this behavior. I consistently counsel males who are so uncomfortable in their own skin, they pop into irritability, frustration, or anger to cope with the discomfort of their anxiety or tenseness. Forgive my gender bias but men feel more in control by being irritated than by being anxious. I talk to them and tell them my conclusions. No one really disagrees with me. Why? Because it makes total sense! Males have been socialized and habituated to cut themselves off from their own feelings. My goodness, they can't even spell anxiety. They look at me dumbfounded and then slowly nod their heads and agree with me. Wives excitedly nod their heads and look excited—like we were on the verge of a breakthrough. This has happened so many times—over the days, weeks, months, and years—that I cannot even count. What a drag! I am so sorry that men have learned over time to cope with stressors by popping into irritability and agitation (grumpiness).

Many men exit anxiety ASAP. It is so uncomfortable for them that they self-medicate (I use that term loosely even though I have been a substance abuse counselor) with anger, substances, or alcohol. I have such compassion for how unnatural it has become for men to identify with their ongoing stress as anxiety. These cyclical patterns of thoughts, feelings, and behaviors result in someone jumping out of their skin (figuratively speaking) from high anxiety to high frustration or anger; it is really not good for them or their loved ones. In these cases, their children learn anxiety and they grow up to be angry adults. This is more proof that each person in the family needs to do his or her part in taking care of themselves, their partner, and family.

GUILT

As a result of committing a "breach of conduct" or an offensive act, someone states that they feel guilty. You are not alone if you think you're the only one who feels guilty. Many clients suffer from harbored secrets, repetitive lies, past misdeeds, and personal failings. Ultimately, if a behavior is pinpointed, the response might sometimes be a spontaneous knee-jerk defensiveness (linked to guilty feelings about the behavior). Most certainly, guilty feelings derail efforts toward salvaging any shred of self-esteem. If you saw them on the street, you would probably call them one of the "beautiful people." You know, the ones who look good, have nice clothes, have the beautiful car, have the perfect life with money in the bank. However, their "Bank of Self-Esteem" is bankrupt! Some therapists might make the comment that the "perfect" persona is an effort to overcompensate for guilty feelings. However, the one thing about being a cognitive therapist is that I have the honor and the responsibility to listen to people's most private thoughts. These include the negative self-deprecating thoughts of the most visibly beautiful people who consistently maintain a barrage of guilt-producing thoughts!

These individuals often think of something from their past. They often think that if other people really find out who they are, they would be rejected and ridiculed for being phony. When I listen to these clients who candidly reveal these inner thoughts—it is all I can do to hold back the tearing in my heart, not to mention my tear-filled eyes. How painful and sorrowful. At the very least, it is a clear example of how polarized their inner life is compared to their outer life. Emotionally, mentally, physically, and spiritually—guilt extracts from their core. An extreme amount of negative energy is spent just trying to cope and live with that negative tape recorder in their heads saying how terrible they are, over and over and over. This chronic perpetuation of guilt is really unhealthy at all levels.

Exercise to Remove Guilt

This is a classic cognitive exercise using your capacity to imagine.

Take a few minutes of quiet away from your cell phone, TV, kids, and dogs. Just close your eyes and breathe deeply. Can you remember the past situation that you repeat often to yourself mentally that results in your feelings of guilt? What was that circumstance? Now, I want you to imagine that instead of you having that experience, it is actually your best friend. See him or her come to you and say that s(he) has no one to talk to but s(he) needs to share a story with you about his or her past. This is your best friend's story to you. I want you to be his or her best friend and see yourself being compassionate and nonjudgmental. This is your best friend! You love them and would never hold this past story against them. Can you see yourself being patient, kind, and supportive while they divulge their guilty feelings to you? How do you feel as you see yourself being compassionate? How do you feel listening to the story? Is it shocking? Are you negative toward your friend? I would take a guess that you are a very good friend. Now, imagine how you feel being a friend without an agenda. How does your friend act in response to your kindness in listening? NEXT

STEP: Take the first step toward self-healing by being compassionate to yourself. When you listened to your friend's story and thought, "What's the big deal?", it puts things into perspective, doesn't it? It is in the past, it happened, it is over. However, your guilt-producing thoughts are constantly giving it life. You have kept that guilt alive by repeatedly feeding it every time you think about that past behavior. Today, it is time to let it go. Please be your own best friend!

SHAME

It refers to one's ability to conform to society's rules because it is an emotion rooted in our social, cultural, and environmental norms and rules. Shame is a feeling related to an individual's sense of personal integrity or character.

In our day-to-day existence, we have the opportunity to experience small natural occurrences of shame in which we might feel different from others or embarrassed for a moment. However, at a deeper core level, when an individual suffers from a wound in their Self, it results in a pervasive and consistent negative view of Self. This manifests in low self-esteem—feelings of being unworthy or self-labeling (stupid, fat, loser, etc.).

Over the years, too many clients would state early on in our sessions that they were "defective" or "damaged goods." Imagine going through life labeling yourself as less than normal. Yes, there are many of you walking around as "wounded souls." However, I really try to steer away from negative labels. Otherwise, you become the label.

Have you been hurt? Yes, probably. Does this mean I am minimizing your pain? Well, let me acknowledge your pain while simultaneously looking you in the eye and asking you this: "What are you going to do about it?" Are you going to wallow in pain and be sure to tell yourself and everyone every day that you have been wounded? Or, are you going to move forward in life? If you remain stuck in the pain, you are refusing to give yourself the opportunity of a lifetime. It means that you have created your own prison and you locked yourself up and threw away the key! That means the chance to grow, evolve, change, learn, and evolve some more is lost to you unless you decide to give yourself another chance. **Your job is to get on with your life right now.** In doing so, only then can you start bringing the BEST OF YOU to all aspects of your life. Thus, you benefit in addition to everyone around you including your significant other (lover, partner, spouse, friend, and soul-mate), who gets the benefit of loving you back! You are worth loving. First, you have to do it for yourself before anyone else can do it back at you.

Exercise to Remove Shame:

#1—You can do the "Forgiveness Formula" mentioned in Part VI.

#2—You can perform the "Reclaiming Your Own Power Back" (described next).

#3—You can do the following 3-part cognitive exercise.

Step 1: Identify your shame (depression, anxiety, shame, guilt, co-dependency). Where is it in your body, exactly? What size is it? Is it the size of a dinner place mat? Is it small like an egg? What shape is your shame? Is it oval, circular, or square? What color is your shame? Is it red, black, or grey? What texture is this shame? Is it solid like cement? Is it gaseous like fumes? Is it prickly like a porcupine? Is it gooey like Jell-O? Does this shape and size impede upon any organs inside your body? Does it impair your breathing? Does it cause stomachaches or diarrhea? Does it cause headaches? Please describe in detail.

Step 2: In this second part, you speak out directly addressing your shame. I provide you with an example of what you might say, but the words should come from within yourself, naturally. This is an opportunity to speak to shame and basically tell your shame that you no longer want or need it to cope; finally, you demand that your shame leave your body, your heart, your mind, and your psyche immediately.

Example: "Shame, I want to tell you that I am very grateful for everything you have done for me for the past several decades. No matter how happy I might be or how stressed I might be in life, I could always count on you to come and be by my side. You have always been my dysfunctional coping mechanism. You have done a tremendous job of keeping me tied to you, shame. Now however, I want you to know that I no longer need you. I no longer need to be anchored to you! I am choosing a healthier way of coping that excludes you from my life and body, and heart and mind. I am telling you right now: "SHAME, I DEMAND THAT YOU LEAVE MY BODY, MIND, HEART AND SOUL—RIGHT NOW! SHAME, LEAVE ME NOW! SHAME, I COMMAND YOU TO LEAVE MY LIFE NOW! BE GONE!"

Step 3: This final section is visual and creative. I want you to imagine that you are a Hollywood producer and you have unlimited funds available to you. You have anywhere from 2-to-22 special-effects engineers. You can create any scene imaginable—a movie! Now, I want you to describe to me a scene that you have created in which Shame is removed from your body and destroyed. Now remember, this is magical and Hollywood. It does not have to be logical or linear. For example, you can have a flying dragon come across the sky and reach down with its talons and clutch the Shame from your body (name the body part where Shame was located and describe the size, shape, color and texture of the Shame removed from your body). As soon as that is done, you are safe and whole. The flying dragon only took the Shame out of you and did not harm you in any way. Now, see the flying dragon continue across the ocean toward China and halfway through his flight the dragon drops the "ball of Shame" (or however you describe it) and it falls 800 feet to the depths of the ocean. It immediately begins to deteriorate because of the ocean's salt water. No fish eats your Shame. No Shame bubbles up to the top of the ocean for someone else to catch it. It is completely dissipated and destroyed. There is not even one tiny spec of SHAME left any-where. Your SHAME IS GONE! Good! Now tell me how you feel right now.

There are many examples from clients. One person described the Star Wars scene where he was standing under a laser beam that disintegrated him. When he emerged, he emerged without Shame (or any other affliction). Another client described a beautiful White

Good Witch of the West (like in the Wizard of Oz), and the Good Witch was illuminated in complete glowing light. With a magical wand in her right hand, she lightly touched my client and the Shame (or depression, anxiety, fear, anger, etc.) went away. There were many more examples. Remember there is no right or wrong way to conduct the exercise as long as your SHAME is completely gone from your body without harming you. Once it is removed from your body, it is destroyed by whatever means so no one else can contact it!

As soon as you finish the exercise, immediately repeat it once out loud—all three parts. An hour later repeat it again. So today, you will have said it out loud 3 times. Tomorrow, you must say it four times and the day after tomorrow (two days from now) you must say it another four times. This means that in the next 48 hours you will have said this exact exercise 10 times in addition to the first time you described it. This ensures that you can quasi-memorize it. This means that you will eventually find a few shortcuts in which you might say a word or phrase and you immediately know what it means—in complete detail. You see it very clearly. Even if you sit inside your car with the keys turned off in a parking garage or at the supermarket parking lot, you need to say it out loud so that you can hear yourself say the words. As time passes, you can think it automatically next time you feel SHAME. You can progress through the three-part exercise silently and quickly advance to the part where you excise the SHAME from your body, heart, mind, and soul. Will SHAME or whatever issue you identified come back? Most certainly yes, you have harbored SHAME for years and years. It will be like a rubber band and come back to find home in your psyche. However, the more you stay on top of it by noticing its presence the more likely it is that you can remove this highly negative and toxic emotion from your life. This is an excellent and very powerful exercise. It is a tool for life!

NAME A NEGATIVE FEELING THAT IS A THEME IN YOUR LIFE

Every time we create a relationship or situation that results in negativity, we lose part of our core Self.

Identify the negative feeling that you want to change. This does not mean you identify someone else who must change. Rather, it is about searching within yourself to identify themes throughout your life that have been circulating and re-circulating in your relationships at work, with the neighbors, your parents, your mate, your family, and so on. What are those issues or negative emotions that trail consciously and subconsciously in all of your relationships? Is it low self-esteem? Is it co-dependency? Is it anger? Is it fear? Is it depression or sadness? What is it? From what place do you operate? Are you overly boastful because inside you feel little and unliked? Are you overly helpful because you fear rejection? Do you stew in irritability and anger more often than not? What is it?

Exercise to Remove Negative Feeling:

#1—Perform the following steps in a private, quiet setting without interruption. Do not do this if other people are in the next room or in another location of your house. Be alone.

#2—Identify a negative feeling that is a theme in your life and throughout all of your relationships such as: Anger, Guilt, Depression, Fear, Low Self-Esteem. Pick one of your own.
Let's say it's Fear.

#3—In your mind's eye, visualize and see directly in front of you that negative feeling. If it is fear, then see FEAR right there in front of you. Either see the word, or feel the feeling (FEAR) and give it a color and see it looming directly in front of you at eye level.

#4—Reach out with both of your arms extended, almost touching the fear. Then, reach out with both arms and fingers pointed as you say out loud the following:
"I reclaim my power back now from Fear!"

#5—As soon as you forcefully say: "I reclaim my power back now from…." Take both of your hands and curl your fingers into a fist as you bring your hands back to your chest touching your heart.

What you are doing at this moment is releasing the Fear and re-claiming your own positive energy back into your heart as your own. This means that you are reclaiming the original effort, time, and energy that are a part of YOU that have been lost—maybe for years. Now you are bringing them back to your core—back to your heart and soul. You've spent a lot of your own core energy creating a negative feeling to cope in life.

This is a way to reclaim your core energy and be whole again.

#6—When you first do this exercise, repeat it at least 40 times! You will feel the surge of energy. If you have more than one negative feeling, try not to do the exercise for more than three feelings. Also, do steps 1-to-5 for one feeling, then start over for steps 1-to-5 for the next feeling.

Do you currently have a series of connected problems that seem to be spiraling into a negative cluster of arguments, multiple negative feelings, or just a lack of joy in a specific relationship? Do you feel uncomfortable in this person's presence or do you feel intimidated by them? Do you feel like you cannot be yourself when you are with them? Or, do you feel abused or constantly criticized? Do you like who you are when you are with them? Do you feel like you are not who you used to be in this relationship? You can also perform this exercise if you have created a problematic relationship or have multiple negative feelings in your relationship with a particular person. If so, then do the following powerful exercise.

STEPS TO HEAL FROM A TOXIC RELATIONSHIP

#1—Perform the following steps in a private, quiet setting without interruption. Do not do this if other people are in the next room or in another location of your house. Be alone.

#2—If you have a specific difficult relationship with one person over a period of time, focus on that person. Say that person's name out loud. See the person's face directly in front of you at eye level in your mind's eye. Do not really stand in front of the person! This is a mental cognitive exercise only! This exercise uses your imagination.

#3—Reach out with both of your arms extended to the person's face you see in front of you. Then, reach out with both arms and fingers pointed as you say out loud the following:

"I reclaim my power back now from (name _____)!"

#4—As soon as you forcefully say: "I reclaim my power back now from (name _____)," take both of your hands and curl your fingers into a fist as you bring your hands back to your chest touching your heart. What you are doing at this moment is releasing all of the negativity associated with this person. You are reclaiming your own positive energy back into your heart as your own. This means that the original effort, time, and energy that are a part of YOU have been lost—maybe for years and that is part of the problem in this relationship. Maybe in this relationship you feel confused. Perhaps you feel like you are no longer who you used to be or you've lost a part of yourself in this relationship. Now you are bringing it back to your core—back to your heart and soul. You've spent a lot of your own core energy creating a relationship to cope in life, but that is not the way to cope. Coping has to come from within you first before you can reach out to someone else. This exercise is a way to reclaim back your core energy and be whole again.

#5—Please note that this is NOT about rejecting this person in your life nor is it about having dominance or power over this person. It is also not about sharing this very personal exercise with them. This is a private individual exercise that you are doing for your own betterment. This exercise is about **you** finding balance within yourself first.

#6—When you first do this exercise, repeat it at least 40 times! You will feel the surge of energy.

#7—Every time you feel out of balance with this person you can quietly take the time to go to the restroom, or go to the backyard, or in your car on the way home from work and do this exercise. It is amazing how it can help to equalize your energy within the relationship.

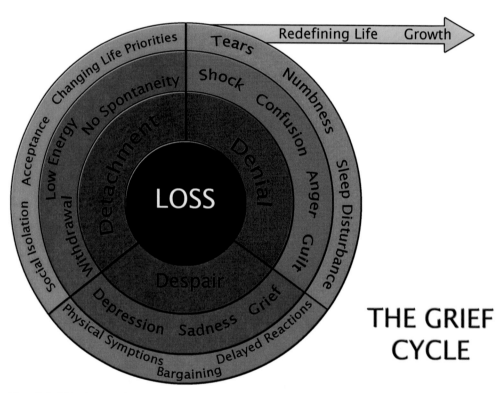

The Grief Cycle

GRIEF

Grief unfolds in stages. Elisabeth Kubler-Ross was the famous Swiss psychiatrist, who in 1969 created the *Five Stages of Grief*. She watched over long-term, terminally ill cancer patients. She comforted them and, in observing her patients, she developed the *Five Stages of Grief*. "Stages" were originally meant to describe Ross's patients' stages of grief as they approached death. These stages have also been used to depict the often overwhelming and confusing stages of grief suffered by loved ones, who lose a family member (spouse, friend) through death. It should also be mentioned that the *Five Stages of Grief* has been expanded to many other arenas where each of us experiences loss and grief for multiple reasons—divorce, job loss, friends moving away, and so on.

The Five Stages of Grief
- **Denial, Disbelief**
- **Anger**
- **Bargaining**
- **Depression-Sadness**
- **Acceptance**

Denial, Disbelief

I usually add the word "shock" to this stage. This is the stage when you are still numb from just hearing the news. Something you might say at this stage is, "I can't believe it!" or "This can't be happening!" This is the stage of being in denial. Your psyche or subconscious can only take in so much information. If it is too painful for you to absorb the event or situation, then you will stay in denial until you can move onto the next phase. Remember there is no formula for dictating how long you stay in each stage. It is a personal journey. The advantage of knowing the stages is for you to be able to identify them while they are happening. "Oh my goodness, I don't even know what to do; I can't think about this right now; my mind is numb; I need to sit here

and try to think." Any one of those statements might represent disbelief and provide insight as to what you are experiencing. "Wow, I'm
probably in shock right now! I need to sit down and just try to be
quiet for a minute." This is not a stage where you are going to start
strategizing logistics or possible outcomes. This is a mind-numbing
phase. Your mind is denying that it is real! So be kind to yourself.

Anger

This is self-explanatory. We've all been there and done that. There are
so many examples I am certain you have several of your own. One
might be that after hearing some shocking news from your partner
(job loss, affair, a secret, poor money investment), you emerge from
phase one into anger. You are steaming mad and you want answers
to questions. You want to know why it happened, when it happened,
what was said or not said. You want to investigate and you are propelled
by anger. The beauty of this phase is that it can be very energizing and
very empowering and very different from the frozen silence of the
shock phase of denial. So at first blush, it feels good to be energized
by anger. The cautionary note is that you don't want to stay stuck in
anger for prolonged periods of time. This stage activates your fight/
flight biophysical chemistry. The prolonged flooding of stress hormones into your system is not healthy. Anger is natural and it can be a
catapult to move forward through to the next stage of "bargaining."

Bargaining

"Let's make a deal!" That's what I call the bargaining phase. This is
the phase where you talk to your Creator and ask for help by cutting
a deal. "I promise to do A, B, C if you'll just bring her back. Please
help me to get through this and I promise I'll never ask you again for
anything else."; "I promise to stop drinking if you'll just help her pull
through this." Whatever your bargaining chip is, this is your time to
deal out your cards while all the time, wishing and hoping for a PASS.
Basically, I'll do this, if you do that (whomever your belief system
relies upon)—promises, promises. This is a less intense form of denial.
At this point, you are starting to strategize and think of options. This

is not the frozen stage of shock. This is the mover and shaker trying to wheel and deal for a different outcome. Obviously, this is energizing the way anger was energizing, but this phase has a more cognitive tone to it, whereas anger was pure emotion.

Depression–Sadness

It should be noted that depression and sadness are two different things. Depression has a series of descriptors that include sadness. Pure sadness or grief does not necessarily result in depression. They have many similar components but are very different in essence. Yet, both of them share this stage of grief. This is the fourth stage of grief. This is an unpleasant place to be. This phase is not energizing. This stage of grief is basically being in the middle of it. This is feeling and rolling around in grief. This is getting in touch with the loss and the pain. Who wants to do that? Why is it important? It is important because this is how you get in touch with your feelings of loss so that you can move on in a healthy manner. If you don't, and you avoid this stage through some sort of self-medication (alcohol, drugs, sex, distractions like being around a lot of people and not processing your inner feelings), then you will delay your journey through what I call "working through" the grief. Whatever it takes, I really advocate for facing the sadness as much as you can—head on.

Certainly, have people nearby to console you or support you. Definitely, if you are feeling very strange—like you are going to hurt yourself or you are exhibiting irrational thoughts—then see a counselor and tell those people closest to you that you think you need help. Aside from signs of depression, pure grief is natural and healthy. Does it feel good? Absolutely not! In the short-term and the long-term you will feel stronger and better if you allow yourself to feel the loss. Then, acknowledge the loss. Talk about the loss. Write about the loss, especially if you like keeping a journal or have no one to talk to. Go outside in your backyard by the apple tree and feel it. If you are having difficulties going to that spot of sadness within yourself, then try to look at something that symbolizes the situation or sadness. Finally, just listen to some very sad and melancholy music or watch a sad movie.

Do anything that can kick-start your efforts in moving beyond this phase to the final phase of acceptance.

Acceptance

First we deny, then we get angry, and then we try to bargain, and then we cry, but at the end of the journey we arrive at the final stage—acceptance. At this phase, the pain is much lessened. They say time heals, and my take on it is, yes, the pain is reduced. The pain retreats to a point that might seem invisible and gone, but it retreats to a point that allows us to go back to functioning and living again. The more "working through" we did in previous phases—by acknowledging each phase and noticing the last phase we just left—the better. Pay attention. That means: SEE IT, SAY THAT YOU SEE IT, TELL SOMEONE ELSE THAT YOU SEE IT, FEEL IT, ACKNOWLEDGE TO YOURSELF THAT YOU FEEL IT, THEN RELEASE IT! Let it go and appreciate the fact that you have moved on, taking a step toward life, love, and the pursuit of your own well-being and happiness. The stage of acceptance is the most energizing phase with the full integration of all the healthy efforts you made happen during your deepest period of pain. You came through to the other side! You arrived at the other end of the tunnel! You made it! What a journey! The more you can do this, the less baggage you will have in life, relationships, challenging situations, and stressful moments. Are you still going to have stressors? Absolutely! However, you will emerge stronger and healthier for all of your efforts in taking care of yourself during your most vulnerable time.

WHAT HAVE YOU LEARNED?

Just to be clear, we all need someone else to reach out toward, but there is another lesson here. The lesson is to learn how to rely upon yourself to take care of yourself. Your job is to check in with yourself and rest—if you feel like resting, talk—if you feel like talking, pray—if you feel like praying, cry—if you feel like crying, and then move onto the next step. In so doing, you will be taking steps to soothe yourself; trust yourself to be OK within yourself. Simply put, if you always default to reaching outside of yourself to feel better—to rely upon someone else to make you feel better—then you are blessed to have those people around you. HOWEVER, I caution you in becoming reliant on others more than yourself. This can be a detriment because over time you might conclude that you can't do it on your own and you will stop paying attention to your inner thoughts and feelings. As a result, you might stop listening and trusting you! This starts out as a simple behavior with others who have good intentions wanting to help you (there are a lot of caregivers in the world). However, you also must learn how to be your own caregiver. Can you do that?

In summary, these "Stages of Grief" are linear, meaning that they are sequential from top to bottom. My client experience has shown that you can go from top to bottom in a split second and then go back down the list in sequence and stay stuck on a particular stage of grief for years. I remember one client who came in alone and was furious. He spoke of his recent divorce and called his ex-wife all kinds of names. He was really upset and was not assimilating into his new role as a divorcee. When I asked him how long he had been divorced (3 months? 4 months?) he told me 13 years. Wow! He was stuck in anger for 13 years—like it had happened yesterday. The goal of course is to get to the bottom—ACCEPTANCE—and feel good.

I hate sounding like a therapist, but when speaking to my clients, I often ask, "Did you work through those feelings?" Actually, what I am referring to is how you are able to transition from one feeling to another. This is especially important because feelings come in layers, and feelings also unfold. In grief, it is imperative to be able to do what you have learned in this book.

Identify your feeling (name how you feel), then acknowledge it by owning that emotion in your heart with the physical manifestation of that emotion in your body.

Example: Sadness can result in tightness in the chest. Release that feeling and allow yourself to move on to the next feeling. This is what I mean when I say "working through" your feelings. You'd be amazed at how STUCK you can become in not moving forward with your feelings or in your relationships when you have not worked through your feelings.

Grief comes in all shapes and sizes. Some people are not familiar with the *Five Stages of Grief*; this short list is really helpful in life because you can point to a stage and say, "Oh, it's a natural grief reaction." The beauty of working through grief allows you to be in touch with your feelings and to heal from the wound, naturally.

Loss is loss. No one can judge you for grieving. We all grieve in our own way. So if anyone says to you, "You should be OVER it by now." Please ignore that advice. It is inaccurate.

As someone who worked in the high-tech sector for 17 years and as a career counselor, executive coach, and psychotherapist, I've heard some terrible workplace examples of how clueless managers or bosses are when it comes to the human condition of grief. I once attended the memorial service of a female friend. The reception was held by her husband in their home. While everyone was sitting quietly around eating and talking, the husband's manager sat at my table and asked him directly, "When are you coming back to work? We really need you." This was on the day of his beautiful wife's memorial service. Unfortunately, I was sitting right at the table; I felt like speaking my mind, but it wasn't my battle.

Also, I had a client years ago who told me that after her husband had unexpectedly died from a heart attack, she returned to work after 3 weeks and was still having a hard time concentrating and completing tasks. Her female manager came up to her after about 3-to-4 weeks and screamed at her saying, "GET OVER IT! HE'S DEAD!"

Believe me, I've heard it all. My opinion is that ignorance is no excuse for being mean. Although I had many emotional and cognitive reactions when I first heard that story, I also wondered what would happen to that female manager when she lost her mate or someone very dear to her. Would she some day remember her harsh words to that employee? I wondered what her life lesson would be that might help her to have more understanding in the future for others.

GRIEF AND INTIMACY

Clearly, being intimate is not just about sex. I am talking about your ability to be mindful of your own emotional and cognitive being. Up to this point, you (the reader) and I (the writer) have been talking about communicating what you feel and think to your most precious partner. When grief descends upon us, it like being in the middle of a dark gray misty fog that swallows us up. Everything is silent around us and nothing really seems to have the same importance. In fact, you can't really relate or understand too much because your inner Self is buried by a deep and all-consuming sadness that just sits there in your heart. All you feel is hurt and pain and sadness.

When this fog of grief surrounds us, our challenge is to "work through" it by acknowledging each feeling, sensation, and thought. To keep working through grief—that is the goal. Our mindfulness is important in helping us to move through grief. This is the healthiest way I know to move forward after a loss.

Unfortunately, some people short-stop the process by self-medicating with illegal substances or alcohol. Misuse of alcohol and other substances only halts the grieving process and stops your growth. Even though over time you might stop crying or even have another relationship, it is quite possible that you may not move through all of the phases of grief. If true, please note that you have blocked your ability at some core level to be intimate with another partner because you have not allowed yourself to be intimate with yourself first. Intimacy begins with Self! If you have not taken care of yourself in a healthy manner to work through the grief, then you haven't taken care of business—"It will come to bite you back when you least expect it." Think of it this way, life hands us lessons to be learned and mastered so we can move on to the next lesson. If you choose not to "deal" with your grief, then the unresolved residue of leftover grief lingers and festers until you deal with it at some future point.

I remember a brilliant doctoral supervisor who once told me, "Unresolved grief is a barrier to intimacy." For years, I remembered

that and automatically assumed he meant being intimate with a partner. Actually, I believe that was his intention. However, over the years I
have expanded its meaning to include YOU! Yes, if you do not resolve
your grief, then you cannot be intimate with yourself, which ultimately
leads to a lack of intimacy with others. I feel very strongly about this.

You'd be shocked at the number of couples who come to me and
one partner would ultimately say something like this, "When my father
died 6 years ago, you were not there for me in a way that I needed you
to be. I have resented you ever since." One particular couple had not
had sex in 6 years. The one who made the statement had been depressed
for a long time; she had performed below standards and lost her job
as a senior executive. Their finances had failed and they argued a lot
or remained distant (avoidance). The one who blamed her mate, also
admitted to drinking alcohol excessively to the point of displaying alcoholic behavior. The other admitted to a one-night stand. Their finances
were in shambles—the list went on and on. These are classic examples of
blocked intimacy caused by grief. How unfortunate that steps had not
been taken sooner to alleviate pain and suffering. They eventually got
divorced.

PERSISTENT COMPLEX BEREAVEMENT DISORDER

There is a diagnosis called "Persistent Complex Bereavement Disorder"
(DSM-5). This serious disorder is clearly evident when there are clear,
reactive symptoms to loss that have extended for years after the loss.
It is important to get professional counseling. I would advise going to
your physician for an evaluation and perhaps considering short-term
medication as an aid in healing from the loss. I do not list them all, but
a few of the most noted symptoms include:

—a prolonged denial about the loss (talking about the deceased
in the present tense, refusal to remove clothing and items of the
deceased after years)

—demonstrating an intense fresh sadness years after the loss
(instant tears)

—physical symptoms around holidays or the anniversary of the death

—a shift in level of functioning after the loss compared to behavior prior to the loss (avoidance of family, friends, or activities)

NORMAL GRIEF VS. DEPRESSION

Normal Grief

- Sadness or emptiness
- Transient physical complaints
- Connection of the sad feelings to the loss
- Acceptance of comfort and support from others
- Displays of anger
- Moments of pleasure and engagement with others
- Temporary guilt and low self-esteem relating specifically to the loss

Depression

- Hopelessness or chronic emptiness
- Ongoing physical complaints
- Inability to pinpoint depression to any particular event in life
- Isolation and refusal of comfort or support from others
- Low-grade irritability (known as irritably depressed)
- Absence of joy or pleasure in life—views life as gloom and doom
- Excessive or inappropriate feelings of guilt and worthlessness

PART IV

Family

TRIANGULATION

When a couple has a fight or argument, it is natural for one partner (or both) to triangulate. This happens when you choose something other than your mate to change the dynamic or emotional energy between you. It could be work, neighbors, in-laws, alcohol, sports, friends, kids, and so on. By itself, the other person (child, friend, in-law) or the other thing (career) can be good. However, when it is triangulated into the relationship as a TRIANGLE—it has a purpose and an outcome. When there is conflict between you and your spouse, the act of triangulating another person (example: you call your mother and complain about your husband being mean to you), changes the intensity of the tension between you and your mate.

Simply put, the tension between a husband and wife when they argue can exist before, during, and after the argument. One or the other might subconsciously divert some of the tension by triangulating someone or something else. Let's say you and your husband have a big fight; your husband might go to work early and stay later or do it for several days following the argument. Even though it is work, it helps him cope and relieves the intensity of the stress he feels at home "walking on eggshells" around you. So the purpose of triangulation is to decrease stress and tension and to deflect that stress and tension between the two of you. The outcome is decreased tension (temporarily) and also the triangulation of something else into your relationship. The unfortunate part of this scenario is that it can become habitual and cyclical. Over time, you include this other person or thing more into your troubles and conflicts, instead of addressing them head-on with your mate.

How many times have you heard that everything in life is about balance? Everything I have mentioned here is a natural part of your life with your partner, your family, and your lifestyle. However, triangulation is the over-involvement of a third entity (person or thing) just at the time of fighting; it is subconsciously used to help the user feel better emotionally. So, you don't consciously say out loud, "Gee, I'm going to triangulate my mother-in-law and tell her what a drag it is to be married to her daughter." No, in actuality, the subconscious choice comes as a natural reaching out to include something or someone else to focus on, so that you can cope better.

It is unhealthy. It is dysfunctional. The classic example—after a fight when the couple is not talking to each other and the mother tells her 8-year-old daughter to tell her father that she will not talk to him unless he apologizes. So the child is the messenger to carry statements back and forth between the couple. Plus, all three of them (daughter, mom, and dad) could be sitting at the kitchen table eating dinner together and the mother instructs the daughter in front of the father! This is clear triangulation.

Over time, psychological research has documented the negative results of triangulation. It is known that specifically with teens, the increase in triangulation (using the teenager to be the messenger and the emotional punching bag, figuratively speaking) for the parents, is not good. For example, the teenager who is consistently drawn into the parental conflict will suffer on the inside and the outside. The teenager is no longer allowed to be a teenager; instead they have to come home and be a referee for yelling parents who can't control themselves. This can result in self-blame. We know that kids no matter what age always blame themselves for the fight, for the separation, and for the divorce. The kids think it is their fault!

The more teenagers are embroiled in this unhealthy dynamic between parents, the more likely it is they can be negatively affected in their relationship with each parent. The parent-teenager

relationship breaks down. Communication with your child is crucial at any age. At the most sensitive time of your child's growth
when they start to outgrow childhood, triangulation can set them
up for poor self-image and poor self-esteem. The challenge for
parents with children is that these parents have to adjust to the
ever-changing needs of their children as they go from infancy to
young adults. Every age is a tender age. In the adolescent phase,
hormones rage and teenagers demand autonomy. Yet, they are little
children in growing bodies. So at this crucial stage, to abandon
your child by destroying any chance they might have of knowing you, loving you, and leaning on you as the adult—is horrible.
You have destroyed your relationship with your teenager by simply
using them as a conduit for communication with your partner
because you don't want to be the first one to open your mouth,
eat humble pie, and talk to your spouse. **This is SERIOUS! Stop
it! Only you can take responsibility for your current relationship with your spouse. So, first take responsibility and,
second, do something about it (without triangulating your
child or others).**

Couple

LOCKED IN A CYCLE…SO WHAT IS LIFE LIKE WHEN THERE IS NO 72-HOUR RULE?

Well, it is a lot of blaming and it is all about the past.

For many couples, this can go on for years and for many of those couples it is 'same 'ole same 'ole'. Can you imagine having the same old argument over and over? Life is not about rewinding. It is NOT ABOUT GOING INTO THE PAST, IT IS ABOUT HERE AND NOW. But, couples have their hot buttons and like to rehash and rewind. So, not only do they have arguments in which they both know their roles and script by heart, but they can each predict what's going to happen next and they watch while they participate in the ugliness. What a waste of time, life, and energy.

The Blame Game is a huge ugly game and it can take off with a life of its own. I equate it to mud slinging at your partner—until the hurts and resentments are piled so high you can't even see each other, let alone hear each other on the opposite sides of the mud wall. The negative ramifications of this are far-reaching and can turn into a habit that continues for years.

As a result, communication breaks down. Who wants to start a dialogue when it will just wind up in the same old argument? Oftentimes, one partner will shut down and do what I call hide behind the rock. The other partner is intent on engaging—all fireworks ahead. "Let's talk." "What's wrong?" Their goal is to lure the other out from behind the rock so that they can play and engage together. Ultimately, with arguments, the greater the chances are that those arguments escalate to real ugliness. Perhaps, one person decides to shut down and make a life behind the rock (figuratively speaking). After many buttons have been pushed, they can't take it anymore and they come roaring out from behind the rock and a HUGE argument ensues. The person behinds the rock loses a huge part of who they are or who they used to be and instead spend life reacting to their partner. The person behind the rock can be anxious, depressed, or fearful. Or, they could simply be hesitant and cautious about revealing their true thoughts and feelings in front of a roaring lion. The loud person who raises their voice yelling at their partner to come out from behind the rock often views life as frustrating and exasperating. They say to themselves, "Why is it I'm the only one who is always trying to communicate? What is the problem? I am so tired of trying." And so the dance begins….

I once sat in front of a couple who was not the usual polite couple on the first night of therapy. In the first 11 minutes, they immediately escalated into blame about the past. They went on for quite a while. I can be very direct and assertive in couple's sessions. However, in this case I listened and observed their dance. After 30 minutes, I spoke loud enough for them to hear me, I asked them, "When was this exactly?" They turned to look at me like I had 3 heads (I think they forgot I was in the room), and they said, "Why 20 years ago of course!" I responded: "WHAT? You've been sitting in my office yelling at each other about something that happened 20 years ago? Well," I responded emphatically, "Listen to me very carefully. You can have the rest of the hour but IF YOU COME BACK NEXT WEEK WE ARE NOT GOING TO TALK ABOUT ANYTHING THAT HAPPENED 20 YEARS AGO!" They immediately turned toward each other on the couch and continued their dance. This chaotic and cyclical type of communication is ingrained and habitual.

COMMUNICATION BLOCKS

Block: Drawing a conclusion without data.
Example: "He's probably worried."

Alternative: Get proof, verify your perception/interpretation. Check in with your partner to find out if you are accurate in your interpretation.

Block: Clichés or overused expressions can be confusing.
Example: "Don't rock the boat."
Alternative: Give specific examples to clarify your meaning.

Block: Generalize.
Example: "It never changes; he never asks me."
Alternative: Stop generalizing. "Check in with your partner."

Block: Blame or Criticism
Example: Finger-pointing or sarcasm
Alternative: Help stop the conflict by refusing to get defensive.

Ask your partner to talk to you in a calm and positive manner without criticism, and you do the same.

Block: Labeling your partner
Example: Rigid, domineering, conservative, mean
Alternative: Describe your partner's behavior to him or her, don't use labels.

Block: Negatives
Example: Don't … Can't … Won't
Alternative: Restate your point positively.

Block: Unrelated issues—focusing on more than one topic
Example: Bringing up an unrelated issue that lacks detail.
Alternative: Stop getting off track when discussing one topic only.

Block: Vagueness
Example: Using an unclear word, phrase or statement, "I don't know"; "Whatever."
Alternative: Ask your mate for more information to help clarify.

Block: Automatic "NO!"
Example: "That's impossible!"; "Out of the question!"; "I can't."
Alternative: First, acknowledge that you heard him or her say no and then provide reasoning.

Block: Questions, Questions, Questions

Example: "Why did you do it that way?"; "Don't you know any better?"

Alternative: You ask a question to extract more exact information. The questions given above are covering up actual judging statements. The questioner does not really want an answer to the question. You might say, "What do you suggest?"; "What were you expecting or hoping for?"

Block: YES/BUT

Example: "Yes that is true, but let me tell you how."; "Yes, but it is wrong."

Alternative: Restate it by substituting BUT with AND.

Block: Contradiction/Mixed messages between words and behavior.

Example: She asks to do it alone then demands help! Or, he acts helpless and then takes over in a dominant manner.

Alternative: Point out what was first stated and then how the behavior of the person is the opposite of what they stated (mixed messages).

MIND READING

As mentioned previously, OVER communication rather than UNDER communication is the goal of this book. Mind reading is not allowed! The reason it is not allowed is because it can be and, often is, the downfall of even the simplest conversation. Mind reading gets in the way. You'd be amazed how often we think we know what our mate is thinking. Granted, if you've been with your spouse for years, does that mean you automatically "know" what s(he) is saying? As much as it is tempting, the answer to this is, "NO!" A relationship does not work on automatic pilot! A relationship does not just float along! A relationship does not just take care of itself! IF you continue to NOT TALK and let time pass in silence, that does NOT mean that you are communicating clearly or truthfully or accurately with each other. You are totally guessing on that one. If I were there to bet you money on it, you'd lose!

I remember one couple—they sat on my couch—both highly educated with two children. They'd been married about 12 years and all the wife did in session was cry. I couldn't get her to talk. I would ask questions and she would sit there and weep. He kept blaming their problems on some medication she probably needed. He "knew" that she loved him. So he devoted his time in session to professing his love for her. FINALLY, I got her very close (after 5 sessions) to coughing up what she was choking on. She almost backed away, but I put more pressure on her at that moment instead of sitting there for another 5 sessions just to get her close enough to talk again. I told her that he deserved to know the truth. I told her that the biggest gift she could give him was the truth. I told her that her tears were symptomatic of something deep (who knows? guilt, shame, fear). Anyway, I instructed her to lift her head, to look him in the eye and to tell him what her truth was at that moment. She said, "I want a divorce." He was SHOCKED! He got defensive and spent the remaining 20 minutes professing his love and telling her that she really loved him and that he "knew" she did not mean it. He did not see it coming at all. Much later, in another session, I questioned his logic in "knowing" that she loved him as much as he loved her. He cited simple things, like when he asked her if everything was OK? Then, she would respond that everything was fine. Or, when he asked her if she loved him and she said that she did.

I'm NOT saying that you need to distrust anything your partner says to you. ABSOLUTELY NOT! I'm saying he was holding on to the words she spoke but did not tune into the vibe or behavior she demonstrated. He heard the words he wanted to hear from her then went about his business. She did not speak her truth to him. She said what he wanted to hear so that she could continue to avoid facing her own reality. They hobbled along like that for years! How many times did I see that on my therapy couch?—too many sad hours helping couples face their TRUTH so that they could start on a different track and start being kind to each other, either while they began infusing their relationship with hope toward future intimacy, or as they began the sad journey toward separation and divorce.

GAME PLAYING—THE NEGATIVE DANCE/POWER STRUGGLE/HIDDEN AGENDAS

Some couple's therapists see their clients as a couple and automatically separate each of them to individual sessions but have them return as a couple. It is a viable theoretical premise to do so. Other psychotherapists only follow that model when and if necessary. In other words, they separate some couples and not others. Some therapists refuse to separate couples, no matter what. It can be tricky and depends on why you feel it is important to see the couple separately. The standard "at risk" dilemma is that when you separate the couple, a few things can happen. This makes coming back together as the couple client awkward or complicated. One reason, of course, is that the individual partner (he/she) would tell the therapist a secret and then you as the therapist become the container of the secret but would be obligated to work diligently when the couple is united in therapy to encourage and engage the partner with the secret to reveal it for the benefit of the couple unit (this gets explained in the individual session prior to any secrets being revealed). However, it can get sticky. Another less complicated scenario is that the individual who comes alone for one session, might see that as an opportunity to bitch and complain and basically dump on his or her partner who is not there to hear it all. The third dilemma is that separating the couple can cause doubt or mistrust of what their partner said to the therapist in private.

The goal of the therapist is to facilitate each partner's ability to communicate their needs and wants to their spouse in a healthy manner. I've done all three modalities and each has its successes and failures. On which approach I use, it depends on the couple, the couple's functionality, the couple's issues, the trust between them—it just depends. In the past few years, I have chosen to not separate couples in therapy. However, there is a real downfall to this. Certainly, it makes it less sticky, but if the individuals are not strong enough to raise their concerns in the couple's sessions in front of each other, then the therapist can really lose out on hidden and unspoken issues (affairs, substance abuse, anger issues, etc.).

When one partner is dominant or physically abusive, this makes him or her not an especially good candidate for couple's therapy. There are wonderful professional psychotherapists who are experts in the Domestic Violence Cycle; it takes an expert to engineer couple's sessions with this type of couple.

In general, the average non-violent couple who is high-functioning (non-abusive) but with your garden-variety of dynamics such as power struggles, hidden agendas, and poor communication skills make good candidates for certain types of couple's therapy. However, the challenge for the therapist is knowing what the issues are for the couple and what therapeutic approach will best fit their needs.

From a therapeutic viewpoint, **the key is to identify the problem from both the couple's perspective and from a clinical point of view.** It is imperative to identify the issues and the therapeutic approach that can intervene in alleviating those issues. As with the fishing metaphor, it is all about the type of fish you are going to catch. Is it salt-water or fresh-water? What pound or weight of fish are you going to fish for? What is the modality (bait, rod, fishing line, weight, etc.)? What region of the country are you going to visit? In therapy, my job would be to identify the problem and then to step-by-step lay out the treatment plan geared toward symptom alleviation (elimination) and improvement of communication skill sets. Then, the ultimate goal would be to move toward an increased intimacy with improvement of trust, respect, and teamwork.

ARE YOU BOTH PLAYING GAMES?

The goal is to feel better about yourself first as an individual. Then, the goal is to put more energy into your relationship, so that each partner feels better about Self, life, and the future together. This is a positive self-fulfilling cycle that gains more traction over time. Basically, the goal is a positive outcome. However, this is NOT just problem-solving. It is helping the couple collaboratively problem-solve together and have them increase their skill set toward future problem-solving when the next stressor comes into play. The goal is to do the work, remember the tools, and find success without taking the therapist home with you (figuratively speaking)!

When there is a power dynamic or power struggle in a relationship, I usually tell parables or give metaphors. Here is one more metaphor: If you and your partner are at a company picnic, one game you can play is the one called Tug o' War. That's right it's war. Each of you is on separate ends of the rope, tugging, pulling, yelling, yanking, digging your feet in the sand—totally committed to pulling until it ends. You will NOT give up! You are in competition with each other. Well, guess what? That is definitely NOT going to work in your relationship. You're going to have to find some other healthier way to communicate. Don't you agree? I tell my couples that the Tug o' War game is a no winner. It is a LOSE-LOSE scenario. All I ever ask of my couple clients is that one of them (I do not care who does it first), just ONE of them decides to do it differently and drop the rope.

As soon as you or your spouse drops the rope (figuratively) then guess what? GAME OVER! That's right, there is no longer a game being played. THIS IS HUGE! I can not emphasize this enough. NO GAMES! NO GAMES! NO GAMES! Stop it now! Please stop playing this game. It goes nowhere except into cycles, circles and loops—it just keeps repeating. Why are you working against each other? Why do you choose to exhibit all of those negative behaviors, feelings, and thoughts AGAINST the person you chose to love, live with, and make a future? To be honest, it makes no sense. So if you are willing to really make changes—ALL CHANGES BEGIN WITH YOU FIRST! And, my hope is that if both of you are reading this part together, my message is this, "Stop waiting for the other person to do it first." I hear that all day long when one person says out loud: "Well, I'm waiting for him to make the first step. Why should I have to take the first step? It's always me who has to take the first step."

My answer to that statement is to stop waiting. Otherwise, you are still playing the game. GAMES ARE NOT AUTHENTIC! GAMES ARE FALSE AND COMPETITIVE! GAMES HIDE THE REAL YOU FROM YOURSELF AND FROM YOUR PARTNER! THERE IS NO INTIMACY IN GAME PLAYING! Please I beg of you, stop now! Unite as one! Do not work against each other. Work together. The world is your competition. Your job is to work together as you face life's challenges. If you want the other person to drop the rope first, then you are cheating yourself and your lover of a future of intense love, trust, and fun! What a waste of energy. All head games,

mind games—any kind of game between the two of you is negative—
energetically wasteful.

I would finish by saying that game playing can be a barrier to
connecting authentically to Self. You have blocked You, at your core.
At this point, you are the tail of the dog whipping around—lost in a
world of falseness. You are afraid to even be with yourself and be connected to Self. So you play a game with yourself first and then loop
yourself into a relationship with a partner who is willing to play along
at both a conscious and subconscious level. Believe me, the years will
pass and you will be so far gone and disconnected from who you really are, you will wonder what happened. You will look around and
be completely confused as to how you got there. I'll tell you how
you got there. You got there because TODAY YOU DECIDED TO
STAY IN DENIAL! When you did not face the truth within yourself,
you started down the path of being lost when you didn't spend 5-to-
15 minutes a day alone and have a conversation with yourself without
being interrupted. You gradually meandered down the path of lost
when you stopped "checking in" with yourself first and with your
partner second.

DO NOT COMPETE WITH YOUR PARTNER!

The goal is for you and your partner to be a team and face life together. Life is the competition, not your partner! Other people, situations, and places will be the challenges you face as a couple—when
you move across the country and don't know anyone; when one of
you loses a job and for the first time in your life you are dependent on
someone else's salary; when your child is born at risk and no one on
earth can understand the feelings you experience in that moment of
helplessness. Together, you are the couple unit that faces life together.
The two of you combine forces to deal with life's ups and downs. Do
not compete with your mate! It is destructive; it is divisive. It will tear
your relationship down.

How do you combine forces if your togetherness is defined by
being on guard, cautious, and defensive? How can you combine forces

if you do not allow yourself to be yourself in a relationship? If you spend your time trying to outdo each other or outperforming each other, then your relationship will suffer. If each of you consistently competes against the other, then the real fruits of the marriage (showing up and being yourself) are lost and buried beneath the game being played. Bottom line—it feels similar to: "Do not trust"; "Be on guard"; "I can beat you this time"; "I'm the winner *(you're the loser)*"; "I haven't forgotten the last time you made me lose!" These might seem like mild statements. From my perspective, they spell separation, competition, aggression, lack of trust, game playing, and being at odds—rather than connected. Believe me, if you just show up and be who you are in the relationship, there are lots of opportunities in life to have differences and to have dissimilar tastes, ideas, values, and thoughts. That alone can be at the very most, challenging, and at the very least, stimulating, as you both work to discover and uncover each other—together.

GAME NAMES

Break up/Make up

This is where the cycle of stops and starts occurs. Couples fight; they make up. They fight and break up and they make up with lots of, "I'm sorry." This is a vicious cycle. It is inauthentic and can be very habitual. It is essential that you do something to stop this cycle. If you are caught up in this game, you might have to see a therapist to stop it, or go to a couple's retreat to help you. However, if you are both strong enough, you could sit down together when you are in a good space, write down some ground rules that you both agree to that would help you take steps toward stopping this Break UP/Make UP cycle! It can be done. You just have to BOTH decide that it is not working for you—then do something about it.

I know of a couple who married and divorced each other five times! So what are your thoughts about that? That obviously is an extreme example, but not different from those who constantly fight and involve everyone else in their drama and then make up and do it again a few days or weeks later. Stop it!

I Don't Know

This is a game. Some therapists might say it is a result of poor self-esteem. Others might say that it comes from a family-of-origin issue where as a little person you lived in a family where you were not allowed to have an opinion. Or, in your family when you were asked a question and you answered, you were criticized, no matter what your opinion might have been. As an adult, you always answer your boss, lover, and friends with, "I don't know." Once again, you are not allowing your real Self to emerge. You are locked in a hiding place. The problem is that you have accomplished this so well for so long that you have actually started hiding from yourself as much as from everyone else. It is a coping mechanism. It is a cycle—a game with Self and others. It is fear-based. It goes nowhere. Again, there are many avenues open to the person who repeats, "I don't know." You could go to therapy, you could have a quiet Self-Talk conversation in which you commit to stopping; you could ask a friend or partner to help you stop; you could correct yourself every time you say it. Upon correcting yourself, you would STATE YOUR OPINION at that moment, even if you have to sit there for a few minutes to figure out what exactly your opinion is. Remember this habit has been going on for decades and it will take consistency and time to heal.

It's Your Fault, Not Mine

This is the game where one person refuses to look within. This is an ancient way for them to cope in life. When in doubt, just point your finger and blame, blame, blame. There is little psychological insight on one side of the couch. The one pointing the finger is the one who is PROJECTING all of their stuff onto their partner and, in reality, it is a reflection of their deepest worries. They cannot and will not OWN IT! Their defense mechanisms are fragile. By that I mean that this is someone I would tread very lightly with in therapy. I would not push them unnecessarily. Even though I can become very dominant and forceful in sessions, it would do no good unless I am just hoping the person will get up and walk out in the middle of the session. This is a tough scenario. This is challenging only because from my perspective, therapy would be a slow go to no go, if you get my drift. My sense is that one or both partners might benefit from individual therapy to help identify their respective roles in this partnership. Also, this would provide an opportunity to help the blamed partner see his or her role and gain strength and insight and help them derail from their position as the source of constant blame.

Also, the blamer would benefit from having individual therapy to help with identifying his or her role in projecting and deflecting so automatically. Over time, perhaps this person will become stronger (in ego) so that they can OWN their part of this negative dance.

Pick Pick, Nag Nag

You see this often as a therapist. As human beings we get bogged down in bad habits in communicating and thinking. In a long-term relationship, it is important to wake up and listen to how we communicate with our partners. IF you observe yourself, then you can begin the process of unhooking yourself from the cycle. The "pick pick, nag nag" drama is one criticism after another. I often see both couples and individual clients come in—usually more women than men—who complain out loud that they feel like their spouse is their third child (they would say this in front of their spouse). Or, they would state that they are tired of telling their partner what to do. The partner, of course, would say that he is tired of her telling him what to do. The challenge in therapy is to make change happen. I challenge either partner to notice that their particular dance is happening again, and whoever notices it first is encouraged to say something. Oftentimes, what this means for the female (who is most often the one who notices) is that she feels resentful because I am asking her to help her partner get on board. Certainly, we could and would try to have the partner who is perceived as doing less, do more without having to ask. However, it is equally important for her to ask for help rather than fold her arms on her chest and refuse to help the situation. What that leads to is a full implosion or explosion where she can't take the fact that she is the nitpicker and she can't stand holding back from her criticism. She says, "Nothing gets done, unless I point out that it needs to be done! I'm tired of it!"

Several options exist and have been tried—everything from a schedule (Wednesday is my toilet cleaning day); Blackberry reminders; notes on the refrigerator; or learning how to ask your partner without the whining, or fury attached—"Hey sweetie, when you get a chance, can you be sure to do the laundry today?"

Many discussions have focused on his perspective, that he did not forget, but he was going to get to it on his time schedule (which did not get spoken out loud), even though it was not agreeable to her timetable (which did not get spoken out loud either). It is imperative that communication be done around what is a priority, what is intent, what is acceptable, how to ask if the schedule slips, and compliments back and forth to support your partner's efforts toward positive change. One thing is for sure, the nagging and the downward spiral of resentment and frustration that stem from nagging do not work for either partner and really looks ugly when viewed by third party family members from the outside.

Example: I remember one young couple with two little children; the wife's biggest concern (they both worked full-time) was that he did not just flop down on the couch right after coming home from work and saying hello. She wanted him to take the laundry basket upstairs while he was on his way upstairs anyway. He was agreeable but forgetful. So we worked out some fail-safe scenarios that would keep him mindful of this one important chore. You'd be amazed how happy they became when the laundry basket was no longer an issue. She felt supported by his efforts to help and he felt good for being supportive. It changed the entire evening between them night after night. Sometimes, small things can make a big difference in the outcome. For that couple, it allowed them to move deeper to the other emerging deeper issues between them. They did the work and they survived and thrived as a result of their courage and love.

I'm Fine, Don't Look Now, but I'm Angry

This is stuffed anger. "Everything's fine," she says, while slamming kitchen cupboards—mixed signals between what she is saying and how she is acting. The vibe doesn't match the words. It is very confusing and very discounting. If my partner is slamming kitchen cupboards and gritting her teeth and telling me that everything is fine, I am going to feel shut out and disconnected from her. I know that she is not telling me what is really going on. How can I comfort her if she will not let me in? How can I change what is upsetting her if she will not let me know what I did wrong or how I disappointed her? If it was something outside of our relationship, I want to be there for her, but I DO NOT WANT TO BE A PUNCHING BAG (figuratively speaking).

Once again, the challenge is to calm down, sit down, and start talking. Stop saying everything is fine if it is not fine! Walk in the door and say, "I am so frustrated right now, I can't even talk about it, but I want you to know that I need a little space until I can compose myself—today was not good." At least an announcement like that gives your partner a "heads up" that you are in a foul mood, that it has nothing to do with him or her, and that you need some space to get it together—you will talk later. I actually love that part! Announce that you are angry! Say it out loud. Don't act it—say it! That is the key (move your mouth and speak). It can solve a lot of unnecessary heartache. As a therapist, I see couples who have arguments on top of other arguments and pretty soon they don't know why or how the argument got started in the first place!

Fix Me. Help Me. I'm Helpless

This is the person or couple who comes to therapy to be fixed. Right away, I inform them that my style does not allow for them to be the victim or to be the person or client who needs fixing. I don't fix anyone. I provide tools, I provide information, I can be your advocate, or I can be the devil's advocate but I do not make you better, and I refuse to call you my patient. That word specifically depicts power over someone. My style is collaborative. It is give and share and facilitate and admonish or advocate. Once that is announced it really puts the client on the spot because they have to decide if they want to work in therapy rather than watch me work to find the answer as to how to fix them. This game is a LOSE-LOSE, essentially, because it would mean that even if I could fix you, the next time there is a crisis you would have to come back so that I could fix you again—which means you aren't really fixed, are you? So the answer to that one is, "I don't look upon people as needing to be fixed." Actually, I view people as getting in a rough spot or getting stuck for the moment and they need help in moving on to the next step.

Now, with respect to this game, HELP ME I'M HELPLESS. It probably has roots in some family-of-origin messages or trauma. My job is to help this person find another role in life that would prove to be more positive and healthy. You'd be amazed if you were a fly on the wall and saw some VERY DRAMATIC CHANGES in my clients once they knew that they could not lean on me!

Example: I remember one client who came in with a long list of ailments. It was an actual list of DSM diagnosis codes as to what was wrong with him. He wept and told me how bad things were for him. My hope was that I could show some compassion, but he was so insistent on telling me how sick he was that I stopped him cold. I told him my thoughts on that. Furthermore, I informed him that if he wanted to come see me in future sessions, he needed to rethink his role in being the victim. I told him that I expected a lot from him and that I would completely understand if I was not a good fit for his needs.

It's a long story but he made a huge 180-degree turn in a few short sessions (less than 6 sessions). He was awesome! It was awesome! It's like he knew it but no one ever called him on it and once I put him "on notice," he blossomed like a flower. He became more aware of his cognitions. His behavior changed and he started to smile. He actually found JOY in his life. There is so much more I could share with you about the dramatic changes he achieved with lots of determination! I still get excited when I think about him. It was so rewarding to be able to see someone take charge of his own happiness. His smile just kept getting broader and bigger and more beautiful.

I KNOW! I Know. I HAVE to be Right, Smarter, Better

This is a competition game. Oh my goodness, what a lot of pressure this person has to be under to always be right or smarter! What a drag! They are so insecure they pretend that they know even though they

might not know. Let me qualify that by saying, this is NOT to say
that people who frequently repeat, "I know"—do Not know! There
are some people who probably know and say "I know" for one set of
reasons, but the point is this—the person who does NOT know and
says, "I know," probably has the same underlying insecurities as the
one who knows.

So let's call them PERSON A (they know) and PERSON B
(they don't know, they are faking it). My sense is that both are insecure, have low self-esteem, and habitually say it out loud; it comes
from a subconscious place. They are not aware that they say it often.
PERSON A wants to prove that they know and strives to keep suc-
ceeding and is very competitive at work and across-the-board in all
relationships. PERSON B has been coping so long in a world that
does not always make complete sense to him. Either through lack of
education or life experience, PERSON B continually states, "I know,
I know." In actuality, they are saying that to feel better, perhaps to be
accepted, or maybe like PERSON A to compete and be better than
the next person. The major difference between the two, of course, is
that one person is knowledgeable, perhaps an expert in their field, and
has been very successful. The other person, (PERSON B), has limited
experience but feels a need to be important and recognized as wise
and right.

Similarly, my belief is that neither one of them hears how they
come across. Their intention might be to compete, but they have been
saying this one phrase for a lifetime and they no longer hear themselves saying it. Each person (A & B) uses this game to operate and
cope with life, people, and events. To them these magical words "I
KNOW," gives them power and propels them forward.

For PERSON B, the words ease their underlying anxiety in not
knowing or wanting to be the best or better than someone else. My
sense is that over time, they probably have convinced themselves that
they do know and they are right. So what might have started out as
method of coping with stress or anxiety, has now evolved into a habit
and a conviction that they are indeed knowledgeable. Perhaps, they
feel that no one will love them unconditionally so that they need to

be good, or right, or better in order to be accepted by others. PERSON A, on the other hand, is trying to be heard by the boss and to be acknowledged as the best. This person wants to be king of the hill and top of the mountain. This person has information, experience, and credibility and also habitually uses this adopted role to cope with wanting more and believing that they deserve more.

The unfortunate outcome of this game, as with all of the games mentioned, is that when someone is entrenched in a game, they are inauthentic. So just like any other game mentioned here in this book and the many more I have not mentioned, these individuals are separating themselves from others. How can you be connected to someone else when you are not connected to Self first? This game results in them being separated from others. How do you respond to someone who says repeatedly, "I know, I KNOW!" Wow! The first thing that comes to my mind is that they don't know, or they want to know, or they're really hurting inside, and they are so shut off from others! My sense is that I am not allowed to be with them or have a relationship with them because they will not let me in; they are too busy knowing it all! They have erected a HUGE WALL around themselves. If this is true, PERSON A might be fine because their goal is to be king of the mountain anyway. We all know there is only one spot at the top of the mountain and it is lonely up there. On the other hand, PERSON B has it harder. If they have adopted this role as a way of coping, wanting to be seen as smarter than they are, the sad part is that whatever acceptance they wanted from others is lost. This is due partly because of the same principle I mentioned previously. How can you accept someone who spends their time in life convincing others that they know? There's that wall again. How can I accept you if you won't let me in? On the plus side, I have seen people move away from operating this way.

THE SILENT TREATMENT

I would have couples come in and tell me that sometimes they would not talk to each other for 5 days after a fight! This is not the kind of silence that is avoidant behavior (not wanting to engage in conflict). No, this is punishment. This is a game called, "I will punish you by withdrawing my love." This behavior only adds to the already-present distancing that has taken place between the couple. I would hear couples still arguing about the silent treatment from the last fight and how it hurt them and confused them and prolonged the painful conflict between them. Silence does not mean that resolution is nearby. If anything, it just intensifies the already-brewing, unsettled atmosphere between each partner. The silent treatment is very hurtful and can erode an already fragile relationship. The couples I saw participate in this mind game had been doing it for years and were shocked by my strong negative reaction to their dance. After all, it is the exact opposite of what I value.

I believe in communication and collaboration and connection. The triple "C" effect! Anything less is a relationship ripe for conflict at the very worst, or at the bare minimum, an opportunity to drift further apart—"hobbling along." There are many couples out there (perhaps you are reading these words right now), who are hobbling along in their marriage or partnership. Is it an abusive marriage? Perhaps not. Is it a disconnected marriage? Perhaps not. Is it a strongly unpleasant marriage? Perhaps not. What is it then? It is a marriage that looks OK from the outside. However, the real core of the marriage is untouched, meaning that there is probably a lack of real intimacy (sincere conversations about thoughts, feelings, and behaviors). There might even be a lack of shared activities (or not a lot of them). For certain, there can be too many unresolved arguments that just get stuffed under the rug without dialogue or real exchange of inner thoughts and feelings before, during, and after an argument. Instead, it can result in lots of yelling, then lots of silence. It sounds chaotic and it often looks chaotic.

Extremes like this in a marriage are not good. The ups and downs of possibly arguing or yelling to get your point across, then hours or days of silence, and then return to normal activity like nothing happened is very unhealthy. It is disingenuous and only adds multiple layers of both behaviors and feelings on top of what is at the core issue for the couple. If it keeps brewing and each of you keeps reacting to the other and then over-react to each other's reactions, nothing really gets better—how can it feel good? How can you build trust? How can you relax and laugh and have fun together? Where do you go from here?

To me, silence is much more than me advocating that you start talking. Most certainly I do, however, I am advocating that you start talking about the silence and how it feels and what it means to you and ask your partner for their feedback and what they are experiencing during that same time frame. Now, you are having a real conversation! The intimacy begins by honestly reaching out to each other. Is there risk in reaching out to your partner when in the past it has not been successful? Absolutely! However, to not do it, or to not try again, or to not try to do it differently than before would be a major loss. To remain hobbling along does not have a good prognosis over time for both personal or growth as a couple in the long-term.

IDENTIFY YOUR DANCE

This is an exercise I did with some couples in therapy. I would give each of them a yellow sheet of paper and have them draw their own dance on the paper as I asked questions such as: "What happened next?"; "Then what happened?"; "What did you do when she did that?"; "What was your first feeling?"; "What was your first thought?" Partners had to identify their role in the couple dance and how each of them acted toward and against the other, before the upset, during the upset, and after the upset. **Can you identify your dance?**

Steps

1. Each partner takes a piece of paper and draws a large circle on it about 8 inches in diameter.
2. Think about the last big argument you both had. Can you remember when that was? Do you remember how it unfolded? If so, use that last argument as a reference for this exercise.

3. Start at the top of the circle and write the word "Argument/ Blow Up."

4. Before you start completing your circle, prepare your thoughts about the sequence of events during your last argument. Write in a workbook or journal the steps that led you up to the big blow up (perhaps on the back of the same paper or on a separate paper—see below for example). What do you notice first in your body or thoughts that get you upset? Write it down. Then, what do you notice as the next step as you get more upset? What is that behavior? Do you yell? Do you get silent? Do you walk out of the room? Write it down. Just before the huge argument, what did you say or do to your partner? Were you in the same room? Were you still talking? Were you crying? What were the words you said? How did you feel emotionally? Name that feeling. What were the layers of feelings (disappointment, sadness, irritation, anger, rage)?

5. Go back to the circle and start at the 6:00 o'clock position. Plot the sequence of events that led up to the argument (it could be three or five phases). Use your workbook paragraphs as a guide to help you jot down the sequence of feelings, thoughts, and behaviors. Write them down with an up arrow leading from one phase to the next.

6. After you reach the 12:00 o'clock position where you have written THE ARGUMENT, continue down the right side of the circle with the down arrow in between and write down three-to-five stages of what happens to you immediately following the big blow up (use your workbook space to identify the sequence of events for you). Are you quiet? Are you alone in a room? Do you cry or yell? What is the phase after that? Do you walk on eggshells and not talk? What's next? How do you feel? What is the sequence of feelings for you? Do you stew over the issue, or do you make up? Do you look at your partner for clues to a make up? Or, do you distance yourself and ignore each other? What do you do and what do you feel? Write it down.

7. After your circle is complete, sit at the kitchen table together (no interruptions) and merge your circles together on a new sheet of

paper so that the circles are concentric (one inside the other). It does not matter whose circle is on the inside or the outside. In this manner, you will be able to see how you behave and what is happening to your partner in response to your action or attitude.

8. Once you have compiled the concentric circles, you can sit and talk about your dynamic cycle. This is your dance! You've just identified your dance. This is how you act and react together as a couple. In stage acting, they call it "foiling" off of each other. This can be tremendously helpful in slowing down the dance on paper so that you can really have an in-depth conversation of what your role feels like while you are able to listen to your partner's description of their experience at the same time.

CONGRATULATIONS! This can be a very powerful tool in helping you identify what behaviors you have and other behaviors you might choose instead. My couples LOVE this exercise! They describe to me that it really helps them to understand the ebb and flow of the upset (argument) and it offers them an opportunity to choose a different way of thinking/perceiving that evolves into different feelings and behavior. They also tell me that they actually felt more intimate with their partner because describing their dance to each other helps them reveal their inner assumptions and hurts. You know how it goes, once revealed, the negative perception and emotions lose their impact and can often be replaced with more positive feelings. Good luck.

THE DANCE

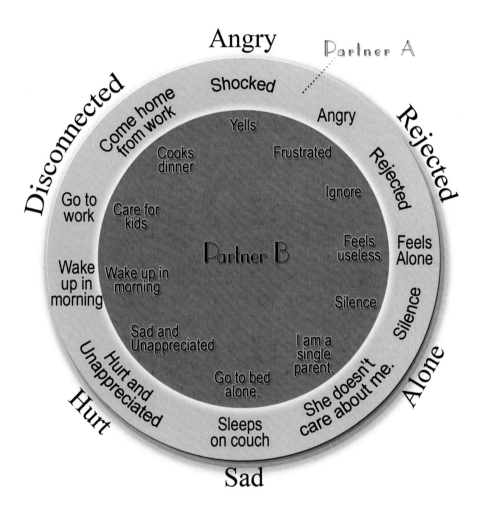

Partner A = Outer Circle
Partner B = Inner Circle

THE DANCE: WORKBOOK EXAMPLE: PARTNER A

Next is an example of writing or journaling a workbook—step-by-step—of the scene as it unfolds. (This is not the circle but the prep work prior to drawing the circle.) It is his version of the scene (he writes in his workspace just prior to creating his circle of emotions):

1. I had just come home. We were in the kitchen, the TV was blaring, she was cooking, the kids were screaming and she said to me: "Don't just stand there, play with Tommy!"

2. I concluded that I wasn't worth a smile and she doesn't care about me, she just wants help!

3. My face got hot (like it was red). Then, my chest got tight. I got really quiet, not that she could tell, she had her back to me.

4. I said: "Fine, hello to you too."

5. Then, I put my briefcase in our bedroom and took off my jacket and came into the living room to play with Tommy until dinner was ready.

6. I felt angry, rejected, and useless.

7. I work hard all day and when I come home, she can't even pretend that she's glad to see me without barking orders.

8. I feel hurt and unappreciated.

9. We had dinner (didn't talk to each other, just spoke to the kids), then, I helped the kids with their baths. She read them bedtime stories; I kissed them goodnight then I changed my clothes and sat on the couch to watch TV. She stayed on the computer while I watched TV, then shortly after that she went to bed. I fell asleep on the couch (like I usually do), woke up at 11:30 P.M. and went to bed.

THE DANCE: WORKBOOK EXAMPLE: PARTNER B

Next is an example of writing or journaling a workbook—step-by-step—of the scene as it unfolds. (This is not the circle but the prep work prior to drawing the circle.) It is her version of the scene (she writes in her workspace just prior to creating her circle of emotions):

1. At least eight out of ten nights, I'm trying to get dinner finished before he comes home. I've been with the little ones all day. At dinnertime they're always out of control because I'm paying more attention to dinner than to them.

2. I'm usually half-way through my first glass of wine before he comes home.

3. I'm doing three things at once—the table is set, the salad is made, the meatloaf is in the oven, I'm mashing the potatoes and he comes in and stands like a robot waiting for instructions! I am NOT Wonder Woman! I need help!

4. I don't even notice what happens but I'm really upset and my forehead feels like it has got a rubber band around it. I am so frustrated! Why do I have to be the Instructor and the Director?

5. Why can't he be a man instead of my third kid? I feel so alone.

6. Anyway, he plays with the kids, I finish dinner, and we eat. I do the dishes, he starts the kids' baths. Then, I read them their bedtime stories. Finally, when they are asleep with lights out, I go onto the computer for about an hour, and then I go to bed alone (he's asleep or something on the couch).

7. I said, "goodnight" but he didn't answer me.

8. It seems like a switch that is either on full strength or I'm switched off and I am exhausted and completely done.

9. I know I probably wanted the kids more than he did, I realize he works hard to provide for us, but I feel like a single parent and I don't feel connected to him at all.

10. I try not to think about it because I get sad and alone. Then I get mad.

Now that you have seen the previous workbook examples of Partner A and Partner B, can you plot their dance in two circles? Does your image match the image I have depicted? Now plot your own dance.

SECRETS, SEX, MONEY

A professor in my doctoral program once told me that the three major reasons couples come to therapy are: Secrets, Sex, or Money. Often, the secrets are about sex and/or money! So that about sums it up, doesn't it? One partner could be charging up a storm in credit card debt and working hard to keep it from the other partner; or taking drugs; or taking drugs and having sexual escapades with others. One partner could have lost a job and kept it from their spouse; or stole something and was arrested (never told); or had long-term affairs (many years) without the other partner knowing (that's debatable in my book). The list goes on. From my perspective, it is a sad list.

It takes so much effort to live a double life. The effort requires thoughts, words, deeds, emotions, all tied up in playing a role in front of your family while behind the scenes there is A BIG SECRET!

I say much more about this in subsequent chapters.

The intensity of the secret is the stuff that creates best-selling movies and books. A colleague (psychiatrist) and I once got into a deep discussion about this topic. It is the anxiety and the obsessive qualities that intensify the secrecy. If the secret is sex, then the intensity is even more over-the-top. It is sex with a big "NO, NO" attached to it from society. Imagine, everything hangs in the balance—your job, your family life, your church, your friends, or your standing in the community. It all hangs in jeopardy. Yet, you continue to indulge in this BIG SECRET!

The obsessive thoughts attached to being involved, then the compulsions (behaviors) that continue to perpetuate the cycle. It can get very sticky. No matter what the secret, it is the same cycle. It starts with being lured (in your own mind) and then conflicted (but not enough to say no). Next, you go to slippery places, which draw you in further. Finally, you take the plunge and for many it is a plunge into an abyss! The plunge takes you to new levels that you have not yet experienced. Immediately, there is euphoria, obsession—more guilt and shame. The guilt and shame are often not enough to pull you back from the abyss. This is the internal conflict that keeps you mentally, emotionally, and physically busy until it reaches a crescendo or breaking point.

What does such secretive behavior indicate about what's missing from a relationship? How does this behavior as a symptom demonstrate a deeper level of pain, hurt, and fear? Basically, a behaviorist would say that the person is self-medicating through their secretive behavior. Rather than deal with the underlying issue, they "act out." They would rather be distracted and do something impulsive and feel better temporarily. The operative word is "temporarily."

Individual clients with secrets have solicited my help in the past because they were so confused. I was honored to help them stop their behavior and upon completion, I referred them to another therapist for couple's therapy. I encouraged them to continue the journey toward redefining their marriage. As deep as many of these individuals were into a double life and a world of secrets, the most important thing for them was to put significant effort into pulling themselves out of the hole they had dug for themselves. It took ENORMOUS amounts of EVERYTHING for them to pull themselves out. Yes, they did it. I just watched. I might have thrown a dose of verbal reality their way, but they gobbled it up and got stronger and stronger (enough to finally make a decision).

Either way, as a professional counselor and as a woman, I will tell you that I really care for all of my clients. In order for me to do my work well, I have to be disconnected from the outcome. I am only the facilitator of their efforts. My clientele are extremely high-functioning. I see a broad range of clients—doctors, lawyers, engineers, CEOs, laborers, the unemployed and permanently disabled individuals. These high-functioning people have had no major diagnoses except for, perhaps, depression and anxiety. Yet, my job is to get them to do what they need to do with their eyes wide open, leaving no room for denial or despair. I care, and although I might not have made the choices they have made, I do not judge them for their choices; I simply help them out of their dilemmas.

We are ALL HUMAN and we ALL MAKE CHOICES BASED UPON OUR THOUGHTS. In the cases I speak of here, it is usually about SECRETS, SEX, OR MONEY, however it could easily be something else. So my role is to either be the one who helps partners achieve whatever goal they have set for themselves, or let them know directly that reality is a few steps over to the left. The honor in working with a client who has made poor choices is that it humbles you as a therapist. This person is so desperate, they come to therapy for help! My job is to deliver the goods! I am there to help not hurt. If I am not the one for them, then I encourage them to find someone else who can help. Bottom line—they are motivated to change. How could I not get excited about helping someone so determined to get it right the second time?

AFFAIRS...WHAT YOU NEED TO KNOW

A recent study indicates that, statistically, 74 percent of men and 68 percent of women say they would have an affair if they knew they would never get caught.

Accordingly, only 31 percent of marriages last after an affair has been admitted to or discovered. Books have been written about this topic, and in this chapter we are briefly highlighting things to be aware of in your attitude about affairs (either as you as the participant or you on the receiving end of infidelity). One thing is for certain: Affairs are complicated and they do not work!

Affairs are based on secrecy, deceit, and lies. Over the years, I have counseled many married female clients who have had long-term affairs. Long-term—meaning years (1 to 20 years). I've seen clients who came to me prior to having an affair and tried to convince me that they should! I've also seen clients who came to therapy to tell me about their 5-year affair with one man and their hurt was because their lover was cheating on them! I could give you 50 more examples of people's choices and behaviors.

I have had many different kinds of couples come to see me over the years: multicultural, multiracial groups, blended marriages (one stepparent), separate religious faiths, different economic backgrounds, and so forth. I've seen all kinds of couples, relationships, and partnerships in all kinds of stages of togetherness.

We all have opinions about affairs, depending upon our reference point.

You might argue it from a statistical outcome, a religious faith-based moral position, a legal argument, or from a psychological perspective. That is why there are many books on just this topic alone! Knowing this, I would like to make a few brief points:

#1—**Once you have an affair, you cannot take it back!** You cannot erase it from your memory. You can't go back to the way you used to see yourself, your spouse, or your life—because you've changed! Once you cross that threshold, you could be confused, scared, excited, guilty, or angry (and a host of other more complicated feelings). Regardless of what happens before, during, or after—once you have participated in an affair—you will be digging out your own heart as well as your spouse's heart.

#2—**The affair is a symptom of what is lacking in your marriage/partnership. It is a symptom of something that is deeper.** It does not take a rocket scientist to see this important point. Whatever you are yearning for more of—love, affection, respect, fun, sex, more conversation—you need to re-examine your needs and go back to your spouse or mate and ask him or her for it first. As soon as you decide to seek it out elsewhere, you have started down a path from which you and most people cannot find their way back.

#3—**I don't believe that "stuff happens." Stuff does NOT happen!** YOU make it happen. You think it, you feel it, and then you act on it. This is really serious. You are affecting your own life and the well-being of your marriage and family life.

#4—**Even if you do not tell your spouse about the affair, you and your spouse are both subconsciously acting out roles that contribute to one of you having an affair.** It is the result of both of your behaviors and how you are connected (or not) that contributes to the affair. That's not saying that your spouse made you do it! I am saying that each of you plays a role in the dance and how it unfolds—even if no words are spoken out loud.

#5—If you decide to tell your spouse about the affair you have to be prepared for your partner to leave you. Just because you can't handle the guilt and shame and you feel compelled to unburden yourself to your partner, don't expect sympathy. You have held onto this secret for a long time and mulled it over and over in your mind and NOW you want to be open and share with your spouse? Be prepared! Your partner is under no obligation to forgive or forget.

#6—Think clearly and fairly about what you are thinking and feeling before deciding to start an affair. I say "affair" loosely. It could be a one-time event or a multiyear relationship. Whatever you might be rationalizing is OK for outside of your marriage—you might want to rethink your behavior. Play devil's advocate and start questioning your justification for making a choice that is lifelasting for everyone! Do you even know what your possible lover's level of commitment is to you? Who is this person? Who do you want him or her to be? Think, then think some more.

#7—If you are going to tell your best friend then you need to tell your spouse. Why on earth would you tell anyone without telling your spouse first? Are you hoping that word will get back to him or her and save you the trouble? I get that you might not have the closest relationship in the world, but that is too cold. If you open your mouth to your sister, your mother, your best friend—then you need to really examine why you've chosen to tell anyone at all, including the one who deserves to hear it from you first!

#8—Different marital counselors have different belief systems. This is an issue of HUGE CONTROVERSY! Some therapists automatically say you MUST TELL your partner and begin the healing process. Others say just as vehemently, "Do NOT TELL!"

If my client is dying to tell, then, go ahead and tell him. I will prepare you through questions and roleplaying as to possible outcomes to be prepared for when you tell all. However, at first blush, this is NOT about "kiss but don't tell." I believe in not having affairs in the first place! However, if it is already a done deal, I would question you in depth to find out what you are thinking and feeling. What are your intentions in revealing this secret to your spouse? There are many questions attached to the "Why would you tell?"

#9—**Different marital counselors approach the process of therapy or their model of therapy based upon the theory to which they subscribe.** In other words, for you the couple client, re-member that one experience with one couple's therapist might look and feel completely different from another couple's therapist. Some therapists might take a long-term approach with an objective, passive role in therapy (more analytical), and others might be more engaged, having fewer sessions and prescribing homework for the couple, in addition to therapy. Many styles and approaches exist according to theory and modality.

#10—**Cyber affairs, cyber-sex, cyber flirting, virtual cheating, (no matter your terminology) are under-reported by couples because many do NOT view it as an affair.** My view is very client-centered. I have told you that I don't judge the person (I qual-ify that statement with this specific topic of cyber affairs—I draw the line at homicide or child molestation). If a couple comes to me and one or both partners are having a problem with cyber exchange of nude photos, then my take on it is—if it is a problem for one—then it is a problem for both! In this instance, as a counselor, I would treat it as an affair. However, if I had a couple (and this is true) who came to me and they did NOT have a problem with his flirtations online except that he was doing more of it and she was concerned, then, I would recommend we have a completely different discussion as to what was really acceptable for each. We would back all the way up to the beginning as to what was originally agreed upon, how long it had been going on and what were their particular values around fi-delity in this specific area. Had they openly talked about boundaries?

Did he share his fantasies with her? How did he know that he had overstepped the boundary? You get the idea. So in the world of cyberspace, affairs can and have taken on new meanings.

VERBAL ABUSE

In the last section of this book, I talk about functional communication also known to me as: Communication 101. I talk about using the pronoun "I" instead of "you." I want to elaborate and emphasize a few comments here. Without getting into a moralistic discussion about swearing, I will say that the cardinal rule is to NOT SWEAR AT YOUR MATE! I really don't care how foul your mouth is, since this is a couple's book, my foremost concern is that you do not swear at your mate. Certainly, if you have children, that needs to stop NOW! But, getting back to your partner, I have been known to be loose with my tongue over the years, but I NEVER SWEAR AT MY HUSBAND! That is a No No! It goes along with name-calling. Some people don't even know they are doing it. "You are ridiculous!"; "That is so stupid!" Excuse me? That means she is stupid, even though you did not put the pronoun "you" in there! "You" is inferred. This is a huge area of discourse in which I need to make myself very clear. Putting your partner down either directly by using foul language or with name-calling needs to stop NOW! It might sound Victorian to you, but as relaxed as I might be in my opinions, when my partner and I speak to each other, it is with complete respect. Even though you have been doing this for years, you might be surprised to find out that when you stop, your mate says it feels more positive and less attacking (even when both of you were swearing at each other). So, one of my cardinal rules is to not swear or name call. I really encourage you to put your best effort into making this happen. Even if you explain it away by calling it a lazy vocabulary you cannot convince me otherwise. This is not OK.

Excellent books about verbal abuse are out there. In particular, I recommend, *The Verbally Abusive Relationship,* by Patricia Evans. The thing about verbal abuse is that it is rooted in a power struggle. It is unhealthy and there is no even playing field. There is an entire dynamic cycling around the abusiveness. In session, clients would admit that verbal abuse did not feel good and they felt stupid, or they felt like they were not good enough. Often, they didn't believe their partner really liked them and the "victim" would be chronically anxious while walking on eggshells around a hypercritical and verbally abusive partner. Other clients just got more worn down—with no joy in their lives—gradually becoming more depressed.

Verbal, mental, and emotional abuse is very demeaning and damaging. It is hurtful and painful. Emotional scars may be invisible to others, but of course as a therapist they are not invisible to me. For example: What if you got a broken arm? Your partner would rush you to the hospital emergency room, right? So, why is it OK to inflict heartbreak and low self-esteem in your partner? I don't believe they are unequal in importance. Your mental and emotional well-being is just as important as your physical well-being. The outside world may not see the bleeding, but just ask your partner how it feels and you might be surprised.

Certainly, verbal abuse goes both ways and does not stick with one gender over the other. This combination of role modeling (those who role modeled for you from your own family-of-origin) and the fact that you are role modeling for your own nuclear family (your children and grandchildren) is very important. OK, I have a Master's degree in family systems theory. I get that we parent the way we were parented and that our primary role models were mom and dad. If both parents yelled, that's what you learned, or if dad was a yeller and mom took it and you're the guy reading this book, then perhaps you have taken on that transgenerational role of male yeller. You tell me, "That's the way I was raised," or "That's how my father treated my mother." I don't care how you want to analyze it or justify it. My take on it is very simple. You are reading this book. You have access to information via the Internet, books, self-help groups, therapy, church, and so on. You know better. You can make a different choice with a different set of beliefs. You are reading this now and I am the one telling you that it is not something to dismiss as OK. It is NOT OK!

The challenge is when couples have been doing a negative behavior for so long they have a certain ritual when they fight. There
is a rhythm to how the argument or fight escalates. Then, there is the
name-calling and the demoralized language that you have accustomed
yourselves to by yelling at each other in the heat of battle. Believe me,
I am not a prude by any stretch. You need to hear me on this. I will
clearly tell you that it is negative to speak to anyone in a way that
demeans and disrespects them! Are you listening to this? The military
might re-program recruits through yelling—3 inches from their noses
telling them how stupid they are. However, this is not the military.
This is your life. This is REALLY UNHEALTHY! I don't care if you
are the golden egg at work and you have achieved the stars in your career. I don't care if you verbally abuse your partner and no one is there
to witness—they really don't know that side of you. My take on that
is—no way! The way you behave to your partner or spouse implies
you have that negativity swirling around you. Even if it is subconscious, other people will get that vibe. Why do you think you haven't
received that promotion at work or that you don't have a lot of close
friends? There is something about you that other people pick up on
and sense about you. So you see, the very behavior that you believe
is a secret is really right out there; everyone else (except you) senses
something that does not add up! They might say, "He's a really nice
looking guy and he's really smart, but I don't know, there is something
about him that just does not add up," or "She is my manager and she
smiles a lot; I respect her for her ability to run our group, but I'm not
that close to her because I'm not sure I like her or trust her. I just can't
put my finger on it." Think about it. You are treating another human
being as if they are dirt, as if they are less than you! You are doing it to
compensate or help you feel better at someone else's expense.

What bothers me the most is that verbal, emotional and mental abuse often do not get noticed. Often, they are diminished or
rationalized—like it's not as bad as physical abuse—and that reaction is
from the one being victimized! We see the broken arm and black eye
and we are horrified. However, the emotional and mental scarring that
takes place from repetitive verbal insults and put downs are insidious

and oftentimes so familiar that they are not even noticed by the person living with it every day. Whether it is the next door neighbor who is in a dysfunctional marriage, or something you've witnessed in your own parents' relationship, or seen in the justice system's dismissal of verbal abuse compared to physical abuse, it is inconsequential—it is not right! It does matter how you speak to each other, and verbal put downs are negative and damaging. They are damaging to the relationship, victim, family, community and society at large. We have become immune to them. We hear them in music; we see them in movies; we see them on TV; and we read about them in e-mails or view them on YouTube. Verbal put downs are pervasive. Please do your part to start taking care of yourself in a healthier manner.

If it comes down to verbal abuse and put downs versus respect, why wouldn't you want to treat the woman you love, the mother of your children, your partner for life with respect? The same equation holds true for your beautiful husband, the father of your children, or your partner for life. If you recognize this trait within yourself and within your marriage, please reach out and talk to someone to balance your perspective. Tools exist that you can use to help you get back on track.

GENDER ROLES

It does not matter if you are in a heterosexual marriage or a same-sex marriage—what matters is how flexible each of you is in your identification of your own role and what you bring to the table. The benefit of role flexibility is that you each bring what you do best to your marriage and hopefully it totally complements the relationship. That's nice. Yet, what if you are in a relationship and neither of you cooks, or you both hate doing the laundry, or you both like working in the garden and hate cleaning the house? That's slightly different because the final decision of who does what based on need can be negotiated, collaborated, or compromised. After all, you both have to eat, right? So, at some point you'll do what needs to be done so you can both eat. Figuring that out could be very meaningful and maybe even challenging in strengthening your relationship as you work together to figure it out. My hope would be that you both have a voice in the marriage and each of you can openly state your preferences and desires.

What I would consider a red flag is when one partner doesn't just advocate who does what, but rather dictates, "the woman's role requires—" or "the man's role determines—." To me this rigid, restrictive role identification by gender can be very negative to the relationship. In case you have not figured it out yet, I am very nontraditional in some ways. So there are many facets of this discussion that need to be looked at. Is the person dictating roles adhering to a rigid religious principle or perhaps a cultural expectation? If so, I honor his or her belief system. Yet, if it is not working in the relationship, I would advocate that he or she conduct research (reading, asking the minister, talking to an elder) to determine what options are available and to determine if the limiting role identification to which one or both are subscribed is understood. If cultural, I would ask which generation each of them is from in relation to their extended families. Other questions would include: Where does their family live (which country)? And, how long have they have been in the United States? Where do they stand in the family system from eldest child to youngest? Are there any other siblings who have paved the way for them to become more flexible in their culturally defined role within their relationship? What would happen if they strayed from their gender-based culturally defined role?

If there are limitations, then they have to decide as a couple within the framework of their belief system what can and cannot be negotiated. After the negotiation, what does each partner want or need and can he or she live with the final negotiated outcome? This of course assumes that even with religious-based, gender-role limitations or cultural expectations that they are allowed to negotiate. What if their religious or cultural defined roles limit negotiations? What if their religious beliefs or cultural roles lean toward men having more voice and women having less? Then it does not matter what they negotiate (if they do) because there is an imbalance from the outset. Again, we all have choices. In this case, I would remain the facilitator for the couple, but the couple would definitely have to educate me at the beginning as to what is allowed and not allowed and if they both agree to that, then I would do my best to advocate for both within that framework. In a session like this, I am very vocal about letting them know my value-based thinking, which limits me from project-ing my mainstream American ideals on them. It gives us all a refer-ence point to be aware of as we continue down the path of dialogue about what it feels like to be in this marriage when some needs are not being met.

In heterosexual couples, the ingrained messages from each part-ner's respective family-of-origin provide the role model of who does what—but again, not across the board. As adults we have chosen to do it differently from the way our fathers or mothers did it in their marriage. My comment on that is—I sure hope so! After all, that was a generation ago. We live in a completely different economic environment. Also, we have been exposed to many more influencers than our parents (war vs. peace; internet vs. TV/news; new age sci-entific and spiritual awareness vs. religion; higher education vs. high school education; American foods vs. ethnic foods, world travel and global perspective vs. community-based ideals, and so much more).

On the other hand, there are some who have adhered to the thought that a woman should do it this way because my mother did it that way, or a man should take care of his wife (because father completely took care of mom). Some of that thinking is valid, but it is much more conducive to a healthy relationship when you can voice your beliefs out loud to your partner and then put it within the context of your partner's beliefs while framing it within today's societal and economic requirements. Ask yourselves this as a couple: Is it working for you? Do you need to modify something? Did it work at the beginning of your relationship, and now it doesn't? Just ask yourself and your partner if anything has changed for him or her. Then, talk about it.

Continuing this discussion with a couple that is same-sex is much simpler from my perspective. I could be wrong but my experience over the years is that there is a beautifully built-in radar screen in most same-sex couples because they are not hung up on the rigid gender role. This is due mainly because they are of the same gender. Thus, they are already forced to think outside the box as to which partner does what best. Most same-sex couples tend to be more amenable to flexibly giving and taking in their marriage. I have observed this based on my experience and the complexity of their couple issues. More often than not, same-sex partners do not get hung up on who does what based upon gender. If one person loves mowing the grass then that person does it. If the other loves decorating the house, then that person does it; if they both love to snow ski then they do it together.

CONFLICT OVER RELIGIOUS BELIEFS

Remember when I said that the hot button topics for couples are: religion, sex, politics and money? Why? Because they represent belief systems connected to values. Religion is a powerful operating principle in many people's lives. My sense is that we all have our different paths and whatever makes you a better person and citizen of society, then good. If you are striving to be a better person and religion helps you achieve that, then you win and I win, because you are helping make our community and our society a better place by your own efforts. My point is that we each have our own path.

Please allow me to have my own path as I allow you to have your own path. So forgive me for projecting my own free voice in believing that each of us has a choice because that is my value system. For one elderly couple I met in my private practice, they did not seem to share that perspective.

This couple (married for 30+ years) was very religious. They were both devout in their faith. So what was the problem? Well, it turned out that the husband had gone behind his wife's back and decided to convert to another religious faith. This was such a huge deal for them that they came to couple's therapy. I was a little confused at first about what the problem entailed exactly. I asked a lot of questions and probed about values, feelings, and recent behaviors. I certainly asked some questions about their marriage. Then, I asked what they wanted from me. He was silent, and she looked me straight in the eye and said, "Make him stop converting to another religion, of course!"

After further examination of the issues surrounding their respective strongly held religious beliefs, I discovered that this might be a deal breaker for them. Now, remember, there are multiple issues here. Although they were both highly educated and scholarly in their own right, she appeared more dominant on this issue. Yet, he had kept a big secret from her. This was his way of avoiding her rage. What might mean nothing to another couple was a HUGE issue for both of them. I did my best to facilitate their efforts at communicating the significance of this deception and the significance of his strong desire to convert. She felt betrayed by his behavior. She felt he was a hypocrite in their religious community. Unfortunately, her desire, clearly stated at the beginning of the session, was for me to stop him from leaving one religious faith for another. I told her just as clearly that I could not do that in my role. I couldn't make him stop that. From that point forward, any discussion we had disappointed her because that was the only reason they had come to see me. Her objective was for me to help her stop his conversion to another religious faith. What we have here is a multifaceted compounded issue around communication, a shift in values, and secrets. I wondered if they had other secrets in their marriage? I wondered if this was the only issue in which she was the forceful one? Why was he not allowed to have a voice in the marriage? Why were they still together? The questions continued. As it turned out, it was a deal breaker for them. He expressed relief while she remained full of rage. What a sad day it was when their love for each other crumbled to divorce over religious faith. You don't want my commentary on it any longer, however, my mind was shocked and my heart was sad for them both. I was a witness to the final stage of their relationship.

There are so many excellent premarital counselors and therapists who will help you discover and uncover your premarital sticking points. In what ways are you similar (beliefs, values, interests, money, religion, etc.)? In what ways are you different and how do you negotiate these differences?

Sometimes, in an example like the one just mentioned, I wonder about the strength of the foundation at the outset of the marriage. How easy for me to judge! I also would question how a beautiful couple could migrate through life decade after decade and conquer the multiple stressors of daily life, only to have it crumble in on account of their deep love for God. In the end, their common value became cemented in their relationship. The value they shared as a couple did not allow for individual growth or change. It is easy for me to be the Monday morning sports analyst after the fact, but to me there seemed to be so much in their lives that they loved together and shared. However, this straw that broke the camel's back was exactly what was needed for each of them to point to and say, "See, there it is, that is the reason I am leaving you!" Looking for a reason to divorce is easy—there are plenty of them out there!

PROJECTION AND FINGER-POINTING

Everyone is so savvy nowadays. You can look up anything on the Internet. I do not mean to insult your intelligence. I am certain you know the term "projection." Just to clarify, projection is a Freudian term that describes an individual's way of coping maladaptively with conscious or subconscious feelings that are too painful for them to hold onto, so they project them onto another person. An individual projects his own feelings or characteristics onto another person because they are too painful to recognize in him or herself. The emotional stressor can be internal (conflicted within) or external (an external stressor). Bottom line—this is the person who extends their arm and index finger with the rest of their hand curled back and they say, "You, You, You...[*fill in the blanks*]." Look very carefully at their extended hand and index finger pointing at you. Now, look at their middle, ring, and baby finger on their same hand. You got it! They have three fingers pointing back at themselves! They are talking about themselves and they don't know it. Now of course, you cannot tell them that, but the power you have is to remind yourself that this is really about that person. NOT YOU! I have to be careful here; I realize I am talking to you, the reader. For the high functioning individual or couple reading this book, please let me say IF you had a paranoid personality disorder or some other diagnosis, I would not say this so blandly. For most of us, when this happens, the key is to not take what the person is saying so personally. This is their stuff. This is more about them than it is about you. When you understand that, then it makes it easier to disengage by not reacting emotionally to the other person's negative blaming, finger-pointing, and projections.

Sometimes you hear people make a comment, "You made me feel guilty." Well, that is a perfect example of the other person projecting guilt, shame, and fear or whatever onto the person who is saying, "You made me feel … this way or that." No one can make us feel anything we don't want to feel. Your task in reading this book is to become more centered and grounded—know who you are. Take the time to treat yourself with respect. Take the time to be with yourself in a quiet moment. Set goals for yourself. Do something that makes you feel good. BUT do not buy wholeheartedly a sack of goods from someone who is only pointing the finger—projecting their emotional garbage onto you. Take a step back and breathe. Let it go and clear a path away from that person (unless you want an irrational and highly emotional argument that goes nowhere).

Projection is unhealthy. It represents the exact opposite of what this book's purpose is focused on—ownership of Self and then execution of new thoughts, feelings, and positive behaviors in the world of love that you have created with your partner. If you take care of number one (that's putting yourself as a priority), and your spouse takes care of number one (that's putting himself as a priority), then each of you can emotionally support the other and you can stop reading this book. Thus, you are NUMBER ONE, your spouse is NUMBER ONE and the two of you together are NUMBER ONE!

PART V

Danger Signs

Why am I even bothering to tell you about the categories that I have included in "Danger Signs"? The answer is because on top of all the other challenges couples face in a marriage or relationship, this is one category that can totally devastate a marriage. You'd be amazed that today, with all of the information at our fingertips, there are still highly educated people living in culturally rich metropolis areas who are still in denial either about their own addictions or those of their partners. IT IS NOT EASIER TO HIDE FROM THESE SIGNS! IT IS NOT! It takes a huge amount of energy to avoid, deny, dismiss, and work around the elephant in the middle of the room. Why don't you just stand up from the couch and admit to yourself, your partner and your family, that WE HAVE A PROBLEM! WE NEED TO TALK ABOUT IT AND GET REAL!

Please examine the following categories and educate yourself. If you are suspicious about someone you love as possibly using substances to excess, or their behavior (or loss of money) does not add up, then something is lurking in the background. From this perspective, I believe in self-education. Get informed, face the facts, keep your eyes open and then either do nothing (that is always an option), or make an informed decision. Doing nothing is a decision. My hope is you choose the latter rather than the former. On the other hand, if we are talking about YOU, then please believe me...YOU DESERVE TO DO SOMETHING ABOUT YOUR

ADDICTION. Don't fool yourself. You are not coping effectively, and ultimately, your addiction will blow up in your face. It might result in health problems. It might result in legal problems. It might result in career or financial problems. Or, it might result in marital problems (divorce). Please, please ask for help and then act on that help. The problem with addicts is that they do not like to ask for help. This can be their biggest downfall.

ADDICTION TO SUBSTANCES AND OTHER THINGS

Diagnosis focuses upon: abuse, dependence, and withdrawal. Clients who come to my office are assessed for frequency, intensity, and duration. In other words—what do they use? How much do they use? How often do they use it? When they are not using it, what is their thinking focused on (where to find their next drink, smoke, or pill)? The following information is synthesized from the *Diagnostic and Statistical Manual of Mental Disorders* (DSM-5).

Substance Abuse

Ask yourself the following YES/NO questions:

#1—Have you used a substance in large amounts for the past year (not daily) that results in you NOT performing or functioning like you used to prior to your abuse of the substance? In other words, does your use or abuse of the substance cause you problems in areas of your life that weren't present previously?

#2—By using the substance, do you fail in meeting obligations and responsibilities (work, home, school)?

#3—Do you place yourself in physically dangerous circumstances while using the substance (while driving, operating machinery, etc.)?

#4—While using the substance, do you find yourself in substance-related legal jeopardy such as arrests, speeding tickets, and so on?

#5—Do you find that you are experiencing both social and per-sonal problems such as physical fights and arguments about the consequences of being intoxicated?

If you answered "yes" to one question, you have a problem.

Substance Dependence

A combination of thoughts, behaviors, and physiological symptoms indicate dependence.

Ask yourself the following YES/NO questions:

#1—Since you first started using substances, do you use them regularly and continually despite experiencing problems that are directly related to your continued use?

#2—Do you have a body tolerance in which you actually crave more of the substance to achieve a higher high?

#3—Do you experience a physical withdrawal or unpleasant bodily symptom when you decrease the amount of substance to less than your regular dosage or amount?

#4—Do you find yourself compulsively having to use the substance even when doing so might be inappropriate (on the way to work, going to church for a baptism, on your way to a job interview)?

If you answered "yes" to one question, you have a problem.

Substance Withdrawal

After long periods of substance usage and dependence, a decrease in the amount of substance used or complete stoppage will result in an individual experiencing a clustering of changed physical symptoms with accompanying cognitive (thoughts) and behavioral symptoms. "It is the development of substance-specific problematic behavioral change (DSM-5)." In other words, the addicted person starts to behave differently and tries to cope maladaptively to deal with the withdrawal. This can affect them in their relationships, their work, or school. Previous levels of functioning prior to the addiction are negatively affected as the addict starts to physically withdraw from the substance.

Whether it is you who is addicted, or someone you know with an addiction of some kind—work, alcohol, food, sex, substances (street drugs or prescribed)—it is a problem. If it causes your finances, your relationships, your health, your peace of mind, or your legal standing to be a problem for yourself or those around you—THEN IT IS A PROBLEM!!

I know it's scary, but if you are an addict, stop reading this book right now and close your eyes for one second and visualize yourself taking the first step toward stopping your addiction. Keep your eyes closed, then say to yourself, "Today, I CAN do it! Today, I take my first step toward being free of my addiction. Today, I want a healthier life filled with happiness." You or your loved one has been self-medicating for so long that you've forgotten what feeling good is really like. Now is the time to reach out for help. This is the first and most difficult step. You cannot do it on your own.

When you always have to go to the liquor store before it closes or look for an after-hours club where you stop by for only one drink, and this pattern repeats itself, then, this is a problem. Or, if you started out popping one or two Vicodin a day as needed and now you are up to 8-to-14 pills a day, then, this is an addiction. Or, if you go to all of the fast-food restaurants in your immediate area and gather four to eight bags of fast food from the drive thru window so that you can stuff your face all in one sitting, then you have a problem.

If areas of conflict center around payday when part of your paycheck mysteriously disappears and your partner wants information, or, you neglect your responsibilities (picking up your daughter at school, going to work, missing a major project deadline at work, skip out on school finals or miss semester project deadlines, or not pay bills, etc.), you have a problem! You are numbing yourself! You need to really take stock of what is happening. Are you and your spouse having more arguments? Do you spend more time alone? Do you spend more time away with friends, partying, than with your spouse or loved ones? Please quit being in denial and face the truth now! This is a slow (or rapid) deterioration of your life. It is real. My hope is that you choose to love yourself in a healthy way.

PRESCRIPTION DRUGS

Prescription medicine abuse, leading to addiction, is on the rise. Usually, it starts out as legitimate—a pain medication prescription for some injury, surgery, or disorder. However, the unfortunate scenario is that either the prescribing doctor may not monitor closely enough the mood and behavior of the patient who is asking for more refills, or, the patient is doctor-shopping until they find more than one doctor who will prescribe what they need. Doctors are very diligent and thorough in their efforts to screen the needs of their patients. Because doctors are, however, not trained in behavioral medicine (mood, thoughts, behaviors), they might miss small clues that could indicate the beginning of substance abuse or addiction. When addicted, patients frequently lie to their doctors! Doctors are, nevertheless, doing their job to help heal and to alleviate pain during the healing process.

An addict will move mountains to get a drug. There is no happy ending to this scenario. They could end up with multiple doctors, each of whom does not know that the patient is doctor-shopping with legally prescribed medications. Or, if the patient is having difficulty getting their doctor to renew prescriptions, the patient might panic and resort to more extreme measures such as raiding medicine cabinets, buying pills on the black market, or shopping online. It is an ugly trail that leads to addiction and illegal activities.

NOTE: The only exception to this would be psychiatrists who are specifically trained as both medical doctors (M.D.) and in mood, thoughts, and behavior (Ph.D.). These specialists are trained in monitoring your behavior, mood fluctuations, and thought content. There are also psychiatrists who have an additional subspecialty in addiction issues and are well versed in both behavioral medicine and addiction issues. They are trained to pay attention to those small clues that indicate progressive addiction in their clients. They are experts at helping individuals properly manage their moods, rather than self-medicating through illegal drugs or misuse of prescription drugs to cope with life stressors and mood fluctuations.

STIMULANTS (Speed, Cocaine, Crack)

What a journey stimulants have taken from the 1960s to present day.

Speed/Amphetamine

Just like in the 1960s, today, it is speed—drop it (drink it); snort it (inhale it); inject it (intravenous needle injection), and smoke it (pipe or cigarette). Speed (Amphetamine) is cheaper than cocaine and smaller amounts have more lasting effects than cocaine. The biggest indicators of speed dependence are the binges that can result in aggressive or violent behavior. When crashing or coming off of speed, the individual sleeps for prolonged hours and then may awaken with a voracious eating binge to compensate for decreased caloric intake during drug usage (only if you don't buy more drugs to continue the high).

Cocaine

Both speed and cocaine can result in short but intense periods of anxiety, paranoid ideation, or psychotic episodes, and serious health problems (DSM-5). Cocaine was very popular in the 1960s but very expensive and more trendy in the 1980s. Cocaine and speed are still in use today.

Crack

For the last two decades of the 20th century, the use of crack was an epidemic of astronomic proportions. We read about crack babies affecting the future of our society. Our health institutions tried to cope with treating newborns addicted to crack and going through withdrawal. These same children developmentally faced major learning and emotional challenges, preventing them from automatically mainstreaming in schools. Additionally, our education systems and health care industries struggled with trying to create effective medical and social programs for treatment. By using this cheaply available substance, adults addicted to crack were losing their teeth, their minds, their material possessions, and their families.

DEPRESSANTS (Heroin, Sedatives/Barbiturates, Benzodiazepines)

In the 1960s, heroin and sedatives were popular; during the 1980s, they took a hiatus—at least from the public eye. Now they have returned in full swing.

Heroin

Heroin—you can smoke it (pipe or cigarette); snort it (inhale it); or inject it (intravenous or intramuscular injection). Some individuals do speed balls (consisting of cocaine and heroin, or speed and heroin) for both snorting or injecting. Heroin has always had an underground aura about it. It has a reputation as a heavy narcotic connected to the street scene. It has never been associated with casual recreational or social drug use.

Sedatives/Barbiturates

In the 1960s and 1970s, sedatives were available by prescription and on the street. Sedatives and barbiturates were widely used by those who preferred "downers" as well as those who preferred speed, methamphetamine, or stimulants such as cocaine or crack. Sedatives were used to help an individual "come down" from the stimulant high that robbed the individual of sleep when they used cocaine, crack, or speed. Downers helped the person switch from staying high in party-mode back to their daily lifestyle. It was really easy to overdose on sedatives. Today, they are still used but usually in conjunction with surgery-related procedures.

Benzodiazepines

Benzodiazepines are used widely today and prescribed as a replacement for barbiturates and sedatives. They are used in routine medical practice with less chance of overdose. Benzodiazepines are also used as an anti-anxiety medication.

ALCOHOL

Alcohol is the socially and legally acceptable drug of choice. It is on TV, billboards, magazines, the Internet, and so on. It is everywhere. It has been in mainstream society for more than a century (even in pro-hibition it was illegal but still present). Found in beer and wine to hard spirits, it has become more stylish and attractive to advertise multiple brands from all over the world. It has always represented being an adult. Alcoholism is a deadly disease that has pervasive negative consequences for individuals and their families. The DSM-5 clearly states that, "In most cultures, alcohol is the most frequently used intoxicating substance and contributes to considerable morbidity and mortality. In the United States, 80% of adults (age 18 years and older) have consumed alcohol at some time in their lives, and 65% are current drinkers (last 12 months)."

Alcoholism is assessed in the same format as substances for abuse, dependency, and withdrawal. Alcohol can impair judgment, in addition to social and occupational functioning. It can result in problematic behavioral change (DSM-5). Thus, under the influence individuals can engage in inappropriate sexual or aggressive behavior or have mood changes. In assessing problematic drinking patterns, the counselor looks for already mentioned criteria—frequency, intensity, and duration. How much does thinking about drinking impact the individual's life? Does the actively drinking individual drink alone or with others? Finally, how much alcohol is consumed? Does all form of thought, feeling, and behavior focus on getting a drink?

I am certain that you do not need me to tell you another story of someone whose life has been devastated because they did not get help, or got help but relapsed, or got divorced, fired, lost custody of the kids, became homeless, or lost their license because of alcoholism.

MARIJUANA

Medical marijuana is currently legal in 22 states. As a person who grew up in the 1960s and the decades that followed on the west coast of the United States and as a professional health care provider, my understanding is that marijuana has been a theme in social/recreational use for a long time. It has never really gone away or even gone underground. It was definitely criminalized by the U.S. government for many decades. Many advocate its use as a non-violent, non-offensive herb that grows in the ground—promoting individual use. Others have presented it over the years as a "gateway drug," meaning that if you smoke marijuana you will automatically advance to heroin. My sense as a substance abuse counselor is that conservatism has died and liberalism has won out. Now it is considered beneficial for certain medical ailments and advocated accordingly (glaucoma, AIDS, antinausea, PMS, insomnia, lack of appetite, fibromyalgia, chronic pain, arthritis, and some symptoms of M.S.)—hence, the emergence of medical marijuana legislation.

PHYSICAL HEALTH

Since the 1960s when President Kennedy advocated healthy living and exercise across the nation, we have certainly become polarized in our all-or-nothing attitude about healthy eating. Overall, we have the exercise jogger, or dedicated gym member who eats healthy and exercises regularly. Their lifestyles are centered around gym classes and even other sports-related activities on the weekend (cycling, hiking, swimming, tennis, golf, etc.). Unfortunately, we have a large segment of society who do not participate in that effort. They either do not believe they can change their lifestyle, or, they choose not to. There is a segment of extremely obese individuals whom you can see in line at the store, or on TV with entire programs dedicated to their problems. Then, you have the average citizen who is not obese but certainly 30 pounds overweight. I'll get off of my soapbox and summarize by saying that we are at risk as a society in that we are exceedingly overweight; our children are becoming diabetic because of unhealthy, fast-food consumption, and couch potato lifestyles that have paralyzed them into eating all the wrong foods—large amounts of it.

The problem is that you can give up a narcotic or drug habit and start living a clean and healthy lifestyle. However, food is required as nourishment necessary for life. For persons who are compulsive overeaters, their struggle to search for that boundary between eating as sustenance and eating as a way of self-medication reaches to the very core of their spiritual being. They haven't got the first clue as to HOW to do it, or where to begin. Imagine trying to reach for food as sustenance without caving into cravings, desires, and compulsions that drive you to eat and eat and eat. How do you use it without abusing it?

It is a tough scenario. In my practice, I have seen many individuals who were extremely overweight and others who were medically obese. Without exploring surgical alternatives, or fad diets that advocate calories versus carbohydrate intake, there are a few basic points that I want to make here.

#1—Like any other addiction, you have to admit you are powerless over your drug of choice (food) and that you have a problem.

#2—Do you know why you overeat? What does food mean to you?

What is it you say to yourself silently about how large you physically have become? What is the tiny voice inside your head telling you every time you reach for a candy bar or a plate of pasta? Let's just assume you are self-medicating some other negative feelings or even depression with your intake of food. Can you find another way to try to feel better without all of that food? Can you stop right now and address what is really going on with you? Are you nervous about money? Are you unhappy in your marriage? Do you think people talk about you? What? Do you believe that you are not good enough? What is it that you say to yourself and believe about yourself that keeps you shoveling food into your mouth? If you can say that right now out loud and you KNOW the answer—then you've just achieved 85 percent of what it takes to turn this situation around. Believe me those are great odds! The time for thinking and eating is over. Now is the time for you to DO SOMETHING ABOUT IT!

#3—You need to take action and set goals for yourself to do at least one thing a day for your own well-being (call the doctor for a physical exam, or go to the doctor's appointment, or join an eating disorder group, or hire a personal trainer to help you with an individual program toward change, consult a nutritionist, go to short-term psychotherapy). DO something!

#4—Make certain you have a personal relationship with your doctor. Really get someone who cares and will listen. Ask for help and ideas. There are low-dosage meds that can help you initially stop cravings and increase Serotonin that will help diminish your urge to eat compulsively.

#5—If you so choose and are open to more natural alternatives, go to a holistic practitioner specializing in: energy work; Reiki; integrated energy therapy; quantum energy healing; healing touch therapy; therapeutic massage; acupuncture; and so on.

#6—I don't know what the best answer is for you, but in addition to reading this book, you need to do some actionable steps every day—set a goal and stick with it. Start by writing down a set of goals, rank them, organize them, and decide which step gives you the most benefit or biggest bang for your buck. You can look at what you've accomplished at the end of each day and say, "I did that!"

#7—Don't tell the world what you are doing. Frequently, my clients say that they told a whole bunch of friends their new plan and then set themselves up by not doing it (failure cycle). So make a plan and make it doable! Do not make it so far out of reach that you feel completely overwhelmed and you self-sabotage! The only person you have to do it for or prove it to is yourself.

#8—Every day you have to be busy and focused on your new goal. Make a 7-day goal. Then on the 8th day, make a 7-day goal and keep it small, short, definable, and measurable. You mark off 7 days and on the weekend, say this: "Look what I did for the past 7 days!"

#9—Identify your weak periods. Are the mornings, when you first wake up, hard for you? Or, are the evenings your most difficult time? Or, is it when you are alone? When your entire family is making popcorn, is that when you cave in after a wonderful day of healthy eating? Pay attention to yourself and take notice of your habits. For example, is it when you are very tired or very bored that you self-sabotage?

#10—As a cognitive counselor, I ask you to identify those negative thoughts that you say to yourself every day that make you your own worse enemy! How about choosing something positive to say to yourself: "I feel fantastic today!"; "I am making a positive change for me today!"; "Every day in some small way I am getting healthier!"

#11—Stop saying negative things about how you hate to exercise.

Even if you don't, start telling yourself that you LOVE to exercise—even if you love it when it is over. Join a Zumba group! Walk around the block three times every morning! DO SOMETHING! Do it consistently. No exceptions!

#12—Identify something that you have always wanted to do but didn't think you deserved to do (massage, pedicure, etc.). Then, set a short-term plan (7-to-30 days) with a gift-to-self that you reward yourself for your efforts (NO FOOD!). Then, set a new goal for the next 7-to- 30 days with another gift-to-self that makes you feel good!

#13—Stay in the now. If you look too far down the pike you will become anxious and overwhelmed, and if you look too far into the past you can become depressed with lots of "should've" and "could've", etc. STOP IT! Just stay focused on what you are doing this morning and what you are doing this afternoon. PAY ATTENTION TO SELF!

#14—When in doubt, tell yourself, "I can do this!"

#15—Close your eyes, see yourself at your ideal weight. See yourself in your favorite slacks or dress. See yourself in a bathing suit—trim and healthy. Whatever it is that motivates you, hang onto the image that you are striving toward. It is a lifestyle change, not a program or diet. You are choosing to put healthy, nutritionally balanced foods into your beautiful body. Let the real you emerge now.

Example

One partner sometimes comes to therapy to gain insight and help for coping with an addicted partner, however, what is staring them in the face is their own problematic behavior. This behavior is invisible to them because they are consumed by their addicted partner's behavior and mood. I remember a client who was really bright and friendly with an attractive face (clinically obese, approximately 450 pounds). She sat on my couch and complained for an hour about her alcoholic husband (not in the session). I gradually attempted to steer the conversation to ask what she had been doing for herself lately? When I gently pointed out that perhaps she was self-medicating her anger and frustration through food, she immediately erupted with some comment about how this session was not about her—it was about her husband! This is the scenario I'm referring to when I comment on how people are disconnected from themselves emotionally, cognitively, and physically. They are lost and their priorities are upside-down. The entire focus of that therapy was to indeed focus on her. She was the one who came to therapy and sought out my services, not her husband. I still have hope that someday she will begin taking care of herself first.

Are You Feeling Denied?

Do you have an attitude because you feel that giving up something is like being denied? If you feel denied, then this won't work for you. It is important that you phrase it with a positive belief that you have decided to make a healthy change in your eating habits because it is time to do that. So do it! Stop reacting negatively to what I suggest and start taking a step forward for yourself. I am here to be your advocate. Take a minute and decide to start loving yourself instead of reacting angrily and negatively. Stop reacting and start acting. Start putting ALL of your energy into taking that first step toward wellness. It is all over the TV and the Internet and on *60 Minutes*: we are obese and we need to reclaim our power back both as individuals, as a society, and as a nation! Getting physically healthy is the first step toward a sharper mind, an open heart, and an intuitive spirit. Get your partner to work with you and set goals together for walks, hikes, salad consumption, and no fast food. **If you really want to do it—you can make it happen!**

GET HELP NOW!

Join the Following or Look Online for More Options!

NA (Narcotics Anonymous); AA (Alcoholics Anonymous); Al-Anon (family members of an addicted person); OA (Overeaters Anonymous); Jenny Craig; Weight Watchers; individual therapy; couple's therapy; group therapy; doctor's appointment. Call your insurance provider and get approved for a 28-day in-house residential treatment program; or, your nearest hospital for an in-patient or an out-patient substance abuse program intake advisor.

Get Help for You and Your Partner

What is the one thing I keep saying over and over in this book? YOU have to take care of YOU, first. When a relationship gets to the stage where one person or both are destroying themselves slowly through alcohol or substances, then it is time for outside professional help. Call your local county mental health hospital for substance abuse or alcohol rehabilitation agencies or programs in your area (or look online). If you are the addict, call your insurance company to find out what your coverage allows and then start looking for a program with available beds to help you dry out. If you don't want to do that, call for an urgent appointment with your physician and tell him or her that you are an addict and that you need help immediately. Sometimes we think we are capable of helping our mates with these serious problems, but the problem is sometimes greater than our ability to provide true help.

LOOK IN THE MIRROR

Who are you? Where are you? Go stare into your pupils in the bathroom mirror for 60 seconds. What color are your eyes? Who do you see when you look 3 inches away from the mirror? Reach down deep to your core and tell yourself that you are going to do it differently, starting today. This behavior certainly has a biochemical component to it for sure (molecular addiction), yet, many have been known to kick a habit with relative ease. Why is that?—simply because they wanted to take the first step. When you decide to do it differently, call someone who is neutral to your addiction (not your drinking buddy, your boss, etc.). Call someone who loves you and will tell you that they're worried about you. Listen to them and GET HELP! Whatever you do, don't sit around for a week or two and "think about getting help"—do it right now. IF you really want to get help and you're scared, that's natural. Give yourself permission to get help. Allow yourself to stop being scared.

SUBSTANCE USE/ABUSE

Addiction Blocks Intimacy

In my practice, I have seen heroin addicts, pill addicts, alcoholics, speed addicts, compulsive overeaters (300-to-400 pounds), and the old socially acceptable standby—the workaholic who might as well have a cot at work. There are too many of you out there walking around trying to numb the pain, spiritually and cognitively cut off from the neck down. Not in touch, not connected to Self. You've waited too long to get help; you've lost a lot of life's years.

When you are under the influence of a substance, you are not emotionally present. It is impossible to connect with Self or with your partner when you are taking something or doing some kind of behavior to numb yourself. I don't care what you've achieved in life and how pretty your white picket fence looks in front of your garden with your beautiful family. If you are popping pills, cheating on your spouse, or drinking too much—you are really threatening your core Self. You are unhappy but you are not taking healthy steps to admit that to yourself.

If you are not the addict but your partner is, then it's an entirely different conversation. Like anything else, the person with the problem has to want to change. What's the saying? You can take a horse to water but you can't make him drink. I regularly get individual clients who want to help an addicted spouse. I say, "Where's your spouse? I need your spouse to tell me he's got a problem and he wants help, otherwise, I can't help."

Habitually using and abusing substances (addiction), not only block or prevent you from being intimate with yourself, but also with others. Developmental studies and decades of dealing with addiction have revealed that chronic use (addiction) of alcohol or any substances can block the developmental growth of an individual. Let's say you have been hooked on a drug (take your choice), or you have been an alcoholic since age 14, then you have the emotional and cognitive coping skills of a 14-year-old! In other words, addiction stunts your growth. A few decades ago, I had a 28-year-old client who had been addicted to Jack Daniels and speed since the age of 12. She literally had the mental coping skills of a preteen. She had legal problems and the naiveté of a young girl. When I spoke to her, a strange sensation came over me as I realized she was really a young girl inside a woman's body. You could listen to her and hear her perspective on life. This is the serious damage that happens to the brain from prolonged use of drugs or alcohol or both. This woman had a lot of growing up to do.

CODEPENDENCY

How do you take care of yourself? Do you even know? You'd be amazed at how many people I've met who are just as numb as their addicted partners—only their numbness centered around putting their partner's needs ahead of their own—lying to everyone about their partner's REAL PROBLEM (not just that (s)he is sick and can't go to work), but also lying to themselves about reality.

This is a classic case of denial. Are you balanced in life? Do you exercise? Are you in therapy? Are you sleeping and eating well? Are you excessively anxious or depressed? Have you had a complete physical exam lately? Why do I keep asking the same questions over and over? Because a majority of people do NOT take care of themselves,

AND if you are living with or aiding/abetting a drug user/abuser or alcoholic then you are DEFINITELY NOT TAKING CARE OF YOURSELF! How can you? You are so tied up in that other person's world of addiction and excuses that you have forgotten to have a life of your own. Your entire day cycles between what kind of mood your friend, partner, spouse, or teenager/adult child is into these days. Are they high? Are they crashing after being high for hours or days? Have they eaten? Will they snap your head off tonight? Or, will they stay out all night or be gone for three days before they return home? Will they stay locked away in their bedroom or in the garage until the early hours of the morning? Is that normal?

This is very serious. If you're getting upset by reading this right now, then you are probably upset for a reason. Why are you upset? Am I hitting too close to home? Is it true? Are you making excuses for someone else's behavior? Please stop. Please stop now! Do you know how to stop? Well, if you get angry or irritated with me now and you just experienced a strong reaction to my statements, that tells me that you are probably not taking care of yourself; you want to deny being an enabler to an addicted person. I realize your job has been to "help" that other person, but my job is to help you first.

I have HUGE discussions with my clients about this. To many, this scenario sounds "selfish," to others who have been care-giving for so many decades, they are completely disconnected. It's become a very bad habit. They don't know what they think; they aren't aware of their own emotions; they are no longer in touch with their bodies (they've numbed out by overeating, overdrinking, etc.). They consistently look everywhere EXCEPT within. I'll tell you that I have worked with heroin addicts, jewelry thieves, alcoholics, obese individuals, obsessive-compulsive individuals, and rage-aholics, from every walk of life—professional to blue collar—unskilled to unemployed. From my experience, the co-dependent caregiver is the hardest compulsion to break. My sense is that the caregiver justifies cognitively their actions in righteousness, which means they don't believe any counterarguments to the unhealthiness of their behavior. Second, they gain some inner sense of control over others who they perceive need them. My answer to that is, yes, the recipients of the caregiver's goodwill needs the caregiver so that they don't have to step up to the plate and do for themselves. It can be habitual on both sides of the issue. The caregiver doesn't know how to do anything differently especially because he or she is getting kudos for doing it over and over. The recipient is in a really great place because he or she doesn't have to do anything except take and take.

PLEASE UNDERSTAND me when I say to you that I am not talking about the wonderful volunteer who gives back to the needy within our communities! I am talking about a mother who coddles her 29-year-old son who sits on the couch smoking weed and watching soap operas while mother works two jobs and cooks and cleans for him like he was in elementary school. He is unemployed, too lazy to go to school, and he doesn't even help with chores around the house. The female care-giving clients I have seen did not like what I had to say. They were so locked into denial about their own behaviors; how could they break through their denial of their lazy son who did nothing and kept his hand out for more? I had one mother tell me, "Oh he's had such a hard life; he was kicked out of a private school for fighting." WHAT? Do you see the difference from being a philanthropist and community activist vs. a slave and habitual caregiver to an able-bodied young person who needs to be accountable and responsible for his or her own behavior? The dilemma with caregivers is that their behavior inhibits the development of the recipient. Care-giving is a wonderful attribute (in balance), however, within the context to which I am referring, the able-bodied person does as little as possible for as long as possible. Why should they change? Life is pretty good for them; they have it easy and their needs are being met.

Both partners on either side of this dynamic are caught in an unhealthy, dysfunctional cycle. My experience with this scenario is that the caregiver (often the wife/mother of the adult son), has completely placed the adult son in the driver's seat. Meanwhile her husband suffers the loss of his marriage and his beautiful wife, who just can't seem to say "NO!" to their son. This is a grave imbalance.

ENABLING BEHAVIORS

Enabling behaviors are the protective behaviors that family, friends, co-workers, employers, and counselors do to shield the addicted, chemically dependent partner from being accountable and accepting the consequences of their addicted behavior (alcohol, prescription drugs, street drugs, etc.).

Ask yourself, what emotion drives you to protect the one you love?

Can you name that feeling? Is it a positive feeling (love) or a negative one (guilt, shame, fear, anger, etc.)? After you protect your loved one, then how do you feel? Do you feel relief? Do you feel exhausted? Do you have hope that they will not do it again? What is going on with you? When you identify what is going on with you, are you certain that this feeling is yours, rather than your reaction to your addicted partner's actions? Perhaps not. That is the challenge—to separate your feelings from the reactive feelings you have for your addicted partner. Can you do that? Do you want to do that? Do you know how to do that?

It is extremely important for you to become aware of what your behavior is in response/reaction to your addicted partner's behavior or mood. Do you know what you do and how you do it? Once you can take a step back and watch what they do, and what you do in response, I want you to stop and write it down. What was their behavior? What did they say; what did they do? Now, write down what you said or did not say or thought, in reaction to them. Even if you got angry at them, unfortunately it does not mean that you have separated from them emotionally. Bottom line—your behavior is HELPING YOUR ADDICTED PARTNER TO REMAIN ADDICTED.

Your behavior is handicapping your partner. You are part of their addiction. How can they possibly begin to change, when things are pretty cool for them? They don't have to tell their boss that they are not coming in (you make that call for them); they don't help around the house because they are too busy getting high, passing out and sleeping late, until they get up and do it again. You do all of the work; you manage everything expertly (clean the house, make the meals, take the kids to their events, pay the bills, you go to work…). So listen up, if you continue your behavior like everything is OK, what makes you think that your partner is suddenly going to see the light? Why should they change? WHY? They have no need to change—they've got it made. They have you!

Please identify the following behaviors and ask yourself some hard questions as to whether or not these words describe you in any way.

Denial
He's not an alcoholic.
He never drinks in the morning.
He only drinks at night.

Minimize
He just drinks too much on the weekends.
He's never had a DUI.
His brother drinks more than he.

Rationalize
He's a lot happier when he drinks and he pays more attention to me.
His work requires him to socialize.
His whole family drinks; he drinks because they drink.

Avoiding Conflict
I don't want to make him upset by bringing up his drug use.
Sometimes, I just ignore him and try to get some space between us.
I walk on eggshells when he is grumpy and tell the kids to be quiet because daddy is resting.
I hope someday it'll change.

Taking Over Responsibilities
I manage the house and the front yard.
I call into his boss to cover for him when he is hung over or sick.

I take care of the kids full time; I don't trust him with the kids.
I pay the bills; otherwise, they won't get paid.

Overprotecting Your Partner
I called his boss and said that my husband was sick today.
I always have dinner ready and waiting after he has been out drinking
with friends.
I'm alone a lot (isolating) and I have to cancel social obligations be-
cause I know he won't be able to attend. We've lost a lot of friends
over the years.
I hide the car keys from him once he starts drinking or using.

Taking Control
I measure the liquor in the liquor bottle to keep track of his usage.
I search for hidden drugs (to flush down the toilet) or alcohol (to
discard) when he is in the shower.
I constantly nag him to stop or slow down on his usage.

Drinking or Using with Your Spouse
I think that if I drink with him he will be happier and I can control
how much he drinks.
If I go to the party with him, maybe he will leave earlier.
Well, if he can do it, so can I!

Situational Excuses
We have family problems.
It's his job—he hates his job and his boss is a jerk.
He's stressed out about our finances.

Overwhelmed and Exhausted
I constantly think about him and what he is doing and what tonight
will bring.
I worry all the time about when it will get better.
I can't concentrate or focus at work—I am so distracted.
I'm exhausted; I can't sleep; I feel blue and hopeless (depression).

It seems like his drug use has gotten worse over the past 2 years and it has prevented him from getting a promotion, or from us taking a vacation as a family together. We can't plan anything.

Stuffing Your Feelings

I cry at the stupidest TV commercials. I don't know what's wrong with me.

I cry alone in my car in the corner of the parking lot after everyone else has left work.

I haven't laughed in a long time—it's been years.

I'm really tense; I wake up grinding my teeth at night.

I heard myself scream at my daughter today, for accidently knocking over the cat bowl. What is wrong with me?

YOU DECIDE

Stop making excuses for yourself or your partner. STOP IT! You want to stop being a victim? Then, take the first step by acknowledging to yourself exactly what you have been doing to contribute to the problem. Stop blaming your addicted partner and take a hard look at yourself first. WHEN you figure that out, you can make some decisions about what you need and what you don't need; what is healthy and what is unhealthy; and what you'll put up with and what is going to stop here and now. As soon as you stand up for yourself, believe me the WORLD WILL NOTICE. They will feel a different vibe from you and once your mind-set has shifted toward a healthier stance, what seemed impossible to you before will simply be the next step in your journey toward well-being. Take the step now. Take action right now. Don't wait. Just do it! When you feel the time is appropriate, ask your mate (sober, not high) if they honestly want to get help because you have done all you can on their behalf. Again, the desire for change must come from within each individual. You cannot force another to stop self-destructive activities. My belief system is that you owe it to yourself to get yourself UNSTUCK and to take that tiny step to move forward. Otherwise, you sacrifice yourself and might wind up sacrificing a lifetime. **Your goal is to work on yourself first. After you get really good at that, then you will get stronger and will begin to see things from a different perspective.**

Everything is a circle. I had one elderly female client who kept the biggest secret ever from friends, family, and co-workers. Her husband was an alcoholic. He started drinking champagne and orange juice in the morning, a Bloody Mary at noon and then beer and vodka all night. He would go to bed by 7:00 P.M. She was a beautiful and gracious woman. Her spouse was an alcoholic; she was a classic codependent. Of course! She was a prisoner in her own home—she did not socialize, she could not go out on her own, she had to make constant excuses for her husband to many social invitations over the years. She was isolated and depressed! Of course! She kept the secret and was miserable. She would sit on the living room couch and tap her fingers on the edge of the couch wanting to go out somewhere—anywhere. She was fearful of his controlling nature and angry mood. He was just functional and alert enough to know what was happening around him and his goal was to keep her right where he could see her. This beautiful, dynamic woman was educated and very much a lady. She was miserable and had been miserable for years and years. She loved him deeply. His health was very fragile and she came to therapy to sort out her thoughts and feelings. As she gained strength in summoning up her courage to make a life for herself (go to lunch with friends, go to the opera with friends, take a workshop, etc.), his health became more fragile and she did not want to leave him in his final months and years—loyal to the end. From my perspective, my goal was not to get her to leave him, rather, I tried to help her cope differently and take better care of herself in a dysfunctional marriage.

ARE YOU THE CODEPENDENT?

If you are the partner to the addicted spouse, then your job still requires you to take care of SELF FIRST. So, that means you attend Al-Anon, a co-dependant's group, individual therapy, or read some self-help books on codependency, so that you can figure out your thoughts and feelings. When clients come to me, my treatment plan is: the stronger and healthier you get, the more choices you have. You can get strong, assert your own needs into the relationship, go to therapy, and join Al-Anon. It might be appropriate for you to see your doctor and get treated with low-dosage medication for depression; you can stay in the marriage but on more even terms (less codependence).

The goal for you as the client in individual therapy is to reactivate your personal growth and evolution. As you get stronger and more grounded about who you are and how you feel, your renewed sense of Self subconsciously challenges the sick partner to come to term with their illness and make some decisions. If they do not, DO something about their addiction. If you choose to do nothing, then it's possible that as you get healthier and stronger you might leave them! This not an automatic, however, it is a possibility. When the addicted partner chooses to take the step toward sobriety, it turns out to be a win-win for both.

THE SUBCONSCIOUS DANCE

However, just as often, the sick partner DOES NOT want to change and will subconsciously try to drag their codependent partner into the same negative pattern they have been living for years. In this case, if you the codependent client gains personal strength and some momentum in your own personal growth, through the steps described throughout this book, then you have a chance to make a difference for yourself first and your partner second. This change in awareness can result in you seeing your partner in a different light. The result? You might choose to leave because going back to your old codependent behaviors is no longer an option, or, you can choose to be in the state of denial—stick your head in the sand like an ostrich. After years of witnessing people take those first steps toward positive change, once you receive the healthy information that educates you to your addiction (or partner's addiction), then you are changed by that information. You can't unknow what you know! Once you reconnect to your own inner core Self and get yourself in mental, emotional, spiritual, and physical shape, you will have the strength to make some choices about HOW TO COPE with your partner's issues.

WHAT ABOUT THE KIDS?

I don't care if you have four kids, you still have to take care of yourself so that you can be a better parent and at the same time be a role model. Kids know what's happening. Kids are brilliant. They are watching both of you to learn how to cope with life's stressors. What is your spouse teaching them? When life gets stressful, take a drink, pop a pill, or get enraged? What are you teaching them? Just be quiet, don't make waves, give and give and give and then become completely depleted and exhausted so that you aren't thinking clearly? What kind of role model is that? NO!

OTHER THINGS

Not to minimize gambling or sexual addictions and many other key disorders—there are wonderful 12-step programs for these. The steps are universal. Admit you have a problem. If you do not admit that you have a problem, you will not be helped. So, if your spouse has a problem—at least you've identified it—you cannot make them go get help! They have to want the help and ask for it themselves. I have had many clients who would say, "My husband has a problem and we need to come in." They would come in together and I would spend an hour with someone who resented being dragged to therapy and who justified his behavior. The person would not say he had a problem and did not think it was a problem. So, I either sat there with an exasperated partner who bitched for an hour to no avail, or I sat there with a partner who froze in fear to say what (s)he was feeling about their spouse's addictive behavior. I would be very direct and give my psycho-education speech, so at least both clients (couple) would be able to leave armed with solid information surrounding whatever the addiction issue was. On the other hand, sometimes it would end with some softening of the immediate and early resistance by the addicted partner. At times, though, it was just a passing of time until they could both leave and go back to their stuck lives. How sad. They did not hire me for the hour to be their friend and to walk softly around the issue of addiction. I delivered it straight and asked all of the tough questions that the partner could not.

SHOPPING, SHOPPING, SHOPPING

STORY #1 I once counseled a couple in which the woman was upset because he only allowed her a $2,000.00 budget for self-expenditures per month! Everyone has their own value system, but for this woman, extreme spending was her addiction. It was a compulsion (a need to repeat the behavior). I often speak of self-medicating anxiety or depression through some maladaptive behavior or substance. There are better ways to cope effectively with your negative emotion that costs a lot less money (talk to a professional about your anxiety, see your physician for low-dosage meds, tell someone that you are feeling anxious, do positive Self-talk, calm yourself down, decrease caffeine, exercise regularly, go to hypnotherapy, or replace shopping with some positive behavior).

STORY #2 I had another female client once who secretively charged HUGE amounts of money for clothes throughout the entire year. Her husband eventually found the credit card bill and it broke the camel's back. He felt that she had mortgaged their four small children's future for college. Regardless of our analysis of her behavior and its intrinsic meaning (passive aggressive payback to her husband, compulsive behavior on her part, or psychopathic personality disorder), no matter how you slice it—it was a HUGE problem resulting in hundreds of thousands of dollars. When you add resentment to anger and anger to loneliness and loneliness to lies upon lies, it becomes a convoluted mess entangled in a web of deceit, resentment, and pain. It's a tragedy of mistakes and poor choices based upon underlying intention to hurt your partner. The sad part is that payback didn't just hurt the husband, the children suffered also.

STORY #3 Years ago, I counseled one young beautiful client who began to tell her story of her compulsive shopping for clothes. The more we talked, the more she revealed that she wasn't just buying "on sale" once in a while. This was ongoing and long-term. Eventually we came up with a behavioral plan where she reorganized her closets into a room totally devoted to her clothes. This was a big change from hiding new clothes from her husband in the back of the closet. Next, she signed a contract in front of me stating that she would stop shopping for clothes for a specific amount of time. I witnessed and we both signed and dated the contract. Then, she got those huge movable racks found in big department stores and started to arrange her clothes from all of the closets in the house into this one room. She arranged them by style (suits, pants, dresses, etc.).

In one of her sessions, she admitted that the majority of items still had the price tag on them. She then added up the cost of all the items in her display room. WOW! You should know that she worked, so her dollar was very important to her. She also liked to have money in the bank. When she uncovered and openly discussed the dollar amount of her "splurges" it was a "coming out" of sorts. She came out to the world (me) and told the truth about her addiction. Anytime she felt like splurging, she would go "shopping" in her home store display room and pick out a complete outfit—shoes, purse, sweater, and pants. This behavioral technique actually worked for more than 8 months. It lessened her compulsion to go out and buy buy buy! It also revealed her previous splurges front and center. Granted, I am only giving you the highlights, but this was a very gradual and healing process for her. My sense was that all of those price tags in one room helped her realize her overspending. She was amazed that she had some really nice clothes in her display room; she could buy a green outfit or a pink outfit anytime she wanted. The display was a turning point for her; it helped to break through her self-destructive behavior.

STORY #4 I once counseled a male client in his early 30s who loved his clothes. He said, "I'm a clothes horse." Everything had to match and look just right. Unfortunately, his love for clothes made him spend more than just his hard-earned dollars. He spent more than he could afford, which led to secrecy. He lied to his wife. Although we explored all aspects of his secrecy's negative impact on his wife, we ultimately worked on his compulsion to spend, spend, and spend some more. He told me that when he got off work early, he rushed to buy clothes. So we came up with different alternatives for him to do ANYTHING (constructive) that would keep him away from the mall and his favorite clothing stores. He decided to go to the gym earlier and work a little longer until he met his friends, rather than spend money shopping. Then, we collaboratively worked on how he could be more honest with his wife about his spending. He decided to organize his clothes rather than keep them hidden in the back of drawers and closets. Finally, we came up with a plan—one that he would stick to for the long-term. Because he INCLUDED his wife in the resolution of his spending sprees, he had two advocates—his wife and me.

What was the plan? Every time he felt the urge to spend, he would call his wife and tell her about his feelings. Then, he would come home (after the gym) and in a big glass jar, put the dollars for the price of what he craved—pants, shirts, shoes, etc. Gradually, his glass jar began to fill up with dollars. He had so much money after 3 months that he was able to pay off credit cards; he continued to put more money in the glass jar. At the end of the year, they had enough money to help with a nice vacation to Hawaii. Behaviorally, he switched impulses and paid himself every time he desired some "thing." Through this strategy, he weaned himself from the "thing" he thought he just had to have and ended up making a return on his investment. First, he stopped charging; second, he started wearing the clothes he purchased; third, he weaned himself from the spending cycle; fourth, he increased his intimacy with his wife (who supported his efforts toward healthy change); fifth, he became debt free; sixth, he saved money for a long-term goal that benefited him and his wife (a pleasurable vacation). This was a huge shift from unhealthy to healthy. Was it an overnight change? Absolutely not. Yet, he did not give up on himself. He was surrounded by those who loved him and he persevered in taking one step at a time for himself and his future.

FYI—NOW DO YOU KNOW WHAT HEALTHY LOOKS LIKE WHEN YOU ARE IN RECOVERY?

Basically, it means facing reality. It means being able to work through the fear and look at yourself—making adjustments, making changes, and then accepting yourself for your failures. It's about trusting yourself—knowing that you are committed to positive change (recovery from your addiction) and that you are OK with you. Perhaps for the first time in your life you will begin the lesson of defining your own space and setting healthy boundaries. This is your biggest aid in setting yourself separate from others who like the "old" you and who want to party one more time. This autonomy (self-actualization) allows you to continue on your journey of getting unstuck from your cycle of repeated negative, self-sabotaging behaviors. Now, for perhaps the first time in a long time, you are able to make decisions, think clearly, have increased self-respect and self-esteem. This is your jumping off point to having a clear sense of Self and in knowing yourself—thus liking yourself. You are able to be intimate in a healthy manner with someone who is equally as healthy. This is the bottom line for well-being and growth. Who was it that emerged from the murky bottom depths of darkness and self-destruction? YOU! Watch out world, here you are and you came to stay! CONGRATULATIONS!

Behavioral Health
Anxiety, Mood, Trauma, Personality

According to the Substance Abuse and Mental Health Services Administration (SAMHSA):

> *The Substance Abuse and Mental Health Services Administration (SAMHSA) found in 2008 that just over half (58.7 percent) of adults in the United States with a serious mental illness received treatment for a mental health problem. In 2012, there were an estimated 43.7 million adults aged 18 or older in the U.S. with adult mental illness in the past year. This represented 18.6 percent of all U.S. adults.*

Please note that the disorders I have chosen to briefly and incompletely describe are chosen only because I have seen frequent cases. By selecting these diagnoses, I do not wish to imply that they are better or worse than any other. Each diagnosis should be taken seriously and it is vital that you consult with your physician, a psychiatrist, a psychotherapist, or mental health counselor to be treated properly. Effective treatment is available for all of these disorders. Treatment helps the diagnosed individual enjoy a quality of life with fewer symptoms.

When one partner of a couple is diagnosed with a mental illness, the impact on both is serious. Life is challenging enough with all of its stressors without piling a diagnosis of any kind (physical or mental) on top of your relationship. In an effort to identify and discuss some of the more frequent diagnoses that I have encountered within my couple clients, I mention only a few.

Within this chapter called Behavioral Health, please know that I definitely have my clinical hat on and it is my duty to be competent in my efforts to help in all ways possible. The following diagnoses are only a few handpicked disorders—the most frequently occurring in my private practice. As a facilitator and collaborator, I see my duty as guiding the couple to feeling better—aiding with communication and problem-solving. As a psychotherapist and practitioner, my role shifts and my ethical duty is to identify, treat, and prescribe resources (physician for meds, psychotherapist) for the partner with an identifiable diagnosis.

Any of the following mental health diagnoses can have a big impact on both the individual with a diagnosis and their partner. Certainly, there is a range of severity within each diagnosis and across diagnostic categories. However, the biggest challenge is when someone suffers an illness and is either not diagnosed (and suffers for years without knowing why) or is misdiagnosed, only to continue suffering without professional assistance. Finally, the goal, of course, is to get the right help, which includes psychotropic medications (anti-depressant, anti-anxiety, etc.) and cognitive behavioral psychotherapy (CBT) to learn how to cope more effectively! Accordingly, the best treatment plan is medication and CBT. The goal is to get better, feel better, and cope better.

NOTE: THIS IS AN INCOMPLETE LISTING OF CRITERIA FOR EACH DIAGNOSIS as described within the DSM-5 (Diagnostic and Statistical Manual of Mental Disorders, Fifth Edition). Each of the following disorders DOES NOT IDENTIFY the complete full criteria to make a proper diagnosis.

Generalized Anxiety Disorder

I find this one very interesting because I have seen individuals and couples demonstrate clinical signs of this disorder, yet, they do not do anything about it. Excessive anxiety and worry (apprehensive expectation) across several areas, activities, or events in life such as work and school are the key elements. The timeline is for a minimum of 6 months! The key word is "excessive." The person with this disorder is on guard, expecting something to happen that will result in more anxiety. He or she finds that they can't control the worry. The worry just takes over. There are both physical symptoms (restlessness, fatigue, insomnia) and cognitive symptoms (inability to concentrate) that accompany this diagnosis. The DSM-5 states: "The anxiety, worry, or physical symptoms cause clinically significant distress or impairment in social, occupational, or other important areas of functioning."

I had one client with a toddler. She was at work and heard a news flash about a 3-year-old on the news in some terrible event. She could not work the rest of the day because she immediately started worrying about her own toddler and obsessed about every "what if" scenario she could think of. This would be termed as "excessive worry."

Hoarding Disorder According to the DSM-5:

"Approximately 80% to 90% of individuals with hoarding disorder display excessive acquisition. The most frequent form of acquisition is excessive buying, followed by acquisition of free items (e.g., leaflets, items discarded by others)."

Clinical Criteria Required for Hoarding Disorder:

- Persistent difficulty discarding or parting with possessions (regardless of value).
- Perceived need to save items and distress associated with discarding items.
- Long-standing difficulty results in congested living space and clutter (only uncluttered when third-party family members or authorities intervene).
- Hoarding causes significant distress or impairment in social, occupational, or other areas such as maintaining a safe environment for self or others.

- Diagnosis not due to medical condition or another mental disorder.

NOTE: Excessive acquisition is when acquisition is not needed or there is no available space.

NOTE: Good or Fair Insight: When the individual identifies or acknowledges that their "hoarding-related beliefs" (clutter, difficulty in discarding items) are problematic.

NOTE: Poor Insight: When the individual is convinced that their hoarding behaviors and beliefs are not problematic when there is clear evidence to the contrary.

Obsessive-Compulsive Disorder (OCD)

This is not to be confused with a personality disorder called Obsessive Compulsive Personality Disorder. This nonpersonality disorder is often referred to as OCD. The two main categories of criteria are obsessions (thoughts) or compulsions (behaviors).

Obsessions are categorized as: thoughts, impulses or images. Without listing the in-depth criteria mentioned by the DSM-5, please note that obsessions are "persistent" and "recurrent" and can be "intrusive," "inappropriate," or indicated by "marked anxiety or distress." Also, obsessions are not simply overly anxious worries about real-life problems. The person actually tries to ignore the obsessions or tries to "neutralize them" (with behaviors or mental acts). Finally, an individual with good or fair insight recognizes that these obsessive-compulsive disorder beliefs are definitely not true or probably not true.

Compulsions are categorized as repetitive behaviors or mental acts. The disorder causes repetitive behaviors (hand washing, ordering, checking) or mental acts (praying, counting, etc.); the person feels driven to performing "in response to an obsession, or according to rules that must be applied rigidly." These compulsions (behaviors or mental acts) are aimed at preventing or reducing anxiety/distress or preventing a dreaded event or situation. Remember! These behaviors or mental acts are not connected realistically "to what they are trying to neutralize or prevent." At the very least, these behaviors/mental acts are clearly excessive.

Obsessions or compulsions "are excessive or unreasonable," and at some point, the individual does recognize that fact. The disorder causes marked distress and can take up a lot of time (more than 1 hour a day), which can significantly and negatively have an impact on the level of functioning—socially, academically, work, in personal day-to-day routine. Neither obsessions nor compulsions are due to physical symptoms directly related to drug abuse, medications, or a general medical condition.

MOOD DISORDERS

This is not an all-inclusive list by exact name of each diagnosis, but certainly by type of Mood disorder:

Major Depressive Disorder

Dysthymic Disorder (low-grade depression)

Bi-polar Disorder (previously known as manic-depressive illness)

Cyclothymic Disorder (low-grade mania, hypomania)

Depressive Disorder and Mood Disorder (due to medical condition or substance use or a general miscellaneous category that does not meet any of the previously mentioned categories).

I will only briefly describe a few of these disorders—not to dismiss any of the unmentioned ones as unimportant. They are all very important to treat for your own well-being and for your partnership! Any mood disorder can be very impactful on both the person with a diagnosis and on their partner. Like any diagnosis, mood disorders can go undiagnosed or untreated. After all, everyone is "blue" or "down in the dumps" once in a while. Such catchall phrases encapsulate a myriad of depressive symptoms and tend to minimize the intensity and debilitating effects of mood disorders. This is not to say that when persons automatically feel blue that they have a diagnosis within this category. I am saying that those with this diagnosis often fall within the "feeling blue today" category, when it is indeed something much more serious and totally treatable. Mood disorders can be effectively treated with psychotropic medicines from either a psychiatrist or your own physician in addition to cognitive-based therapy that helps to alleviate symptoms.

NOTE: An INCOMPLETE listing of criteria for each diagnosis follows. All quotes are from the DSM-5 (*Diagnostic and Statistical Manual of Mental Disorders, Fifth Edition*).

Major Depressive Episode

This is a very serious disorder. There are two kinds of depression— endogenous and non-endogenous. Endogenous depression is a mood disorder that is considered to be genetic. When I see clients with an "off-and-on" history of depression since childhood, preteen years, teenage years, college years on upward, in addition to a family history of depression, then I consider that endogenous. Non-endogenous depression is more situational. Perhaps a person got laid off and they became depressed, perhaps, for the first time in their lives. They may adjust to the lay off, start exercising, get a job, and they don't get depressed again. I consider that as situational depression, rather than a biochemical genetic predisposition to ongoing depression. Remember do NOT blindly accept my thoughts as a firm and accurate diagnosis! In my practice, I also see many new mothers who have been diagnosed with postnatal depression. Depression can range from mild to severe and, thus, is treated with pharmaceuticals and with psychotherapy. If a new mother is breast-feeding, alternative methods should be considered, unless a physician specifies otherwise.

Clinical Requirements of Major Depressive Disorder

This is **not** a complete listing of criteria for **Major Depression** More often than not, at least one (A or B) occurs:

A) Feeling depressed or sad.

B) Loss of interest/no pleasure in activities.

- Depressed mood most of the day, nearly every day (feels sad, empty, hopeless)
- Markedly diminished interest (no pleasure at all) in all or almost all activities every day, nearly every day
- Significant weight loss/weight gain (5% in one month)
- Sleep too much, too little
- Feelings of restlessness/or being slowed down
- Fatigue or loss of energy nearly every day
- Feeling worthlessness or excessive/inappropriate guilt nearly every day
- Can't think, concentrate, make decisions, nearly every day
- Recurrent thoughts of death (not just fear of dying); recurrent suicidal ideation with a plan/without a plan; or a suicide attempt

C) Symptoms cause significant distress or impairment in social, occupational, or other important areas of functioning.

Bipolar Disorder
According to the Substance Abuse and Mental Health Services Administration (SAMSHA):

"At least half of all cases start before age 25. Some people have their first symptoms during childhood, while others may develop symptoms late in life."

According to the DSM-5:

"More than 90 percent of individuals who have a single Manic Episode go on to have future episodes. Approximately 60 percent to 70 percent of manic episodes occur immediately before or after a Major Depressive Episode. The lifetime risk of suicide in individuals with Bipolar Disorder is estimated to be at least 15 times that of the general population. Bipolar Disorder may account for 25% of all completed suicides."

Bipolar disorder is a biochemical disorder that results in mood fluctuations beyond the normal ups and downs and highs and lows that everyone experiences in our daily lives. It was once called "Manic-Depressive Disorder." This illness is hereditary. This disorder can severely impact the quality of life of the individual and their loved ones. Relationships suffer, school performance suffers, jobs or careers are erratic and problematic. Those with mild symptoms may appear to be especially happy and upbeat and filled with energy on some days or mildly depressed on others. Those with a severe diagnosis can demonstrate psychosis (distortion of reality), or be sleepless for days with excessive energy, or irritable/angry and/or crash to the depths of depression and be suicidal. When diagnosed early (this is not often the case), this disorder can be properly treated with medications and psychotherapy, and those with this illness can move forward in leading productive lives.

Clinical Requirements of Bipolar I:

- Manic Episode (more severe)—at least one episode is required
- Hypomanic Episode (less severe form of mania). This may precede Manic Episode or follow the Manic Episode
- Mixed Episode (experience both Manic and Depression at the same time-one week)
- Major Depression (one or more episodes). This may precede the Manic Episode or follow the Manic Episode

Clinical Requirements of Bipolar II:
Hypomanic Episode (at least one episode) + Depressive Episodes (one or more)

This is **not** a complete listing of criteria for **Manic Episode**:
Distinct period of abnormally and persistently elevated expansive or irritable mood, and goal-directed activity or energy, lasting at least one week. Presents most of the day, nearly every day.

- Inflated self-esteem or grandiosity
- Decreased need for sleep (feels rested after 3 hours sleep)
- More talkative than usual (pressure to keep talking)
- Feels like thoughts are racing
- Easily distracted (attention drawn to unimportant stimuli)
- Increase in goal-directed activity (social, work, school, sex); or non-goal-directed activity (psychomotor agitation)
- Excessive involvement in activities that have high potential for painful consequences (unrestrained buying sprees; sexual indiscretions; foolish business investments)

There is a marked impairment in social/occupational functioning (or hospitalization may be required to prevent harm to self or others).

During my pre-doctoral internship, I remember a young college student with bipolar disorder who told me after she was accurately diagnosed that she felt relieved because she always felt she was "different." She said that she had such highs and lows that she would often become extremely irritable—she'd "fire all of her friends." As a young college co-ed she then wanted to be with her friends (who'd left her) and she would feel depressed. Her cycle ranged from "high" and "feeling on top of the world" to "depression" and "irritability." When she did hit what we agreed to call "baseline" (normal) she was bored because no crisis was developing in her life. Luckily, she had loving and attentive parents who supported her completely. She took her medication, was successful in maintaining her attendance in school, and she was able to modify her scholastic goals accordingly. Unfortunately, too many individuals go undiagnosed for years and terminate friends or jobs terminate them. It is a very up-and-down existence with lots of confusion; life does not seem to be as smooth sailing like everyone else's. If you are someone who has this diagnosis, please see a doctor (preferably psychiatrist) and get on the right medicine—the right dosage of that medicine and keep taking your medicine even if time passes and you feel good. This is a lifelong disorder.

Post–Traumatic Stress Disorder (PTSD)

Due to a growing awareness in our society at large and our country having experienced war and peace, the DSM-5 has distinctly and strategically placed PTSD under the category of "Trauma and Stressor-Related Disorders." This important distinction and its revised (expanded clinical) definition is timely and needed.

Clinical Requirements for Diagnosis of Post-Traumatic Stress Disorder—DSM-5:

There are five distinctive areas or categories in which clusters of symptoms present. Overall there are certain number of items that must be identified in each of the categories in order to make a diagnosis. However, I did not specify that number, nor have I offered a complete listing of symptoms/behaviors. This is informative only and INCOMPLETE.

A) Exposure to actual or threatened death, serious injury, or sexual violence:

- You experience the trauma.
- You witness the event as it happens to others.
- You hear about it as it occurred to a close family/friend (violent or accidental death).
- You experience repeated or extreme exposure to details of the traumatic event (that you try to avoid; this can apply to first responders such as CSI investigators or police officers who are repeatedly exposed to details of child abuse).

B) Reliving the trauma:

- Intrusive recurrent distressing memories, thoughts, or images of the trauma.
- Recurrent distressing dreams (nightmares).
- Flashbacks (conscious).

- Internal or external cues that symbolize or resemble an aspect of the trauma.
- Physical reactions to either internal or external cues that symbolize or resemble an aspect of the trauma.

C) Avoidance:

- Avoiding (people, places things, activities, situations).
- Erase the memory (don't talk, emotionally numb).
- Relationships suffer (even with children relationships become strained).

D) Negative changes in cognitions or mood associated with the traumatic event:

- Can't remember an important aspect of the trauma.
- Persistent and exaggerated negative beliefs or expectations about oneself, others, or the world. Example: "No one can be trusted." "I am bad."
- Persistent blaming of self or others due to distorted cognitions about either the cause of the traumatic event or the consequences of the event.
- Persistent negative emotions (such as fear, horror, anger, guilt, or shame).
- Diminished interest/participation in significant activities.
- Feeling detached or estranged from others.
- Persistent inability to experience positive emotions (happiness satisfaction, or love).

E) Marked alterations in arousal and reactivity associated with the trauma:

- Reckless or self-destructive behavior.
- Anger issues (easily irritated with little provocation).

- Difficulty sleeping.
- Difficulty concentrating.
- Super alert or watchful on guard.
- Startle response.

Borderline Personality Disorder

This specific personality disorder is a composite of instability across several areas—relationships, mood, impulsiveness, and self-image. The DSM-5 states it as: "a pervasive pattern." This disorder begins in early adulthood and is identified by the criteria that follow (this is an INCOMPLETE listing of criteria. DSM-5 states:

- Frantic efforts to avoid real or imagined abandonment (if you are late for lunch, it means you have abandoned them and believe you have "left" them for being bad).
- Pattern of unstable/intense relationships (the individual idealizes and devalues the same person—you are the best therapist in the world/you are the worst therapist in the world).
- Persistently unstable self-image (personal appearance, career goals, values, etc.).
- Impulsive and reckless in spending, sex, substance use, driving, eating.
- Recurrent suicidal behavior, gestures, threats or self-mutilating behavior (cuts wrists, thighs, arms, breasts, stomach, etc.).
- Mood instability (lasting for a few hours or a few days: irritability, anxiety, dysphoria).
- Chronic feelings of emptiness (client says, "I have an empty black hole in my belly."—I heard that a lot).
- Inappropriate intense anger, difficulty controlling anger.
- Paranoid ideation, severe dissociative symptoms (stress related).

Individuals with borderline personality disorder suffer deep within. They present with cognitive distortions and overreact to simple everyday occurrences; they believe it directly relates to them. There is a range of functionality with this disorder. Even if you worked with someone who did not meet the criteria for this severe disorder, you would still probably find them to be a difficult personality to work with. These individuals lead lives filled with drama and chaos. There are a lot of relationship changes and upsets. They hop from one intimate partner to the next to avoid being alone. There is much more information not provided here that can not be adequately covered within this small paragraph. There are some excellent behavioral-based treatment programs specifically for individuals with borderline personality disorder. Schema therapy is a specific type of therapy used in the treatment of personality disorders and most commonly for borderline personality disorder. Depending upon which psychological theory you subscribe to, many mental health professionals aspire to the theory that borderline personality disorder (as well as other similar personality disorders) is the result of childhood and adolescent trauma.

Narcissistic Personality Disorder

Once again, the DSM-5 uses the word "pervasive pattern" of "grandiosity in both fantasy and in behavior." Need for admiration and lack of empathy. DSM-5 states:

- Grandiose sense of self-importance
- Preoccupied fantasies (success, power, brilliance, beauty, ideal love)
- Sense of entitlement
- Requires excessive admiration
- Believes to be 'special/unique'
- Takes advantage of others (interpersonally exploitative)
- Lacks empathy
- Envious of others or believes others to be envious of him/her
- Shows arrogant, haughty behaviors or attitudes

The classic example I give of the narcissist personality is illustrated in a description of my recent accident. I tell my friend that the ambulance came and the police showed up. I say, "Oh it was unbelievable! I am really shook up." My friend says, "Oh that happened to me once and I was on my way to get my hair done and when the accident happened it was shocking. I had just gotten off work early and the ambulance came and I cried and…and then another time… I was on vacation and…." All of a sudden, my story turns into her story. If you listen carefully, you will begin to see signs of how it is all about them. They have a difficult time being empathetic and seeing a situation from the other person's perspective. They can become very irritable when wounded by criticism.

Obsessive-Compulsive Personality Disorder

This is not to be confused with "Obsessive-Compulsive Disorder" (as previously mentioned). The key adjectives as with all of the previously mentioned personality disorders are the words, "pervasive pattern." The DSM-5 states:

> *"A pervasive pattern of preoccupation with orderliness, perfectionism, and mental and interpersonal control, at the expense of flexibility, openness, and efficiency."*

This disorder begins by early adulthood.

The DSM-5 states the following:

- Preoccupied with: details, rules, lists, order, organization, or schedules so that the major point of the activity is lost.
- Shows perfectionism that interferes with task completion.
- Excessively devoted to work and productivity (excluding leisurely fun activities or friendships—not due to economic necessity).
- Overly conscientious, scrupulous and inflexible about morality, ethics, or values (not due to cultural or religious identification).
- Unable to discard worn-out or worthless objects—even though no emotional or sentimental attachment.

- Reluctant to delegate tasks or work with others unless they submit to exactly his or her ways of doing things.
- Miserly. Compelled to hoard money for future catastrophes.
- Shows rigidity and stubbornness.

Overall, across all categories, the individual with obsessive-compulsive personality disorder is a rigid, rule/regulated, orderly and detailed perfectionist who has a difficult time being a team player or follower. They will be late on deadlines because their perfectionism instills within them a feeling that the paper they wrote for school is not perfect enough to hand in, or that report is not just right and so therefore they delay handing it into the boss at work. They cannot "see the forest for the trees," or, in this case, they cannot see the trees for the leaves. This can be a serious disorder and very debilitating (as are all personality disorders).

Physical Abuse/ Domestic Violence

PUSHING, CHOKING, HITTING, KNIFE, GUN

General Information

I once counseled a young couple who politely listened while I gave them my standard discussion on NO VIOLENCE. As I described what exactly that meant, by providing examples, they looked at each other and then at me. He said, "Well, I only threw her down on the bed and choked her." Of course, I stopped everything right there and asked some very detailed questions. "Yes, that is indeed VIOLENCE!" He genuinely looked confused and repeated that it happened a long time ago (one year ago) and that he only choked her for a few minutes. "After all, it's not like I hurt her," he said. For all of my readers, I would like to know your thoughts on that one? Based on his answer, it was only considered violence if she actually suffered injury or death. She, of course, sat there in silence.

I do not take on couple's therapy with violent couples; I refer them instead to therapists who only see violent couples and no other clients. My premise is that my short-term results-oriented therapeutic model does not fit with the totally focused intensity needed for ongoing care required for this special type of volatility.

To help both partners, a multifaceted interdisciplinary approach— psychological, medical, financial, legal and child-focused (to mention a few)—is needed. It is a subspecialty that is desperately needed and not widely available. It is quite usual for a couple's therapist to uncover self-reported acts of violence, either while doing an intake or throughout the course of the sessions. Depending on the same criteria for addiction, I think any therapist would determine keeping the couple or not (even if was not a subspecialty) depending upon certain factors unique to that couple such as how many times the therapist has seen the couple and where the couple is in their journey of seeking help (just beginning, making strides toward change, etc.). Much more detailed information is required up front regarding the physical abuse (last time? how many times? the nature of abuse etc.). What were the medical injuries and psychological injuries sustained at that time? Then, moving along to a dual diagnosis of both substance abuse issues/addiction and violence— Were either set of parents in a violent dynamic? What are the legal ramifications of these violent acts (arrest, restraining orders, etc.)?

These are difficult cases with ups-and-downs throughout therapy. Such specialized therapy is very directive. Such couples are not well suited to a passive approach of silence after asking the key question: "Tell me how you feel...." We live in a world of specialization (cardiologists, pharmacologists, psychiatrists, etc.). Of course, within the world of psychotherapy as I have previously stated, there are also subspecialties.

Questions and investigations about physical abuse could easily take up an entire book. The bottom line is that the negative dynamic is identified, explored in detail, and handled effectively by either someone who specializes in the area of domestic violence on a day-to-day basis or by a couple's therapist to determine if gains are being met based on the type of aggressive act and the genuine motivation of both partners for change.

Safety

The most important aspect of all is the victim's safety. Once the existence of a physically abusive relationship has been documented, the victim's safety is the primary focus. This could mean everything from having an immediate safety plan in case violence suddenly occurs, to having a long-term plan for extracting the victim to a permanent and

secret place of safety and financial freedom. The immediate plan usually includes having a bag packed with change of clothes, toiletries,
keys to the car, money, and so on—hidden and available in case of a
crisis. If there are children involved, it means having all of the necessary things for them as well (bag of clothes, toys, etc.). It also means
having someone trustworthy available to the victim to call when the
crisis happens—a place to go to and someone else who knows about
the crisis and the victim's intent to leave. It is a good thing to have a
detailed plan that accounts for adjustments if needed. If 911 is called,
the victim should always have a back-up plan for exiting. Safety can
not be overemphasized! Safety is especially important for those who
either feel they cannot physically leave or for those who do not feel
emotionally strong enough to leave. Individual counseling or visiting
a non-profit in your area that specializes in domestic violence is a
comprehensive way to get the resources needed (counseling, shelter,
financial, legal). Do not delay! Get help now.

Violence Escalated

It's a very complicated topic. Both partners can be violent to each
other. I have heard stories about women who were silent and com-
pliant, but after a few years figured out that it would never be good
enough; they started to fight back. There are books available for you
to read that will educate you about the cycle of violence. I highly
recommend Lundy Bancroft's, *Why Does He Do That: Inside the Minds
of Angry and Controlling Men*. Bottom line, it escalates over time in intensity (from pushing to choking, to knife, to gun) and in frequency.
Instead of once a year, it advances in stages—more frequently and
closer together—monthly, then weekly, then three times per week.
Finally, the duration is the length of time the event lasts. Over time, it
lasts longer and takes a longer time to calm down. For example, one
female client said: "Things used to be good for us in between his upsets, but now they happen more often and they last longer." The cycle
of violence is a syndrome—a cluster of behaviors, cognitions, and
psychological attitudes. This syndrome is the violent dance between
each partner.

In my direct and up-front approach, I fall short of telling any person in psychotherapy, "You should leave him." The ONLY EXCEPTION is when there is violence! In this case, I am vocal, direct, and outspoken. I remember one young couple who came to see me. Over the years, I have become very adept at recognizing who the perpetrator might be. For me, it is the creepy feeling I get around my shoulders and neck when I am in the presence of a perpetrator of violence. I always physically feel it before I clue in to what is happening. I am certain that other therapists have their own indicators. The dilemma is that you have this very nice-looking man sitting, smiling, and being very cooperative, but there is a cloud in the room. As I watch how he behaves and I listen to his words and watch his style, his wife sits like a mouse—very still.

Control and Dominance

Even so, after a little bit of time you can clearly see that his persuasive style is exactly that. He's trying to sell me something and she is so prickly she looks really uptight. Another clue for me is his choice of words. "My wife and I…."; "Well, my wife…"; " I tell my wife…." The therapeutic impression is that control and dominance is the name of that tune. This is very indicative of the abusive relationship. As the renowned author Lundy Bancroft clearly points out in his comprehensive book, *Why Does He Do That; Inside the Minds of Angry and Controlling Men*, the male aggressor takes power and control over his partner by first getting inside her head. He consistently tells her what to think, what to do and slowly but effectively erodes her own perception of Self. She begins the downward slide of doubting herself, second-guessing her own abilities, and believing his manipulative statements. He masterfully corners his prey and strips her (figuratively) of all self-esteem or any sense of Self. Thus, she becomes the victim while the physical aggression rises. It is a two-pronged attack—psychological and physical.

One couple who were physically separated came to see me. She had taken the children and moved in with a relative. It actually turned out that he had cheated on her—all too common.

He was so upset he kept claiming his devoted love to her (except that he was spying on her). Even though he had no physical proof, he accused her of cheating on him. To fast forward, I will say that our couple sessions were over after that first session. He decided that he did not want to come back to therapy. Eventually, she got a restraining order against him and then later wanted to rescind it—not possible. "I still love him," she said. She wanted him restrained but she didn't want him punished—a seesaw of the violent and volatile couple.

STATISTICS FOR DOMESTIC VIOLENCE

Recent Data Confirms That . . .

Nationally, one in four women reports intimate partner violence. The average number of times an abuser hits his spouse before she makes a police report is 35. In the United States, the top two causes of women's death during pregnancy are domestic homicide and suicide, often tied to abuse. Thirty-four percent of rape and sexual assault victims by a family member are under the age of 18. Chances that a gay or bisexual man experiences domestic violence is two out of five (similar to heterosexual women). Ninety-two percent of homeless women with children report having experienced domestic violence. The number of men who experience intimate partner violence is one in seven (this does not specify female to male, or male to male). Men who as children witnessed their parents' domestic violence were twice as likely to abuse their own wives than sons of nonviolent parents. The stats are very depressing. There are statistics by gender and by race, but according to nearly all data sites, data is inadequate due to unreported violence.

As much we want to believe that we have evolved technologically, philosophically, politically, economically, socially, and/or spiritually, these statistics give pause. Like any other social ill, there is no difference across economic or social boundaries. When it is wrong, it is wrong. For me, as a clinician, the challenge—and the internal alert system that percolate when seeing clients—is paying attention to their behavior (mood, thoughts, actions) while simultaneously checking within myself for my own reactions to the client, my clinical sense of the client. The most important question is "How am I reacting internally to the story that is being told and to the story that is not being told?" In other words, do I have a bias? I can say boldly—without hesitation—that I did not specialize in domestic violence couples for this reason.

Women vs. Men

As you can see from these statistics, domestic violence is NOT gender-specific. For sure, I had multiple females who were physically violent against their husbands. I can honestly say that in each one of those cases, when the husband called the police even with a bloody nose, a broken jaw, or a black eye, the wife told the officer that the husband was the perpetrator. In every single case, the police believed the female even though the husband who called the police claimed to be the victim. The men were arrested or charges were brought against them and each man had to spend large sums of money to hire an attorney to defend his name and on their battle for child custody/visitation without supervision. It was a tough, costly battle that resulted in those with little money ending with less or nothing and those who had labored to build a family and a wealthy lifestyle completely financially decimated!

In the cases I am referring to—where the woman was the aggressor (violent abuser)—the observable difference was that the men (no matter what physical type) almost always presented as passive, quiet, and dismissive. The female partner, on the other hand, was vocal, loud, domineering, and articulate. Much more information, however, is needed before one or the other is determined to be the aggressor or the victim. **Please note: These are generalities to which I am referring. This is not true on a case-by-case basis.**

Men vs. Women

No matter which way you slice it, it is an ugly story. Domestic violence is a significant social problem staring us in the face, but there still is so much silence that surrounds this issue. According to the Bureau of Justice Statistics, Female Victims of Violence, up to 99 percent of all criminal assaults are perpetrated by men. The "Power and Control Wheel" is not "gender-neutral" specifically because of the above-mentioned statistics. Men are socialized to violence at an early age, whereas, women in general, are not. When a woman becomes violent, it is more often in reaction to the perpetrator's initial violent act toward her first. Women are not emotionally, socially, or physically engineered to violence, which is socially more acceptable for men—in career choices, sports, or in early role-model identification.

Same-sex Partners

It is known that the cycle of violence for same-sex couples looks very similar and holds many common characteristics as the heterosexual couple. However, same-sex couples operate from within a larger framework of being disenfranchised and oppressed by mainstream society. Specific stressors can alter the dynamics of each domestic partner within their identity framework. What am I saying? Because they are discriminated by society at large and view themselves as "different" from mainstream norms, the pattern or evolution of their cycle of violence takes on a new meaning. Because they often view themselves as a couple within a smaller social circle of like-minded individuals, they can be less reliant upon community mainstream resources during a time of crisis. Overall, this changes their dynamic. They might be more inclined to not reach out for help, thus, remaining doubly isolated in their violent environment.

VIOLENT ACTS

I have always taught my couples that throwing pillows and slamming kitchen cupboard doors are all acts of violence! Certainly walking in the front door after a terrible day at work and kicking the dog and yelling at the kids is NOT OK! In graduate psychology programs, they teach budding therapists to help clients release anger by experiencing anger or by becoming genuinely angry in session. Over the years, I have started to subscribe to a different way of thinking about anger. It is really best to release the anger the way that you would release unforgiveness and resentments. Or, perhaps it is about reaching out to forgive rather than stew in your resentments and anger. You can do that with several of the cognitive exercises I have given you in various sections of this book, most specifically under SHAME, GUILT, and FORGIVENESS.

As they say, "At the end of the day, you have to live with yourself." However, remember that you have a partner or a family that has to live with you also. So you know what I am going to say, right? Yes, every time you take healthy steps toward healing yourself, everyone else that you love benefits too.

To my male readers, please hear me when I say this: "Whatever you've achieved in your careers by working hard and advancing within your profession to provide for your family is tremendous! That makes you a good man in many ways! However, that is NOT the end of the line. There is much more to it." I've heard many of you say, "Well, I'm a good provider!" Yeah, and what about you being hard to live with in your moodiness and volatile anger spells? One does not outweigh the other. Or, perhaps they do. In other words, your working hard does NOT compensate for any anger rages, verbal abuse, or physical violence. Further, any anger rages, verbal abuse, or physical violence **does negatively eliminate any good you might have achieved** in other productive areas. There is no such thing as, "I hit her because she's stupid and she made me upset! But, I make a lot of money and I am the king of this castle and she's lucky to have me. I am a good man!" That is not how it works. You can't explain away your violence for ANY REASON! NO! As fathers, and as partners, you have power and influence over other family members. You are their role models. Your sons are learning first-hand how to treat their wives and daughters when they grow up to be fathers. Your daughters are growing up and learning from you that this is how a man is supposed to treat a woman; you are their role model. At the very least, you are creating the next generation of anxious and angry adults. I would also point out that you, the aggressor, are also suffering on the inside. You have chosen a maladaptive, dysfunctional, dangerous and angry-impulsive coping style based upon Control and Power. STOP IT! Please get help now.

DID I TELL YOU ABOUT YOUNG BOYS EXPOSED TO CHRONIC DOMESTIC VIOLENCE?

Years ago, I remember telling a female client that although she insisted on waiting until her son graduated from high school before divorcing her husband, she was living in an explosive home environment with a violent, alcoholic husband, and she was imprinting violence on her son's psyche. She didn't get it. I explained to her that if she had ever decided in the middle of a crisis to leave and take her son with her to a domestic violence shelter, that the shelter would open the door to her and ask her the age of her son. When she explained that her son was 12 years old, they would explain something to her and then close the door. Certainly, they would admit her, but NOT her 12-year-old son. WHY? Because when a young boy has been chronically exposed to violence at home, the premise is that the 12-year-old male child has already been instilled with the formula for violence in his subconscious. He could be the sweetest most protective young son around. However, he has been exposed and programmed by a violent father to go forth into the world. One of two things will happen. He will either grow up and become a violent perpetrator himself or he will choose to become a victim. Why on earth would you wait for the kitchen to be remodeled or wait until he graduates from high school or wait period! GET OUT NOW!

DOMESTIC VIOLENCE IN SUMMARY

Domestic violence can result in either death or major physical debilitations. It can end up with psychological trauma, nightmares, mood disorders, and post-traumatic stress disorder (PTSD). It can end up with children without one parent or without both parents. The story can end up with one person in prison and in financial devastation. Everyone suffers. The court systems are filled to the brim with entire departments specifically devoted to family services including mediation services, child custody evaluations, child support advocacy, victim rights, psychological evaluations, and social services. District Attorney offices are devoted to the entire legal drama that unfolds once the police arrive at your doorstep due to a domestic violent call.

What does this mean to you? It means your municipal and county government have resources available to you. It also means that your local and countywide non-profits and mental health practitioners are trained professionals who are qualified in this specific area. Please make the call.

DOMESTIC ABUSE INTERVENTION PROJECT
202 East Superior Street
Duluth, Minnesota 55802
218-722-2781
www.duluth-model.org

The Power and Control Wheel

THE POWER AND CONTROL WHEEL

By The Domestic Abuse Intervention Project, Duluth, Minnesota

The Power and Control Wheel was developed by battered women abused by their male partners. The Duluth women's shelter conducted educational groups that fostered the inception of both the Power and Control Wheel in addition to the Equality Wheel, created by the women participants attending the educational group.

I have used this Power and Control Wheel for years in my private practice, providing handouts that generated much dialogue between my individual female clients and me. I would often meet a new female client who would tell her story as to why she was seeking my services. It always started out a little fuzzy as to what had happened or what she needed from me. Then, as I observed and listened some more, she would provide small examples of what her spouse had said or had done. My ears would prick up and immediately I would sense that he was an abuser. Next, I would gently ask specific questions as to their history together and probe for other examples of his behavior and how she reacted to it. Then, I would clearly and calmly deliver my feedback to her that his behavior fit a profile of a "domestic abuser." I would give her the handout while we further discussed whether or not he really fit the profile. At that point, the female client would either become very silent and tense and acknowledge what I suspected, or, she would begin to open up and energetically provide more examples of what her relationship at home was really like.

The following is a commentary on each segment of the Wheel. Take a moment to determine if this fits for you as well. You will find that every aspect of the circle is an overt example of both behavior and mind control, ensuring power over a female partner.

Using Intimidation

This is a composite of violent behavior toward her physical, emotional, and environmental well-being. He violates her physically by his actions, looks, and gestures. He could touch her (push, beat, harm), or he could look and gesture a threat that he has the right to intimidate her at any time; she better beware because it can happen at any time. He is in charge. He is the ruler and the enforcer. He can damage her personal property (rip her clothes, smash her belongings, throw out her make-up, kick her dog). He often will display weapons in a threatening way (spread them out on the bed, set them next to him while he sits in his recliner in the living room).

Using Emotional Abuse

This is another huge aspect of control. He puts her down and calls her terrible names. One minute he makes her feel guilty and the next minute he destroys her self-esteem. He plays mind games to control her and dominate her. For example, he might say one thing but does another so that she can't gauge what he wants or when he will strike. It keeps her constantly on edge and makes her uncertain about her own thoughts and feelings. This is the part that wears her down inch by inch. "You are an ungrateful bitch!"

Using Isolation

He keeps her a prisoner sometimes in a subtle way and other times in a not so subtle way. In the early part of the relationship he might not tell her directly that she cannot do something. He would create an obstacle or he would complain about her friends who he doesn't trust. Or, if she brought a friend over, he would treat her friend(s) very rudely so that they would not come back. Over time, he would be more direct and forbid her to go somewhere, put her down and say that she hasn't performed this task or that task, or that they cannot afford it. Finally, if she were to go, he would make her pay for it emotionally and physically upon her return. Talk about negative reinforcement! The message is loud and clear. Do not talk to your mother or sister, do not go anywhere, and do not make friends!

Minimizing, Denying and Blaming

This is the indirect manner of confusing her and making her uncertain. At first, she might see that he is dismissing her perspective on the abuse. She might express that she does not like it and does not deserve it. Then, he slowly undoes her justification by twisting the reality by blaming her, denying his actions and even saying that the abuse did not happen. He claims he did not do what she says he did! This is ongoing and does not happen once in a while. It is an underlying foundation of the abuse cycle. This is so typical, "You are always making mistakes and all I try to do is help you to be happy! When I point out something you have done wrong, it is for your own good!"

Using Children

Children are definitely a vulnerable point for her. He uses them as weapons against her psyche! He gives them messages to tell mom (triangulation). He makes her feel guilty and makes her question her own mothering skills. He threatens to take the children from her and she will never see them again. I had one female client whose spouse would take the girls to the side and tell them terrible lies about their mother and undermine her own relationship with them.

Using Male Privilege

He defines who does what. He views himself as "King of the Castle." She is not viewed or treated as his queen—only as a servant or slave. She will never be good enough. He is smarter, he makes the money, and she is nothing. This is why he controls all major decisions and even small decisions. "Why did you buy this brand of mayonnaise? You know I hate this brand!" Even though the last brand they used was that brand. In this manner, he whips her with words. One female client cooked, cleaned, and took care of the kids, and he went out and spent enormous amounts of money eating and drinking with the guys (and flirting with the girls) at a bar. She was like Cinderella at home.

Using Economic Abuse

If she is fortunate to have her own job, he will take her paycheck and perhaps give her an allowance. He will monitor the on-line banking ATM balance for everything! He will go through her wallet and purse and sneak to find out any trace of activity about which he does not know. He might prevent her from getting a job. I had a female client whose boyfriend e-mailed the VP of a company who was getting ready to send a written offer to my client. The boyfriend slandered her and sounded crazy. Needless to say, she never got the offer!

Using Coercion and Threats

He can talk about making threats in the future, or he can actually threaten her right there. He can use what I call the deal breaker threat when he says he'll call her boss and tell her that she uses drugs. Or he threatens to call her probation officer with a lie. He forces her to drop the charges against him, or he will take the kids, or leave her penniless, or he will beat her to a pulp.

DIVORCE ATTORNEY? COLLABORATIVE MEDIATION? LITIGATION?

All of the three above mentioned are choices you might decide upon. Please make the choice after gathering information so that you can make an informed decision.

When an individual client comes to me thinking of divorce and describing months of marital arguments that threaten "divorce," I would advocate being a good scientific investigator. My sales pitch is that you cannot make an effective decision until you have all the data, sift through the data, and then make an informed decision. Thus, I would short-circuit all of the complaining and strongly advocate that my client (male or female) go see an attorney, only paying the 1-hour consultation fee. In other words, pay the $250.00 to $650.00 fee for 1 hour only. Do not sit in the attorney's office and cough up a $5,000-to-$20,000 deposit to hire him or her as your divorce attorney during the first visit. The goal is to go there and ask every single question you can think of regarding your marital status. I encourage the client to bring as much financial data to the attorney to calculate who gets the BMW; the vacation home; payment for their child's college; child custody arrangements; alimony; cost of a divorce; and your total income after separation of assets.

Clients who complained the loudest were frequently the ones who usually dragged their heels about going to see an attorney. Granted, my agenda was manipulative. It was not to receive an overabundance of thank you letters from various attorneys for my referrals. Rather, it was to give my clients a reality check as to what it was like to actually sit in front of an attorney and to hear themselves speak out loud about an actual divorce. Sometimes, it scared them straight back into the arms of their spouse. Other times, it helped them realize that they could make it financially. Either way, it was an empowering exercise.

I do not advocate seeing an attorney to push my clients into a divorce. My purpose is to help them either stop complaining and threaten divorce, or to go through with it. Do it or don't!

Ongoing verbal threats of divorce during a heated argument is a game. If my individual client suffers from a spouse who is doing the threatening at home and my client is frozen in fear, I advocate seeing an attorney. This is so that the next time their partner says, "I'm going to divorce you and you won't get anything!" after consulting with an attorney, my client could silently say to themselves, "Hmmm, well actually that is NOT true because I know my legal rights." This alone, could be very empowering and help my client to stop being a victim and move closer toward some actionable steps which would be to their benefit (even if they stayed in the marriage, they would learn to become a stronger partner, informed partner and to make healthier decisions, rather than frozen in fear with no real information at their fingertips).

Litigation today can cost you the price of your home (and we all know that's not worth what it used to be). Long gone are the days of the 1950s and 1960s when you hired an attorney and went to court and litigated for divorce. Today, with attorney fees and court costs, the price of a full-scale fight in court can be astronomical.

I had one female client who hired an attorney; her husband also hired an attorney; and the two attorneys faxed each other back and forth for 3 weeks prior to the first court appointment. The faxing cost more than $17,000.00, and nothing was accomplished (no restraining order, etc.) from 3 weeks of faxing. Now, don't get me wrong. For some reason, I like attorneys. I like the way they think and as clients they have challenged me big time (so of course I had to challenge them back). However, unless you have a lot of disposable income, many of my clients could not afford the traditional litigation attached to fighting for divorce in the courts.

Thus, the current day outgrowth of a crowded court calendar and mushrooming courtroom costs is the role of the divorce mediator. This is a fascinating and very tangible method to achieve legal representation along with a facilitative approach to mediating as to who-gets-what, without the large attorney fees of litigation. Family law as an umbrella over the mediation alternative started in the 1970s.

> *"There are many reasons why parties choose mediation over the court system, including: the desire for a more relaxed environment and process, less formalities of law, the ability for the parties to communicate freely and participate more in the process, the cheaper cost of mediation, and its shorter duration."*
> (J. Abraham, 2009).

Various models of mediation exist. I only mention three models that I advocate for my clients: One is for each partner to get legal consultation on the side with their respective attorneys to determine what their rights are and to identify their own needs and wants for the final disbursement of funds and property. Then, taking the document or "wish list," each partner would meet together in a third attorney's office (neutral to each of them) who would help them negotiate or mediate their individual differences, while inclusively identifying their mutually agreed-upon commonalities.

In this setting, even if more than one session is needed, the idea is that any changes or modifications made could be agreed to in that setting or each partner returns to their original attorney to discuss the suggested modifications. After that, each partner takes their respective document and notations from their attorney and return together to the mediator's (third attorney) office for final negotiation. Once full agreement is reached, then both parties sign. The mediator (attorney) then files the paperwork for both parties. Both parties return several weeks or months later for signing of final court documents filed by the mediator.

Another model called, "Collaborative Divorce Mediation" is very effective and takes place in a law firm office. Each partner (couple) shows up at the same law office conference room and each has individual personal legal representation (an attorney from the law firm), unless they already had a personal attorney who accompanies them. In addition to each divorcing partner, and their respective attorneys, there would also be a facilitator or divorce mediator. This mediator is someone with a licensed psychological background (licensed social worker, psychologist, or licensed marriage therapist), who is certified and trained in mediation. In this model, the facilitator manages the emotions and facilitates each partner's efforts toward agreement. The attorneys in the room legally represent each partner's individual "wish list" or most desired outcome. This model uses a multi-level approach which acknowledges both the legal and negotiated outcomes, while the mediator who is trained in both psychology and in mediation is responsible for toning down extreme emotional displays from either partner. By helping all four members, the two attorneys and the two divorcing partners, the facilitator's goal is to help everyone move forward in a non-threatening and non-abusive format to reach a successful legally negotiated contract without emotional upheaval.

In other similar models, there are two facilitators (one male and one female). In this manner, each divorcing partner has their own emotional facilitator and their respective attorney representing their legal needs. The goals of the sessions are the same.

These are just three of many mediation models available to you. The most important thing to know is that it is a much briefer and more cost-effective choice of action than court litigation. From my perspective, the goal is to achieve a holistic approach to divorce with less emotional upheaval (if that is even possible during a divorce). In other words, the goal is to not inflict more pain on each other, but to treat each other with respect, move through the process and have compassion for your soon-to-be ex-partner.

You are still spending the fees for each attorney, the mediator(s), and for the filing fees. In the end, it is much more cost-effective, however, than the alternative.

PART VI

You!

LOVE YOURSELF FIRST

I tell my clients, I may have a doctorate in psychology, but this is NOT rocket science! My belief is that you've heard or read this before. So much of it is commonsense. However, the thing that fascinates me about life is that I have books in my library to read, and for some reason, I don't read some of them for years. From time to time, I walk right up to an unread book and realize it is exactly what I need to know and understand at that particular point in my life. How timely! With that introduction, what I am about to say you've heard before, yet, my hope is that once again, this is a timely statement that you need to hear right now in your life—on this day and at this time. Here goes….

In any relationship YOU are the most important person. In order to love someone else, you need to love yourself first. How can you take care of someone else's needs or wants unless you attend to your own first? How do you take care of yourself? How often? In your hectic schedule (kids, work, church, commitments, soccer, PTA, dinner, laundry, etc.), do you take time out for yourself every day? Do you actually carve out 15 minutes each day for you alone? It could be your early morning cup of coffee before anyone else gets out of bed! Think small, but think daily. Think doable and think regular.

If up to this point and time you have not made the time to be supportive of yourself, then do you know how to begin? When will you start? Are you already starting to make excuses or doubting your follow-through? Please don't—just say it like you want it and then decide how to make it happen. Don't commit to something HUGE like joining a gym (when you know you won't go), or say "I'll do it at 5:30 A.M." when you are not a morning person! That would be setting yourself up for failure.

Making yourself a priority might even be setting aside one full day per month for only you—go out shopping; take a long lovely bath; go out to lunch with a friend(s); go to a movie; have someone watch the kids all day; go browsing at the bookstore; go to the ocean; go hiking. You can even name the day after yourself! Mark it on the calendar and call it "Pat's Day." This effort that you put back into yourself will reap you many rewards. In addition, those who love you will also benefit because you will be aligning yourself with healthy behaviors that give you back positive energy.

Sometimes, when statements like, "Loving Self" are said out loud, everyone nods their head in agreement. This is commonsense, but sometimes it is not easy to switch gears and do it. Does that sound right? Perhaps, you need to be reminded of some very important essentials in relationships. The core foundation in any relationship begins with the relationship you have within yourself. You are the most important person in the relationship. Actually, you are the most important person in the Universe! How can you begin to love someone else if you have no love or respect for yourself? What kind of gift do you give to the other person you love if you don't love yourself? "I love you so much I give myself to you. Oh by the way, I don't really like myself, nor do I love myself, but I just want to give myself to you. You are really important to me." Thanks, but no thanks would be my answer. To my readers who are more traditional, I would wonder how you confidently profess that your body is a Temple yet, you continue to treat yourself and your body with disrespect? Are you hearing my concern?

You know when you fly in an airplane and the flight attendant gives the safety speech that if anything goes wrong, the adult needs to put the oxygen mask on first before attending to anyone else (even a child)? Guess what? If you don't, you'll pass out from a lack of oxygen. Your challenge is to love yourself without condition.

So in this context, what does loving Self really mean? It means having an intimate relationship with yourself. It means being mindful of your own thought processes. It means taking care of yourself physically, eating right, exercising, and losing weight, if needed. It means asking for what you need from others. It means putting yourself first once in a while. If you find yourself cycling through negative feelings like frustration and anger more and more, please stop for a moment and ask yourself, what thoughts do you have that result in such a negative emotion? Can you name that thought? If you can, good for you! What is the feeling connected to the thought? How can you take care of yourself right now, to start feeling a little bit better? Do you know how? You could start by saying something else to yourself that might result in a more positive emotion than frustration and anger. Good. Now, you can take a small positive action for yourself. Sit down and rest, go for a walk, go to the doctor's, go get your hair done, go out to lunch with a friend, talk to your partner if you feel the urge to discuss something important, and so on. The list goes on. Just do SOMETHING for yourself instead of someone else. Just for this moment, breathe (inhale and exhale slowly—for about 3 seconds). Now, you have begun the path toward paying attention to your own needs instead of someone else's!

PUT BALANCE BACK INTO YOUR LIFE

Balance in life is always the key! We all run around so crazily—we don't have time for ourselves; we don't have time for others; we don't have time for this or that. We rush and rush and rush—at the end of the day, we are scattered, exhausted, or just plain spent! So how do you find balance for yourself? Time just doesn't appear out of nowhere. Actually, you have to carve out time. You have to make time—you have to schedule time and then stick to it. Whether you use your Blackberry, or Outlook calendar or your paper and pencil wall calendar—the point is you cross out a time span and when people ask you to go shopping or do something else, you reply, "I'm sorry, I have a commit-ment!" It's just like when you go to the dentist or when you make a doctor's appointment and wait 3 months for it, you are NOT going to cancel that appointment at the last minute. I recommend that you choose a time slot that is best suited for your energy level. Are you a late-night person who loves to read and focus when the world is asleep? Or, are you an early morning riser who loves to get a head start on the day? Years ago, I asked a friend in my doctorate program when he had the most energy to sit down, concentrate, and commit to reading his journal articles and write his dissertation. He told me, late afternoon from 3:30 P.M. until 7:00 P.M. There you go! Just schedule it, and stick to it and do it. He did, and he did. His dissertation was finished in about 8-to-9 months (he worked in spurts prior to that, so everything was in place for him to finish it).

Time for Self could be 5 minutes a day, 30 minutes a day, or 2-hour slots Monday, Wednesday, and Friday—whatever—just make it happen. You can sit still and breathe. If that drives you nuts, then take a walk around the block or join a gym and make that your time to improve yourself. I have no idea what you like or want or what would be pleasing to you, but you do, so go make it happen on a regular basis, so that it is integrated into your overall lifestyle. This is not like start-ing and stopping a diet. This is about integrating a new life-pleasing activity (or non-activity) just for you alone. It could be free and cost nothing. Or it could be that you sign up for a yoga class for 6 weeks. The idea is to keep at it and make yourself a priority. This is what I meant earlier when I talked about feeling better within yourself and then as a result, having more energy to put back into relationships.

PERSONAL APPEARANCE

From our thoughts, to our emotions, to our behaviors, everything we are is manifested in how we present ourselves to the world. Unfor-tunately, we judge and are judged by external criteria—cleanliness, beauty, skin color, age, and so on. Everything manifested externally extends from within us to outside. Call it image, call it fashion, call it style, it is the composite of how we express ourselves. It can be directly connected to our values, creativity, self-esteem, cultural background, and how much money we choose to spend on such things. More important is the love we have for ourselves and how we respect ourselves through our efforts to please both ourselves and our partner (Self comes first).

Personal appearance can be simply an external representation of how good or bad we feel in a given day, by what colors (or not) we choose to wear, or how big our closet is and if it contains this season's wardrobe (or not). Personal appearance could also mean cleanliness and grooming rather than style and a closet full of clothes.

Personal appearance could also be connected to how you feel about yourself in general. Check out the Internet, medical journals, health magazines, and TV; media is harping on about how fat and unhealthy we are in America. In addition, many of the subchapters in this book have referred to eating healthy, performing exercise, and so on. Personal appearance might be something that you DO FOR YOURSELF; it could even be a sign of respect for yourself. Do you take care of yourself?

You might be young, physically fit, and beautiful. What gifts! However as you age, you learn that the abuse you ignored earlier—what you put into your body and the quality of ingredients you used to cook, really do matter when you are older; the body just can't take the abuse anymore. Yes, you can respect yourself by paying attention to what you put inside your mouth, just as you can argue that respect for Self begins with what you say to yourself (Self-Talk). Either way, it starts with YOU!

I also think it goes both ways. Society is very gender-biased in its slant toward "the distinguished gray-haired gentleman" versus "the older lady." Tell me if I got that wrong. I don't think so. I believe women are making great strides at age 50—wearing longer-styled hair, working out and looking terrific. I also contend that there is a built-in bias—men can age and get away with it a lot easier than females. Is it fair? Well, fair has nothing to do with it. It is what it is. What's more important is what are you going to do about it?

Despite what I have mentioned about society's view on gender and the leeway between the sexes in aging, I still think beauty is in the eye of the beholder. Certainly, throughout time (centuries), and across cultures the idealized value of what is considered socially "beautiful" has changed and evolved. Your value system is directly correlated to both your societal influence as well as your personal preferences. Whether you look like Venus de Milo or Twiggy (male or female), your health, grooming, and appearance dictate your message to the world—this is me. If you can't fit into one airplane seat, you have trouble bending over to tie your shoes, if you huff and puff as you climb a short set of stairs, or if your upper thighs rub so hard together when you walk that you get a rash, then some changes need to be made. Eat less and exercise more. If you have a medical condition, all the more reason for you to pay attention to yourself. Some tips that you may find helpful are next.

Healthy Tips for a More Beautiful YOU

#1—When was the last time you had a complete physical exam with urinalysis and blood work at your primary doctor's office? If it has been more than 1 year—then you are overdue for a complete physical exam.

#2—Once you commit to being healthy, then the rest is easy. Everything follows your thoughts. If you think it will be hard, it will be hard. It does not matter if you have to lose 5 pounds, 55 pounds, or 150 pounds, if you don't think you can do it—then you can't. If you really want to do it and you are convinced of that, then you can take the weight off—you WILL DO IT!

#3—The most natural way to do it is to eat healthy and exercise more calories off than the calories you ingest.

#4—If you feel like you need emotional support—THEN GO GET IT! Whatever you need—don't say it won't work, go make it work. Don't start crying, "Poor me!" Reach out to your doctor or program or counselor. Do it! You CAN make it happen.

Example: Let me tell you a story about food, weight, and thoughts. When I worked in sales, I once received a 10-pound box of chocolate (one huge bar). Always a chocolate lover, I took it home. One day, I decided that I needed some of that chocolate. Because the bar was about 14" x 9" and 1-inch thick, I took out an ice pick and a hammer so that I could cut off a chunk of chocolate. I remember that day clearly. I broke off a piece and I started to chew on it. As I was savoring the thick piece of chocolate, I kept saying to myself, "I'm eating this and enjoying it and I will be the same weight when I finish eating this. All the fat from this chocolate will literally melt off of me and my skin will be clean and clear. I will be zit-free!" Guess what? I ate it, I enjoyed it, and nothing happened. I did not gain an ounce of weight and my skin was blemish-free.

Now of course, this is NOT a scientific experiment! About 3 months later, I decided I wanted to eat some more chocolate. So, I got the ice pick out and the hammer and started to chip out a large chunk. Now I don't know if I did it around the same time of my menstrual cycle or a different time of the month, I don't know if my body had changed in how it metabolized chocolate, but I will tell you this, as I chewed on my large chocolate chunk, I said to myself, "Oh, this is going to be terrible, I know I am going to gain 10 pounds! I know that my skin is going to be messed up big time for at least 3 weeks! Why am I eating this? I shouldn't be eating this! I can feel the weight on my hips already!" Guess what? I ate it and broke out with pimples all over the right side of my cheek. The blemishes lasted a good 10 days. Then, I weighed myself and I had gained 5 pounds in one chocolate sitting!

What is the moral of the story? You tell me. What have I been saying? What we think is what will happen. So pay attention. If you really commit your mind and heart to changing your life around by wanting to look good and feel good and wanting to have a loving partner, then start CREATING a path of happiness both inside of you and outside of you. YOU CAN DO IT! You will shock the world. They will look at you and say, "WOW! Did you see how she changed? Did you see how he changed?" Yeah—watch out world. Here you come!

WHAT EFFECT DOES YOUR APPEARANCE HAVE ON YOUR PARTNER'S ATTRACTION TO YOU?

The answer to that question is—a LOT! When you are part of a couple, your personal appearance can play an important part of your intimacy. If you decide to "let yourself go" after pregnancy or menopause or because you have rationalized that you've got your man, you've paid your dues, or that you don't have time to take care of yourself, then you will be setting yourself up for more disappointment. Why does your personal appearance matter? It matters for your own well-being and for your relationship with others (intimate and professional). It is something very personal and very integral to your own outlook on life. How you present yourself can have a very strong impact on the vibrancy of your marital relationship. If you are pleased when you look in the mirror at yourself, then quite possibly your partner will be too. The effort that you put into looking good and feeling good can spread positively between the two of you. When it comes to paying attention to yourself and to each other in ways that are self-nurturing, this is a great area in which to set goals that benefit both the individual and the couple. You can exercise at the gym together, take hikes in the mountains together, or short walks around the block together before dinner.

You are on a life-long journey. You don't get married or move in together and then get to eat candy bars and potato chips all day and tell yourself that you've got your mate so you don't have to try anymore. Actually, the opposite is true. You have to strive toward new goals both internally and externally to achieve your own growth and your growth as a couple. Life does not stand still just because being married was "The Goal." The goals keep changing and evolving. It's called life. It's called growth.

BODY IMAGE AND SEXUAL RELATIONS; BODY IMAGE AND SELF-ESTEEM

Of all the issues that couples talk about when they come to see me, sex is most often the primary complaint in men's minds. After much exploration (lots of questions), I have discovered an underlying theme for the lack of sex in certain couples—openly admitted in many cases—by the female partner. Specifically, she suffers from a cognitive distortion regarding her body image. There is an actual diagnosis called Body Dysmorphic Disorder, when the individual is preoccupied by a "slight physical anomaly" either imagined or real as identified in the *Diagnostic and Statistical Manual of Mental Disorders* (DSM-5). In this case, the female (some of them athletes) feel less than adequate in their body size or feel they have a defect in their appearance. They feel ashamed, insecure, and are obsessed about this failing aspect of image. As indicated in the DSM-5, the individual (male or female) is significantly distressed or impaired in social, occupational, or other important areas of functioning. Their mental mantra of "I am fat" (when they were trim and fit); "I have ugly ears" (when ear shape is almost invisible to others or insignificant); "My breasts are too small" (when the husband professes how beautiful she is to him) all debilitate the marriage. The more the female withdraws from physical touching or sexual advances, the more her mate becomes frustrated and openly confused. What to do when you have a great partner, a beautiful home, healthy kids, good jobs, and one partner is consistently preoccupied with a distortion of body image that destroys their sex life?

I often hear, "I feel big and overweight"; "I don't feel like being touched because my stomach is puffed out"; "I don't feel sexy but he just doesn't get it." Well you're right about that. He doesn't get it. He wants to understand. He wants to help. He is confused about what he is doing wrong. He wants you to hear him shout from the closest mountaintop that, "YOU ARE BEAUTIFUL TO ME!" He desires you and wants to be physically close to you.

This disorder is not to be dismissed as something minor. It can cause significant distress or impairment in "important areas of functioning"—such as sexual intimacy. In this case, the partner with the distorted body image needs to be supported by a multifaceted treatment plan. The only alternative for the diagnosed client is to recommend a complete physical exam by a physician, possible low-dosage medication (to help with the mental preoccupation), and individual psychotherapy or counseling so that he or she can have a safe place to discuss innermost thoughts and feelings about body image or perceived "defects" (without having a partner present to proclaim their beauty).

A loving partner can profess all day long that their mate is beautiful. However, the reality lodged within the individual's mind is different. He or she sees a defective body attribute. Couple's therapy is adequate or even appropriate at the early stages of identification of this to help diagnose the disorder accurately in front of both partners. This will help the spouse have an increased understanding of the diagnosed partner's internal struggle with body image. For the partner with the cognitive distortion, individual therapy is essential to recovery. Once progress is made in this area, then perhaps, couple's therapy would be more productive later on. To dismiss the diagnosed individual as ready to negotiate increased sexual relations, only puts more pressure on the partner with the body image distortion. In this case, that partner cannot negotiate sex, personal space, nonverbal affection or any kind of closeness when they cringe, fear, or reject any gesture toward sexual intimacy because of their own distorted self-image and low self-esteem.

PERSONAL GOALS AND COUPLE GOALS

Setting goals together is very important. Also, it is about talking about individual goals and individual desires and how they have an impact on you as a couple. So many of the couples I saw would come to therapy to discuss some development that evolved over time into their relationship. When I started probing about what their discussions were about the topic, I would get this shocked and embarrassed look when they revealed that they hadn't really discussed it before. Oh, let's see, you didn't discuss the finances, work schedule, career impact, time spent together, household chores, and other implications, before one of you decided to quit your 6-figure-a-year salary, go back to grad school, have a baby, or decide to move out of state and be 3,000 miles from both sets of parents and grandparents. The list goes on. Talking it out—the pros and cons—and dissecting the budget (looking at before and after scenarios) is really important if you choose to make a life decision with your eyes wide open.

Many couples avoid talking with each other because it is either an emotionally charged topic, or they don't feel they possess the tools to talk and be heard or to collaborate in the discussion with their spouse, without a huge blow up. As humans, we sometimes find comfort in hiding, avoiding, and perhaps hoping it works out. If you are a couple then act like a couple. Talk to each other and figure it out together. Do you have enough strength within yourself to speak and to be heard, then to supportively listen wholeheartedly to your mate, while you expect your needs to met at the same time? Challenging? Yes. Impossible? No. Do other couples do it? Yes, every day by the millions. They have worked at finding the niche or path that works for them and they have enough of an ego (I mean that in a good way). They have inner core knowledge of Self to negotiate through the path of divergent views and another person's needs and wants. So a dialogue means speaking, listening, and negotiating differences within the bubble of love and good intentions through collaboration rather than dominance or abuse.

MANAGING CHANGE BEGINNING—MIDDLE—ENDING

There are many books written on this wonderful topic.

William Bridges comes to mind. His profound concept is that every ending is preparing you for a new beginning. How can you begin something new without ending what you've just started? By allowing yourself to advance through both personal and relationship changes you will begin to see over time that there really is a beginning, a middle, and an end. The unfortunate part is that we often "fall in love" with lots of beginnings and avoid the "other stages." You might see more starts and stops and perhaps lots of beginnings without a middle—just starts (beginnings) and endings (more like unfinished endings, or endings that never really got started in the first place). If you advance through change both as a person, as a couple, and as a family, you will see that change has stages; we take on new information and assimilate it with more emotions, and then we continue on the journey. Each member of the family advances through individual changes and the entire family advances through growth changes—as a twosome or as a group.

Our fear of facing change can be stronger and more negative than what is actually required. Change is the next step in the journey of personal and couple growth. For example, if you have children, then you know that if you continually treat your 15-year-old daughter as if she were eight, she would let you know by her thoughts, words, emotions, and deeds that such treatment does not work for her. You would be very much challenged to acknowledge that your 15-year-old is no longer 8 years old. In facing the facts, and dealing with your environment and embracing your relationships in the spirit of growth and change, you make the adjustments necessary and advance to the next step.

Think of the beginning as the first new cycle of change; it might help you as you migrate through the phases of change. The stages of change are directly related to your marriage or partnership as well as your individual evolution. As a couple, what happens when you read a book together, or go to a workshop together, or set new goals together? You get information, you think about it, talk about it, learn something from it (even if you disagree with it), and then make decisions based upon your conclusions. Isn't that what we all do? Most certainly you could apply those same stages of change when you set personal goals for yourself.

New Beginnings

New beginnings are usually a time of action and activity. They can be a time of increased momentum and heightened energy as you are naturally stimulated to propel yourself forward—identifying your goals, strategizing, and then committing to achieve them. At this point you are advancing toward the execution of your goals. This period of time can have an underlying emotional tone that excites you or makes you anxious. Every one of us experiences mixed emotions as we embark on new beginnings. There can be a lot of passionate talking and HOPE. Think of the space shuttle with its HUGE flame and fire underneath the rocket raring to blast off! The energy is all-consuming even though the rocket has not yet left the launch pad.

The new beginning phase can be one in which as a couple you commit to doing things differently between you. You decide to abandon certain behaviors and to start doing more of those that are agreed-upon. This can be exciting and anxiety producing. What if you fail or you both fail? Remember, "what if…." is an anxiety-producing question. It is natural to be anxious, but not so that it paralyzes you from moving forward to the next step.

Middle Phase

This is just after the rocket has left the launching pad. My sense is that there is a beginning, middle, and end phase to this middle phase as well.

Beginning of the Middle Phase

At first, it is a major shift from blast off to silence as you launch into unknown territory (space). In other words, as you realize that everything you have anticipated is now up to you as you begin to implement change—the quiet drifting phase where the rocket ship is silent and steady but headed in which direction? Each of you tries to organize, schedule, and prioritize what needs to be done and confirm the direction you are going. At this phase, there could be increased communication, a lot of creativity, and high energy about getting it right this time around—a feeling of confusion and fear of the unknown. "Where are we headed? If we don't get it right this time, then we will fail for sure." The emotions can range from anticipation, relief that you've finally started on your goal, and perhaps some impatience and frustration to get started.

Middle of the Middle Phase

Now you have migrated into the center of the center. It is the middle of the middle phase in the entire spectrum of change. You might be in the midst of gathering more last-minute information.

You might be trying to assimilate information while you are trying to implement new changes. You could be communicating actively as a couple as you each try to define what you are doing and whether or not it is working. The feedback loop is working overtime as you advance, analyze, provide feedback on its effectiveness and re-execute the next step. At this point, you might experience saturation level where you start to second-guess your goals. You might have fear of the unknown. You might conclude that things aren't happening quickly enough. You might both feel a little bogged down—paying attention to yourself as well as being mindful of your partner. It is a lot of work (or so it seems)! You begin to wonder if you bit off more than you can chew, or how come things aren't moving as smooth or as fast as you had hoped? This can result in frustration and self-doubt.

Ending of the Middle Phase

At this point your rocket ship is on target but still very much in the middle of the ride (the end is not near but not so far away). You realize how much work has been accomplished between the two of you but at the same time you realize all of the past errors, and you know there is a lot more work to do. You still might not trust the new behaviors and changes that you have both implemented so far. You are tired—perhaps angry and stressed out. This phase has several stops and starts and the stops are more frequent and of longer duration. This phase holds less hope and if you are slipping backward, there are fewer conversation and "check-in" sessions. You start to think negatively and begin to feel stuck: "Nothing changes; it just gets worse."

I would caution you to examine closely how much effort you have achieved with sincere effort toward change. If you think back to where you were when you first started, then perhaps sit down with your partner to discuss what steps you have successfully taken so far, it would help relieve some of the pressure. This would help the two of you take an objective look back on how it felt then when ABC needed to be done, and how it feels now that AB are done but C is not yet completed.

What behaviors did you not have prior to this goal? Has it improved anything? Are your conversations more frequent and smoother? Do you like talking to each other? Check it out with your partner. Be sure to acknowledge what you've accomplished so far. Perhaps, reflection and re-evaluation at this time will show how far you are from your end goal and what steps still need to take place. This would be a good time to make slight modifications as you head into the home stretch. You can both determine what is a reasonable period of time for the final phase of change. Making slight modifications to your end goal does not mean you are quitting or cheating; it means you are making necessary adjustments to grab the brass ring at the end. Do not give up!

Ending

You made it! You are staring at the end of this cycle. You are surprised and shocked that you are near the end! It's like you suddenly and silently slipped into the final phase without any fanfare. Now is the time to be especially observant of Self and partner. This is not the time to self-sabotage by quitting before you've come down for a complete landing. It is natural to feel grief and loss. You might be at a point where you both have less work to do on the marriage or on yourself since many of your goals have been achieved or are very close to being achieved. It is also natural to slow way down, because subconsciously you do not want to finish your goals. You might become angry or deny what you've achieved. You might become perfectionistic about what is wrong and should be done better.

What will happen when you are done? What is next? What is it that you fear by ending this project together? You might conclude that as long as "we are both working on it then there is hope, but if we end?" Let me tell you. You never end. It is a continuous cycle of growth, change, evolution, learning—and more goals. It is called life! Give yourselves permission to reach your goal in this phase in your life together! Acknowledge your efforts and your partner's efforts out loud.

> *"Thank you for your hard work and being such a great team partner on successfully achieving this together! I love you so much. I wouldn't choose anyone else to be by my side, right now and forever. You are the best!"*

Wow! Now enjoy this time and realize your greatness. Then without too long of a pause, talk and set new goals for yourself and for the two of you as a couple. GOOD WORK! You have just created a healthy new cycle of empowerment and positive change.

WHAT IS YOUR GOAL? TO HAVE A HAPPY RELATIONSHIP? TO FEEL GOOD ABOUT YOURSELF?

So, what if I asked you what your life and relationship would look like if it were better? Do you know what it would look like? Can you describe it? Take a moment right now. **Can you name your goal?** See that goal in your mind's eye right now? What if I told you that you could have that right now? Would you go for it? Would you reach out and grab it? I know I would. What do you have to lose? Now, if you tell me you want it, and you can see it, and that you can feel it, good for you!

Now, what if I told you that since you're the one reading this book right now, or because you are the one who is making the decision to go for it right now, then you are the one who has to drop the rope (from the tug of war game), and start being your authentic true Self, right now? If you are confused as to why I say that to stop playing any game you need to start paying attention to yourself, the answer is simply this: You need to identify what you need. Once you get clear as to your own needs, ask for what you need from your partner. Otherwise, you will keep waiting and subconsciously blame him or her every time you are disappointed because they did not automatically know what you needed!

Start identifying your own thoughts, start naming your own feelings, and start deciding to act on those positive thoughts and feelings by making healthier choices such as: exercising, losing weight, eating properly, taking time for yourself, taking up a hobby, taking a class—whatever—just do something for yourself. Treat yourself just like you would your best friend. Then start treating your partner like your best friend.

I frequently hear partners tell each other in session that they feel like they can never do it right: "You are always critical of me. You are unhappy and I don't know how to make it right and when I try to do something, it seems like you don't notice or care. No matter what I do you're never satisfied, I am so tired of trying." You have the power to stop this cycle of blame, disappointment, and unhappiness.

TAKE THE RISK

Do you want to break the cycle? Yes! Then do this.

#1—Start taking care of yourself as best you can (yoga, walking, journaling, art lessons, pedicure, etc.). Then, as you start feeling a little more empowered, you will start feeling positive and good about life and stronger as an individual.

#2—Then, you can assert yourself into the relationship by asking for what you need.

That might be as far as it goes. The outcome of your efforts depends upon your partner. Your spouse might be relieved that you told them what you need. Your spouse might jump at the chance to give you what you need. Your partner might tell you, "Hmmm. I never knew that was so important to you, let me get back to you" (that's a maybe). Or, it could be that your partner listens to you and after you got up all of your courage to ask for what you need, your partner clearly responds with a big, "NO." There are no guarantees with this. That is the BIG RISK. However, let me ask you this; if YOU don't identify what you need, how is your PARTNER going to identify it? It is important for both of you to talk, talk, and talk some more.

MEDICATIONS

As much as I believe in holistic alternatives, I have seen miracles happen when the correct dosage of the right medication was prescribed and administered to a client who was 'clinically depressed' and could not engage in life or was so visibly anxious that he or she could not sit still in the room, let alone go home and get a full night's sleep. For the record, I advocate medicines (not prescribe them personally) because I am a short-term therapist; I have seen hundreds of cases where both cognitive behavioral therapy and low-dosage medications were the best treatment approach. I have been fortunate to witness many suffering individuals and couples become transformed after getting much-needed Serotonin.

I have seen people who were on "probation" at their job emerge as shining stars and professional leaders who contribute to the team's goals in a positive way. I have seen people get promoted at work (not literally—I was told about it). I have seen people start having fun in their marriage again. I have witnessed others able to make career decisions about whether or not to go back to school for a graduate degree—after bouts of depression. I have seen mothers re-engage in their children's lives as well as their own. After you've seen this a few times, it is really easy to become a believer.

For those who absolutely insist on NOT taking any medications, I honor their choice and inform them that the holistic approach is a more inclusive approach, requiring effort in order to work. In this situation, both the client and I agree that if they do not do the complete holistic approach consistently over time, then they must opt for the medicine as a treatment plan because to do nothing is unethical. I can no longer treat them if they refuse to do their part of the work (especially when I knew that medications would work).

The agreement is: They HAVE TO EXERCISE diligently; they have to STOP or decrease their use of certain foods (caffeine, sugar etc.); they have to eat balanced, nutritional foods; and they have to use the cognitive STOP SIGN diligently. I also strongly encourage them to use an herbal approach (St. John's Wort, Omega-3 Fish Oil, etc.), after consulting with their doctor about the risks and benefits of taking herbal supplements. Also, I have them consider acupuncture therapy, massage therapy, energy healing, healing touch, and yoga classes, or, to hire home help for relief with the kids—whatever works! Plus, they can't just choose one thing and do it for a few days and quit. They have to do at least 3 things simultaneously and consistently—a slam dunk approach to conquer depression, anger, or anxiety.

Either one of two things happens. Clients are so scared about taking any medicine, that they diligently perform all of the holistic options—and it WORKS! They feel better and stronger and more like themselves. Or, they start and stop and fail, and are still depressed! They return to therapy and complain about feeling lousy, and they finally agree to take the medicine.

THEN, the miracle occurs! They smile. What beautiful smiles my clients have. Sometimes, it would be the first time I had ever seen their teeth. They were re-engaging in life. So either way, it was a Win-Win! They won, their families won, and I won because I got to see the real them.

I met many really nice and good people, suffering for long periods of time. I would tell my clients that before medication, it's like mountain climbing. The mountain is at a 45-degree angle uphill. They climb, and hike, and they climb, and hike. They NEVER give up. They are determined to get to the top of the mountain. Will they? Of course they will, but they suffer the entire way up. They are not just exposing themselves to life's stressors (car breaks down, kids late for school, husband on a business trip and they are single parents, etc.), but they encounter all of that AND DEPRESSION AT THE SAME TIME! They are doubly down in the dumps—struggle, struggle, struggle. When they are functioning at full tilt and the depression, anxiety, and anger have dissipated, they can actually cope with life—their mental outlook is much more positive—whereas before, a negative thought would take them down the trail of tears. Now a negative thought comes to them, and they say, "Nope, not going to go there." And the negative thought goes away and they continue on their merry way for a positive day.

There is NO SUCH THING AS A "HAPPY PILL." However, there are some wonderful "designer drugs" that have no or low side-effects. One female client told me that she did not feel a thing (negative side effects) when she took her medicine. She felt better by taking the medicine, with no physical symptoms. That was good! If the drug and dosage are correct, you shouldn't feel a thing. You'll just feel better and more like yourself than you have in a long time. Clients would tell me that the medication helped clean out the cobwebs; they were starting to think more clearly and were more focused on task completion. Of course!

Taking medicine is a personal choice. If clients are severely depressed, I see them a few times and refer them to someone else so that they get the continued, consistent care in regular therapy that I don't provide. I am a short-term therapist with a deliverable outcome. Due to the large size of my private practice, I am unable to provide the personalized individual attention that someone who is really depressed needs. For the high-functioning individuals and couples who come to see me, the various cognitive tools and behavioral prescriptions that I advocate (and the visit to the doctor's office for medicine), are often the final answer to a drawn-out period of time with no diagnosis or treatment. Clients are finally doing something for themselves; they are under a doctor's care and they are happy—all due to their efforts! They have finally made their own happiness a priority and are feeling positive! Life's a lot easier when you feel good and are free from pain.

Family

I would venture to say that 98 percent of my clients have at least one child under the age of 6 years and if they have more than one child, the youngest is in diapers. This is a huge life change! Children can change the dynamics and increase the stressors in a marriage—increased responsibilities, less time for yourself as individuals, less space in the house, less sleep, perhaps change in double income to single income. Even though many of these changes are choices—and happy choices—it is still stressful. The body and psyche do not know the difference between good stress (Eustress) and bad stress (Distress). Cortisol floods your system. Cortisol is a stress hormone that the body produces in times of fight and flight. So obviously, there's a lot going on in a partnership when new members of the family start arriving.

CHILDREN

Children are like thermostats. They register everything including when their parents are not as close or intimate as they used to be. When children have problems in school "acting out," or when they begin to display major behavior changes, it can usually be directly linked to parents. As parents, you are either not unified as a parenting team (in other words, one parent does all the work and the other is uninvolved), or you have issues as a couple that you need to address—poor or no communication skills.

PARENTAL CONTROL, RECLAIM YOUR POWER BACK NOW!

When parents have lost control to children, then you as parents need to sit down and re-define the following:

"RULES OF THE HOUSE" (take out the garbage, clean up room, pick up toys, do the dishes, etc.).

"EXPECTATIONS OF THE PARENTS" (help with homework, give allowances, go to little league practice, help in the school bake sale, etc.).

If needed, with older children, you should have written contracts signed and witnessed with the requirements, obligations, and responsibilities of everyone involved, filled out and clearly identified. This contract negotiation should be collaborative by including the teenager's input on the rules with both parents present—NO EXCEPTIONS!

In reuniting as parents you will reunite as a family, and this cannot happen until the role of each individual is clearly identified. Once parents allow children to overstep their boundaries the results can be harmful to you as a married person, to you as a parent, and to the child/children involved—TO THE WHOLE FAMILY.

BLENDED FAMILIES

Blended families, those with either half brothers/sisters; step-brothers/sisters; step-parents; or even adopted children can encounter an entirely different set of difficulties or problems, as a result of the adjustment of each individual to the new and expanding family. This is a dilemma for either the child (the new addition) or for the step-parent (new addition). This is also a life-changing scenario for pre-teenagers or teenagers who were previously the only child and now have to share their mother or father with additional siblings or with a new step-parent. The transition can be compounded if the child's personal space (bedroom) now has to be shared with new family members (step-siblings). It is a complex topic filled with complex logistics and multilayered emotions attached to the merging of people, families, houses, cultures, and finances.

Obviously, time helps everyone adjust. Feeling loved, as well as reciprocating that love, helps unite families. However, all family members according to their status (parent/child/sibling) must be treated equally and fairly. This is accomplished through constant communication and sharing of time, feelings, and activities as well as an equal participation in carrying out family responsibilities—easier said than done.

Family theory research has long advocated that step-parents NOT immediately step into the role of an authority figure. They have to start out as friends with mutual respect and gradually work into the role of parent. This is a very complicated topic. Many of the couples I saw in therapy had plunged into the merging of families without a lot of dialogue and discussion as to role definition—a major flaw in the family dynamic.

Example: A step-mother has been automatically cast into the role of "mother" without a family meeting or a meeting between biological father and child alone followed by another meeting with the step-mother to discuss roles and expectations. This is a situation potentially full of resentment and jealousy. How can the step-parent state, "Do your chores," to a teenager who thinks, "You are NOT my mother"?

A biological father tells a step-mother you have the authority to discipline my daughter; the father, however, frequently undermines the discipline by whispering to his daughter that she does not have to do what her step-mother wants. This leads to a HUGE uproar between the couple, between the step-mother and step-daughter, and the rest of the family members. It is a very sticky situation and, unfortunately, long-term.

The most important factor in all families—blended or natural—is to remember that sincere communication is never too late. I encourage you to read more about this issue if it applies to you and your family. As a couple, both partners should read this book or other books on the topic of blended families, then discuss it as you read it.

Your discussion can strengthen your relationship and the entire family as a unit.

COMMUNICATION WITH CHILDREN

Good communication habits should not begin when your child is 16 years old. Rather, real communication should start when your child is a toddler (2-to-3 years), and continue throughout their development. If your child is a preteen or teen and you have not had a close, communicative relationship—it is not too late. This means that you and your mate are going to have to work harder to connect with your child. You must sincerely start the communication process. Let your child know that you care for him or her, take an interest in them (not police them), and start asking/listening to their viewpoints/opinions/ideas/feelings. This will help build your child's self-esteem and will help make your relationship closer.

SOLID TOPICS FOR DISCUSSION WITH YOUR CHILD

Sex; sexually transmitted diseases; birth control; school; teachers; grades; tutoring; college; goals; topics of interest; friends; sports; music; activities; interests; drugs; and alcohol (etc.).

I once had a coworker at a high tech firm tell me about her 12-year-old daughter. I had my master's degree in counseling at the time but was still working full-time. There was something odd about the way she referred to her child. I bluntly asked if her daughter was on birth control. She did not get angry but was mildly defensive when she asserted that she totally trusted her daughter who was not on birth control; they had not talked about birth control. I listened and said nothing. I knew it was forward of me. I was NOT her therapist, but there was something that gnawed at me the way she spoke about her child. We ended the conversation. To my dismay about 5 weeks later, the same woman and I happened to take that same afternoon coffee break. She quietly looked me in the eye and told me that she should have listened to me—she had just found out that her 12-year-old daughter was pregnant. I have never forgotten her depression and devastation. It rocked me and I was just a coworker!

There is nothing more to say except even that when you think you know what's going on, you might not! As the parent, you owe it to your children to dig and explore and pay close attention to them as they grow into adulthood. That incident was more than 20 years ago! Nowadays, with the increased pressures on both parents and children from the Internet, it is even more important to have an up-close and personal relationship with your child!

PARENTAL CHALLENGES

#1—You no longer have the luxury of parenting the way your parents parented you! Times have changed! You have to do it differently.

#2—You need to question your children every day to determine what is going on in their lives. As a parent you are not the only one who influences your child (friends, teachers, neighborhood, school, etc.).

#3—The opportunity for young children to be children is passing as society pressures them sexually. In my opinion, this pressure skews their natural development—not allowing them to advance through the necessary stages of childhood—from teenage years to young adulthood. It puts too much responsibility on them at too young an age to cope with all of the pressure (peer, sexual, societal, etc.).

#4—It is your responsibility as a parent to educate and prepare your children to face the responsibilities of living independently through role modeling. Your challenge is to give them every chance to be responsible back, for them to demonstrate they are responsible. Give them a chance to prove through their behavior that they are adjusting to the stressors of life in a healthy adaptive manner. You can see this by the decisions they make, the friends they choose, and so on. It's a balancing act, isn't it? Your job is to be the adult and their protector at the same time.

#5—Kids give mixed messages. One minute they want a hug and to tell you their deepest problem; at other times, they are standoffish, moody, or distant. Your job as the parent is to read the tea leaves, pay attention to the ups and downs, be consistent, and not react negatively to their moods—be the grounded adult to help guide them through rough waters. Keep the lines of communication OPEN! When in doubt, keep the lines of communication OPEN! You are not their best friend, you are the adult!

#6—You cannot rely on schools alone to educate your beautiful child to the realities of sex, birth control, and AIDS. You have to do this! If you cannot, at least encourage them to talk to an aunt or uncle or a health professional who can check in with them and make certain they know the truth (not myths and falsehoods). You owe it to them.

FAMILY RELATIONSHIPS

This is another important aspect of balance. I do not conduct family therapy, but I have told my couples, "If I represent anyone at all during the session, I represent your child." I am there to give their child a voice. Why? Because the tension, anger, and volatility that exist between partners (whether or not it is verbal or silent) transmits to their child either making them anxious children today or angry adults in psychotherapy tomorrow. What a choice! Working on the couple relationship is powerful for the entire family!

Each parent must have a balanced, personal relationship with each child. Both parents must spend time with the entire family unit. This can be achieved through family outings to the park, a drive to the ocean, a trip to the movies or theme park, a camping trip, or a family bicycle ride. It could be as simple as having family dinner night at home—every Wednesday—no matter what. You'd be amazed at how healing this can be for everyone. Turn off the TV and Blackberries. Do not text during dinner! Talk to each other. Find out how everyone is doing. Have everyone pitch in and cook certain parts of the dinner together. One person can chop carrots, another can make the salad, and the little one can set the table. MAKE IT HAPPEN! Make a special dessert that everyone loves (or buy it at the bakery). Be a family. This is good stuff. Wednesday nights at home—eating and talking—will be special and memorable.

SINGLE PARENT DATING

The single most important issue for a dating single parent is to look at your significant other and understand clearly what his or her views are with respect to your children. It is very important that you also talk to your children about their views of your new partner. Then, it is important for you to observe both your new partner and your children as they interact.

Communication with your new partner?

Have you talked to each other about this issue? Are you listening to improve your understanding of your partner's expectations toward your children? How flexible is this person? Does your significant other accept you and the kid(s) as a unit, or does your mate accept only you—the single parent—setting your children to the side? Are you flexible about your new partner's role in the family unit? Have you and your partner had a candid discussion about each other's role in the family? Do you allow your new partner parenting privileges and, if so, have you discussed with the family what those privileges are over your children? Or, do you as a single parent set your relationship to the side—separate from the children—keeping your relationship private?

Do you ask your partner for feedback about your children? Do you listen? This can be a powerful exercise in increased understanding. When you ask for information, it is your responsibility to listen and acknowledge what you have heard.

Communication with your children?

Are your children neglected as a result of this new relationship? Have you spoken to your children individually about your intentions regarding your new partner? Or, did you just bring Mr(s). Right home with you and say, "Hi" to everyone?

Do you ask your family for feedback about your new relationship? Do you listen? Be sure to have one-on-one talks with each child so that you can hear their concerns and then acknowledge what you heard. In this way, they will feel like you are listening to them.

If you have recently been divorced, remember this is a trauma to your child and that you need to allow each child to grieve the loss of their home life with their father and mother—the way it used to be. This takes time. Your children need time to grieve the loss of the missing parent; it would be premature for you to expect your kid(s) to automatically accept your new partner. Just because you are ready to start over does not necessarily mean that your family is ready. If your previous marriage was not the best, it still might mean that your child needs time to grieve what life might have been like with dad or mom if you had stayed together. Now, that fantasy is gone. Acknowledge their feelings with respect to the past, present, and future. You have a better chance to be united as you move forward together.

Has your behavior changed due to your new love relationship?

How do you as a single dating parent accept this new person into your family unit? Also, do you switch from partner to partner and bring them all home to meet the children? This can be very threatening and confusing to both young and older children. Research suggests that the best scenario is for you to hold off from early introductions with a new partner. In simple terms, DO NOT BRING THEM HOME TO MEET THE KIDS UNTIL IT IS DETERMINED TO BE A SERIOUS RELATIONSHIP (not a one-month relationship)! Even then, it would be best for you to introduce your child in a setting that is conducive to meeting this person (an outing at a theme park or some event). Bringing your partner home is a MAJOR event; some recommend waiting for a period of 1 year before doing so.

Do you spend more time with this new mate than with your own children? How do you deal with everyone's jealousies? These are very important issues to explore as a single parent, with yourself, with your child, and with your new partner, as well as in a family group setting (a family meeting that includes your new mate).

SUMMARY

What have you learned in this section? Your children need an opportunity to have a voice! If you don't provide that opportunity through your one-on-one talks with them, or in family therapy together, then at least allow them a voice in their own school counseling, or in individual therapy. If you move too fast without including them and their needs in your efforts to start a new life, then you are probably not meeting your children's needs. If you do not allow your children to "work through" their own thoughts and feelings regarding this new life transition, then, it will only resurface at some other developmental stage as negative behavior. You know how life works. If you don't deal with the problem head on now, then it will come back later, when you least expect it—at an inopportune time. The same holds true for your children. Help them learn early on to be real and to face life without stuffing feelings and avoiding responsibility for their behavior. Look at the life lessons you are teaching your child today!

PART VII

Couple

BE FRIENDS FIRST

You can talk yourself into anything you want—even a divorce—if that's what you want. Yes you can! What we say to ourselves can be very powerful. If you start focusing on all of the differences between the two of you, believe me, you won't run out of things to focus on. The more you do it, the more you notice things to focus on—how terrible this is, how frustrating that is, and so on. You get the idea. If you go down that trail it only leads to a trail of tears. I'm not saying you should sugar coat everything and ignore your frustrations—just the opposite. You need to pay attention to how often you feed your psyche with negative comments, conclusions, and judgments about your mate. Pick and choose which battles are most important to focus on. It is really easy to build a case for separation and divorce. Anyone can do it. However, the challenge is to learn how to give and get and to voice your frustrations knowing that your partner has good intentions even though he or she frustrates you sometimes. It is about acknowledging when he or she does something small that is really thoughtful and a statement of love. These are the building blocks of a relationship. Couples forget how to be kind to each other and to be friends! If you are friends first, then you have a strong foundation to fall back on when the love gets crunchy.

BALANCE FOR PARTNER/SPOUSE

You'd be amazed at how often one partner within a couple resents a partner having an outside interest. An entire book could be written about the dynamics of this scenario—the result of jealousy, time spent away from spouse and children, money spent on one person and no one else, or lack of time devoted to "couple activities." The list goes on. Balance means that you BOTH get to have time alone without interruption!

It is vital for you to encourage and support your partner in having some downtime away from you and the family. My hope is that BOTH PARTNERS give this gift to each other.

COMMUNICATION 101

I have my own brand of interaction with couples. Although I do not keep statistics, I have a high rate of success. I **continue** to get thank you cards and photos of babies and families who are expanding in love. I see more validation of the effects of the tools that I impart to my clients. To know that what you gave to others is growing and evolving into healthier forms of communication, intimacy, and love—is very gratifying.

Usually in the first session, I am a stickler for some effective communication tools. Remember in the first paragraphs of this book I stated that I am results-oriented and interested in deliverable outcomes? Well, simply put, that means that my obligation to you is to give you something you can chew on, think about, practice, use if you will, and see the empowering effect of your efforts toward change for yourself and your partner. So, I give my couples a yellow pad and pen and I ask them to write a few phrases down on the page. I provided them with what I call, "**COMMUNICATION 101.**"

EXERCISE #1: First, with paper and pen, write the pronoun "YOU" on the page in big letters. Then, draw a circle around the YOU. Then, X out the circle so that the YOU is crossed out. It is imperative that you stop saying YOU to your partner. You is a blaming pronoun!

People say, "You this…you that…you, you, you…." "You" pushes your partner into a corner and it immediately starts an argument.

"You" blames them and gives them no voice in the relationship. This is not a dialogue! A colleague once told me that she tells her couples that when "you" is first spoken, the argument has already begun. Yes indeed, those are fighting words!

EXERCISE #2: So, you know what to do instead, right? Please write the first person singular "I" on the page and write the following: "I need"; "I want"; "I feel"; "I think"…etc. Write any sentence you want as long as it starts with the pronoun "I." For example, "I am really frustrated and my hope is that we can make time to talk it over. Do you have time now, or can we talk later?"; "From my perspective, I feel like we don't have enough time to be together."; "Do you feel that way too?"; "What do you think about what I just said?"; or, "Sometimes, it seems to me like you don't want to be with me anymore." To be clear, it would sound like this: "I need more time with you, I feel scared that we are drifting apart." This is clearly stating what you feel, what you think, what you need, without blaming your partner. Speak for yourself, not for the other person. Blaming would sound like this, "You never spend time with me!"; "You always put your friends before me!" Do you see the difference?

In couple's sessions, my job is to find out if there is a hidden agenda (like a secret of some kind or an affair) or, simply to help the couple define what each of them wants. I do not save their marriage. I do not believe in making them stay together no matter what. I certainly respect religious beliefs, but I also point out that I might have a different opinion. I feel duty-bound to let them know my frame of reference for our sessions together. I do not fix couples, rather, I help them do the work. I HELP THE COUPLE FIGURE IT OUT. My job is to facilitate their efforts in clarifying and crystallizing their own needs and be able to communicate them effectively to each other in a safe environment. They might come into couple's therapy and get closer to each other—or fall back in love. Or, they might come to therapy and one or both would find the courage to say, "I want a divorce." The whole process would re-engineer their partnership one way or the other. It is NOT my call; it is always their call (there is only one exception to that rule, read on).

A couple I counseled years ago—both highly accomplished individuals in their respective careers—came to see me because they might divorce. It turns out she was further along in the thought process than he was. Even though they were senior executives, she became silent in front of him as he kept speaking, starting with the pronoun "WE." He would say, "We this…." and "We that…" We, we, we… I stopped him and told him that language is very powerful and that by using the pronoun, "we," he was speaking for her and not giving her a voice. He began to argue and justify his reasoning. He had good intentions, but he wanted to take care of her and protect her.

To make a long story short, because of his desire to steer the session in a way that would allow him to protect her in the same manner that he had been doing, he was simultaneously trying to usurp my power in the session and take over. At that moment, I realized that if I did not take the session back from him, then none of us would be doing therapy and I would NOT be doing my job. It was totally symbolic of how he treated his wife. Believe me when I say that's probably about as analytical as I get in this book. Anyway, I made it very clear that this was not going to work unless he allowed me to share my viewpoints without him being defensive and argumentative.

In those days, it took me longer to get them both to the core of the issue. It was about 6 weeks before I got him to speak for himself—for her to have a voice and that he would LISTEN to her. He was busy trying to make it right for both of them, but he was basically suffocating the marriage. The reason it took so long to help him change his approach was because he was firmly set about his good intentions and felt he was doing it right. I remember saying this to him, "Let me guess, I bet I know what you do for a living. You're a salesman, right?" He confirmed. I told him that he was an excellent salesman, but what works at work, does not necessarily work at home (in fact it does NOT). I told him that at work he was good at closing the deal or making the sale. With his wife, he needed to connect to her and INCLUDE HER, NOT EXCLUDE HER by talking at her and speaking for her. It was a journey, but it turned out well. Eight years later I received a card letting me know that they still loved each other and they were doing well together. Bottom line: **LANGUAGE IS POWERFUL!**

Talking to Your Partner

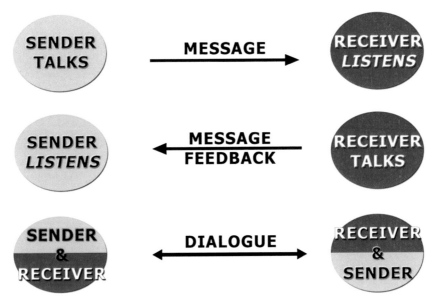

SENDER AND RECEIVER

Sender

In communication, the Sender of the message, also called the Initiator, is responsible for sending a clear message by:

- focusing on only one issue at a time
- describing what you want
- expressing your feelings and thoughts
- avoiding blaming and name-calling
- identifying your own inner truth (take a risk to speak or discover your truth).

The challenge for the Sender is to be able to tolerate or sustain their own truth in the presence of the Receiver (who might have a different opinion).

Receiver

The Receiver is also known as the Listener. The Receiver is responsible for:

- listening
- clarifying
- mirroring/reflecting back to the Sender
- acknowledging what they hear
- not over-reacting emotionally
- not interrupting
- letting the Sender complete his or her thought
- clarifying by asking a question if something is not clear, or reflecting back to the Sender by saying, "What I heard you saying is…." "Are you saying this or that…?"

The magic of this interaction is that both the Sender and the Receiver get to switch roles. As soon as the Receiver starts to mirror back to the Sender, the Receiver becomes

the Sender and the original Sender through listening is now the Receiver.

This interactive back and forth is very important to communication. Over time, the couple learns to find effective shortcuts that do not sound so therapeutically stiff or formal. The key is to identify what you are hearing the Speaker (Initiator/Sender) say. This is especially true if you have a strong emotional reaction to what you just heard. Can you identify your own feelings and then identify the thought tied to that feeling? Once you have done this, then the point is to "check in" with your partner to find out if you got it right.

For example: I always used to tell my couples, before you ACT angry, do a couple of things:

#1—Identify your feelings to yourself. "I am so angry right now."

#2—Announce that you are angry. "I am so angry right now!"

The point is to NOT ACT out your anger, it is to announce it. "I am so frustrated right now!"

#3—Check in with your partner to verify or clarify if your anger is your own or a response to something your partner said.

For example: Let's say your partner said, "I don't want you to go to school." You conclude (in your own mind) that you heard him say that you are stupid and will fail at school. Before you get extremely hurt or very angry or display some other strong feeling, check in with him to find out what exactly he is saying to you. Then, if he is saying indeed that you are stupid, well, that is another conversation.

However, if he is saying, "I am worried about money. I want you to go to school, but I don't think this is the right time or..." Then, you have an opportunity to not over-react, take a breath and keep dialoguing until you find a collaborative solution. Check-ins are very helpful in avoiding conflict and misunderstandings.

A common example of an erroneous conclusion or a distortion of what the Sender is saying would look like this:

S—"I don't want you to go to school."

R—"I'm NOT stupid, you don't believe I have what it takes, do you?"

S—"What are you talking about?"

R—"You always do that. You get the final say."

S—"Why do you do that—blame me—when I want what's best for both of us?"

R—"Best for both of us, give me a break."

A different scenario, same discussion about school:

S—"I don't want you to go to school. I know it is important to you and I want to be supportive, but I want to discuss the finances with you, like how much would it cost? How long would you go? And, would you continue working? That's a lot to take on all together. I've been kind of worrying about it all. Can we talk about it?"

R—"Yes, I do want to talk about it. I have gathered some information about all of that, and I think it will work. I heard you say that you're worrying about it and I don't want you to worry, sweetheart. And, I am glad that you want to be supportive because I want to do this for me and for us. This could really help us long-term in our income stream as I progress further in my career. This is really important to me and I feel really emotional about it, but I am glad that you are open to hearing what I have to say. When do you have time to talk? Do you want to do it now, or would this Saturday be better for you?"

S—"Well, I guess now would be good. Do you have the time and energy? I know it's getting into the evening. I am interested in what you've found out so far. But if you want to wait until Saturday, that is fine with me also. I'm open to either one. What do you want?"

R—"Well, how about Saturday? Thanks for saying you'd be willing to do it tonight, but Saturday will allow me to gather a couple more bits of information for you, and I know I would feel better Saturday morning rather than now—it's been kind of a long day already."

S—"That works for me."

R—"Me too, thanks…it's a date" (smile).

This interchange can be slow going at first, which is good.

"I heard you say this … is that what you said?"

Then, the next person says, "Yes that is what I said." Or, "Well, that's most of it, but actually my main point was this…."

Then, the other person states what they heard.

When each partner reflects accurately what they heard to each other, it is a connection point of intimacy! It is like a tiny bridge that keeps reaching over from one to the other—one sentence or paragraph at a time. At the end of the conversation, the couple feels the flow and exchange of ideas (even if there is a difference of opinion). A lack of ARGUMENT empowers them to feel more confident. There is hope for positive change. At the end of their discussion, their bridge is stronger and bigger and more connected than before.

You'll notice in the previous examples, that the second example clearly has more language to it. My motto has been: It is better to OVER communicate rather than UNDER communicate. You'd be amazed at how many couples really had many benefits working for them, yet, in communicating they would speak fragmented thoughts (partial thoughts) or conclude incorrectly. I once advised a female to talk a little less, or perhaps NOT BE THE FIRST ONE TO TALK, and I advised her partner to continue to speak in declarative sentences, with dependent clauses attached. In other words, instead of speaking in short statements, I encouraged him to add more words to the sentence so that there was more information for his listener to hear and understand his full thought process.

Example: "No, I don't want to go to that restaurant tonight… (because, I went there for lunch yesterday, or because I was really feeling more like Mexican food tonight, because…"). Do you see how a little bit more language can help clarify the simplest of statements?

WHAT HAVE YOU LEARNED?

Don't say YOU, say "I."

Speak in complete thoughts with a focused idea.

Be respectful; make eye contact; don't swear at each other.

When spoken to, listen, then send it right back to your partner,

"I heard you say …" or "So, what you're saying is this … is that right?" or "I'm a little unclear, can you say it again, I don't get it."

Practice, practice, practice with each other, with the people at work, with your kids, and with your neighbors. You will be amazed how natural it becomes over time and how it will really help you.

AFTER YOU TELL ME, I'LL RESPECT YOU MORE

Throughout my years of private practice, I've discovered that people are often afraid to tell someone else what they honestly think or feel. Perhaps it is fear. It could be fear of hurting someone, or fear of being rejected, or fear of the outcome. Instead of acting out of avoidance, not wanting to hurt your partner, try focusing on speaking honestly about your feelings as THE TRUTH. No one can tell what you do or do not feel. No one can discount you for what you feel and when you feel it. Those feelings belong to you and they are the Truth.

If you are paying attention to yourself and your partner, then you know when there is something not quite right. You won't feel as connected, you observe them acting differently, you observe them as withdrawn, or you might even be picking up mixed messages from **what** they tell you compared to **how** they behave. This is all-powerful information for you as a partner in the marriage.

DISCONNECT BETWEEN WHAT YOU HEAR AND WHAT YOU FEEL

I am clearly saying that communication consists of words, type of words, tone, eye contact, lots of conversation and maybe explanations, spontaneous expressions of affection, many non-verbal cues (standing, sneering, smiling, cringing, etc.) and finally, the vibe you get off your mate. If you want to talk about what we know and don't know, let me tell you the one thing I know for sure—the vibe. If you want me to be more specific, I would say "energy" or vibrations" that I pick up from my partner.

So, what am I saying? Well, when there is a disconnect between either what you are hearing your partner say and how he or she is acting around you or even or you just feel like its "off"—then my suggestion to you is to, CHECK IN WITH EACH OTHER. It's really simple to ask a few of the following questions. "Ya' know I hear you saying that you love me, but you don't look happy. It seems like we haven't talked in weeks and that you spend all of your time away from me and the kids. I am feeling more disconnected from you and right now you are not even making eye contact with me. What's happening? Tell me what's going on with you? I am confused because it seems like I am getting mixed signals from you. I want you to be happy...please talk to me, OK?"

Be silent. That is the hardest thing. Be silent. Please do not fill in the blanks anymore. You made your point. Now let him or her answer. The biggest mistake we can make is to let partners walk away without talking or fill in the blanks for them. Let your partner speak. Perhaps, part of the problem is that by over-talking or not allowing your partner to talk—you don't allow them a voice in the marriage. You have to be silent and pause. Do not let them off the hook. Any one of the sentences above would work in the example that I just described. Please do not bombard your spouse with 99 questions. Just state how you feel and say what you've observed and ask them how they are feeling or what is happening on their end. Keep the lines of communication open and fluid. If they answer with, "I don't know," it is important that the TV is off, the kids are gone, that it's NOT midnight on a work night, that you are both sitting at the kitchen table, or on the bed, or on the couch. When you get the, "I don't know," just say something like, "What do you mean? Can you tell me more? I don't understand." Or, "How are you feeling right now?"

Just say anything that keeps the focus on them and the fact that they have not offered an answer. If you keep pouring your heart and soul out to them and they don't speak, what do you know for certain? Not much. You need information from them in order to make it a "dialogue."

I could go on and on and analyze all of the sub-plots going on with the couple I just described above. However, it doesn't matter. It always takes two to tango, right? You bet. So, your job is to do your part. You do the best you can do and if you don't see any movement in the partnership, then you have some choices.

CHOICE #1) Let's just say you went through great strides to make positive changes in your own behavior. That's wonderful. AND… that might be just the ticket for your partner to see how hard you have tried. Your partner wants to make similar positive changes. Good for both of you!—no hidden agendas and lots of positive behavioral changes. It feels better, you both feel closer, you talk a lot more—the fun and sex is back! CONGRATULATIONS! Now, the downside might be that you commit to making all of those positive changes but your partner doesn't notice, doesn't say anything (no acknowledgment for your efforts), or doesn't believe that he or she has anything to change—that it was all your problem to begin with. Or, perhaps, your partner just does not make the effort toward change like you have put forth. It just depends. It could be that things feel better because you are the one doing all of the doing. However, that is not going to work for the long haul, unless your partner is slow to change. It is possible that by observing you serve as a role model, then they decide to do something too. It does take time—just not forever.

CHOICE #2) If after all of that, there is not really much change in the relationship, and your needs are not being met, then, I hate to sound like a therapist, but some couple's therapy would be a great kick-starter in making change. In other words, no matter how much you love your partner, you can't love him or her enough for the both of you. Change, motivation, energy, positive efforts, behaviors, and new thinking have to come from both parties.

CHOICE #3) If your partner refuses to go to couple's therapy, you could try a couple's weekend workshop, a communication class, a self-help couple's book that you read together 15 minutes a day, or, perhaps even a non-therapy, joint activity to make the reconnection happen. For example, take a long walk on the beach just the two of you (or a mountain hike) and talk; go sit in the front seat of the car in the driveway and talk; or go do something fun that you both haven't done in a long time and spend the day together—just the two of you.

CHOICE #4) If you're still feeling stuck and there is a string of empty promises on your partner's end but no action, then perhaps individual short-term, problem-solving therapy would allow you to sort through your own thoughts and feelings so that you can figure out what the next step is for you. It could very well mean that you live with what you've got and make the best of it. It could mean that you try in more creative ways to take care of yourself outside the marriage. You might remain married, but take a class to stimulate yourself in functional creative ways. Or, it might be a deal breaker for you. Only you will know the answer to that.

In summary, the biggest failure would be to not try for yourself first, and then for your partner. The next biggest failure would be to make the positive changes on your own behalf, but then eventually get frustrated, angry, and resentful toward your partner and then blame him or her for no change. Please do not do that. Make change for yourself first—regardless of the outcome.

WHAT HAVE YOU LEARNED?

#1—If you feel a vibe from your partner, say so.

#2—If you are getting mixed messages, and you are uncertain or confused, say so.

#3—If your feelings have changed toward your partner for a long time now, but you are continuing the relationship out of fear from saying anything, please take steps toward helping yourself (therapy, workshop, or this book). Short of a violent reaction from an abuser, my view is that if you feel disconnected, your partner is feeling it too. Work through your fear and speak own your Truth.

#4—The sooner you say your Truth out loud, the better you will feel.

#5—If you need to, find time alone when no one else is in the house and go stand in front of the bathroom mirror and practice saying out

loud a sentence or two over and over. Practice it 40 times out loud
so that you can hear yourself say it. Oftentimes, the shock of what we
want to say is that we've never heard it out loud. When you do face
your partner and say it out loud for the first time, it is a shock—your
emotions surface. However, by practicing it out loud, it desensitizes
you so that when you deliver the message you are more composed,
less emotional, more poised and in control. It is for this reason that
people are encouraged to practice answering questions before a job
interview—they are less emotional.

I am talking about speaking out loud about your feelings and
thoughts rather than holding back THE REAL YOU!

BE REAL WITH YOURSELF FIRST AND THEN WITH
YOUR PARTNER. In doing so, you are creating intimacy between
each other. This is really powerful.

What also matters is how you say it, when you say it, your intention
by saying it, and your clear definition of what your desired outcome
is by saying it in the first place! When you surround any big statement
or revelation in LOVE and tenderness, then it goes a long ways to a
healing outcome. When you tell the Truth to strengthen your LOVE
for each other—then guess what? Your love is going to get stronger.

In my doctoral program, my professor told us about a couple who
dated each other and happily shared many activities together, especially
football. They went to games and to friends' houses to watch games
together. After they married, the wife revealed that she hated football!
How could she do that? My professor stated that scenarios like that
were all too common. As he continued to tell the story, it turned out
that her hating football was one thing, but after the marriage, she
demanded that her spouse give up going to the games and playing
fantasy football. IT WAS A BIG DEAL!

If she had said, "I need to tell you something and it affects something that is really important to you. I need to let you know that I was
not entirely honest with you about one thing …" Maybe that would
have been a start. She hid her true Self from him and then revealed
it with a punch after she had the ring on her finger! Our professor
said that she took it one step further. She DEMANDED that he stop

watching football both live and on TV (at home and with friends) just because she hated it! This was a game she was playing. Her spouse didn't hold back who he was (in this instance) or what he loved doing. He married this woman for love and for her love of football (something he loved). So it was something they shared. Then, she not only took that shared promise from him, she demanded that he stop doing what he had always loved doing! Wow! She played a game with herself first and then with him.

I wonder if he would have married her if she had revealed her true Self to him prior to the marriage? Who knows? I do know, however, that he deserved to make that choice for himself, rather than for her to make it for both of them without dialogue or discussion. In my view, relationships are hard enough without clouding them with falseness, deceit, and secrecy. Please note, I am talking about your soulmate and friend for life. I am talking about your husband and your wife and partner for life. I am not necessarily talking about your boss at work. I am talking about an investment in your intimate partnership. That is why Truth can be so powerful because it is the binding— stucco and cement— that holds the building blocks of trust, love, and respect together. There is really no other way to do it and still call it FUNCTIONAL communication unless you speak your Truth!

ACKNOWLEDGMENT DOES NOT MEAN AGREEMENT

One major assumption between couples is that acknowledgment means agreement. It does not! Acknowledgment does NOT equal agreement. Acknowledgment of what you hear your partner say is so powerful.

Receiver: "I hear you saying that you're thinking that we can not afford for me to go back to school at night. Is that what you're saying?"

Sender: "Yes."

Receiver: "Well, actually I have a different take on that. Let me explain how I think we can handle the finances while I attend school at night."

Differences of opinion can be minimized when acknowledgment is present in conversation. Acknowledgment goes a long way to defusing the high emotion attached to a different point of view.

NON-VERBAL CUES TO COMMUNICATE EFFECTIVELY

HOW, WHEN, WHERE (some commonsense tips)

HOW

How do you approach your mate when you need to talk or discuss an issue? Do you make eye contact? Are you both in a connected space (on the couch, in the bedroom, away from the kids)? Do you give yourself time to think through how you want to approach your partner? Is it going to be a collaborative discussion or just a brain dump on him or her?

DON'T

Don't use the pronoun, "YOU."

Don't speak in incomplete thoughts or sentences.

Don't try to force a discussion if your partner has stated that he or she does not want to talk right now.

Don't make a list of all the things wrong. Keep it focused.

Don't label or swear at your partner. It is NOT OK to swear at each other.

WHEN

Choosing when to talk or the right time to talk is vital to making certain that you are both ready to share and communicate. It could mean knowing when to approach your partner. Make arrangements for the children to be somewhere else for a couple of hours. Create a positive environment. Sit down at the kitchen table across from each other and make eye contact.

DON'T

Don't approach him when he just walked in the front door with his briefcase exhausted after a 12-hour workday.

Don't tell your spouse about your big need to talk when he is rushing
   out the door late for work in the morning.
Don't try to have a talk when your spouse is burdened by major
   financial stress, work stress, or health problems.
Don't try to talk when your partner is doing something personal for
   him or herself (watching TV, reading, etc.).
Don't try to start up a big discussion if you or your partner are high,
   drunk, or even emotionally very tense or angry.

WHERE

Where do you choose to discuss deep personal issues or issues packed
with emotion? It should be somewhere without interruption or distraction. You can take a walk together around the block. Or, go to
the park and sit on a bench and talk. You can choose to go to nature
(ocean, river, lake, mountains). You can go to your bedroom or any-
place quiet. For example, you could even go sit in the front seat of
your car in your driveway.

DON'T

Don't talk in front of the kids if it is a couple's issue.
Don't talk in a public restaurant.
Don't talk at parties.
Don't talk at family gatherings or in front of neighbors or friends.

POSITIVE COMMUNICATION

The mind is very powerful and you can control the mind to be either
negative or positive. WHY NOT GIVE YOUR MIND POSITIVE
THOUGHTS? IF you really truly change negative sentences into
positive sentences, and you really want to be positive, you will find
major changes taking place in your life.

   Is your mate negative or positive? If your mate is negative, why
don't you through your own positive thinking try to encourage positive thinking in a gentle manner without putting him or her down?
You will find that positive thinking has a rippling effect on your entire
life—relationships, work, goals, health, spirituality, and so on.

1. **I LOVE YOU**

   Tell your mate "I love you." Sometimes you might not feel that you show it, so say so and be sure to include the words, "I love you." Say it aloud with sincerity. Positive communication can be both verbal and non-verbal. It means being emotionally, verbally, and behaviorally supportive to your partner—hugging, smiling, making eye contact and time together to talk, being empathic if he or she is worried. This also includes compliments that suggest, "I love you." There are so many more things. It could mean saying your favorite endearments such as "sweetie pie, honey, babe," and so on. It could be romantic gestures. When was the last time you bought your spouse a card and put it in his or her sock drawer? What about flowers? Have you gone to your favorite bakery lately and bought your sweetheart her favorite lemon bars? The list goes on. Sometimes we get into bad habits, or we get busy and we forget what we used to do early on in the relationship. Do not take each other for granted! You cannot put relationships on automatic pilot. Every relationship requires attention and nurturing. What would happen if you just ignored your boss and didn't pay attention to him or her? That wouldn't last very long. If you put one-third of the same energy you put into work into your relationship instead, you might not even need to read this book!

2. **COMPLIMENTS**

   How often do you give your mate compliments? If you never hear anything good or positive from your mate, then it is difficult for you to say something nice or positive back. This is a major technique in reorganizing the communication cycle between you and your mate. By using this exercise, "I Love You," you change your old communication habits. Give a compliment now and then!

3. **HUGGING**

   Hugging, embracing, kissing, holding hands, caressing—all are very gentle, symbolic expressions of love and gentle communication. This is very important and necessary to any relationship! There is more to a relationship than going to bed and having sex—it is talking to each other and sharing precious moments outside the bedroom.

4. ROMANTIC GESTURES

When was the last time you gave your mate flowers, a card, or jewelry? These outward simple expressions of affection can strengthen any relationship. On the other hand, if in the past your mate expressed affection in this manner and you made a negative comment, "I don't like candy" or, "Flowers just die in the vase," then no wonder he or she stopped trying methods of romantic expression. This is a form of rejection. Be considerate of your mate and the reasoning behind the gesture.

5. BE POSITIVE

Have you ever listened to what you say to other people or to your mate? Have you ever taken the time to listen to your inner thoughts (words that run across your mind)? Are they negative? Practice the RED STOP SIGN.

6. SMILING

Have you ever looked in the mirror and saw yourself frowning, and you didn't know it? Smile. It makes you feel extremely good, confident, and positive. Also, it can rub off on your mate, children, friends, and co-workers. What a difference a smile makes.

7. MAINTAINING INTEREST

If you played sports together, read books, played games, listened to music, enjoyed the theater, took walks and so on prior to having kids, then you should make certain that you still take the time to do those activities you mutually enjoyed. Your relationship will grow as a result. There should be enough balance in all facets of your family life to ensure equal time for the kids and for your mate, as well as for yourself.

In addition to maintaining long-term interests together (things you discovered about each other when you first met), as a couple you can both find a new project or activity that you enjoy doing together now—for the first time. This will strengthen your relationship. Just as a tree grows new leaves, a relationship requires all the necessary ingredients important to promote new avenues of growth.

8. BALANCE

Balance is the key. That means if one of you travels excessively due to your job, and the other mate works, while staying at home with the kids, when the traveling partner returns home, an adjustment must be made by everyone. It probably feels good for the traveling partner to stay at home and play house with his or her mate and family. However, the traveling partner should consider their mate's desires too. Maybe the home partner would like to go out to a movie, dinner, or vacation once in a while (since he or she always stay at home when not working). The key to communication is to look at it from your partner's perspective—the traveling partner is exhausted and wants to stay home, but the home partner might be frustrated, bored, lonely and eager to go out. Remember, balance is the key!

Balance means that since you have had kids and all you talk about are the "kids," then, perhaps you should make a point of picking current event topics from the newspaper, news, or Internet and discuss them as a couple. Have an adult conversation about anything but the kids. This will help round out your interactions. This exercise in communication will change your communication patterns and therefore add growth and stimuli to your relationship. Always look at the patterns! Do you always talk about the same old thing? CHANGE IT!

9. RESPECT

Respect your mate by including them in decision-making issues. Do not speak for your mate when asked to attend a party, dinner, lecture, or event without discussing it with that person first. That might mean you don't decide until you discuss it, or it might mean that you have a blanket agreement between you that the social calendar is open—anything you choose is fine with your partner. Do not commit your mate without their say so. This will eliminate petty hassles and unnecessary arguing. You cannot speak for your mate.

INTIMACY WITH SEXUAL ATTRACTION

Below is a list of individual questions that I would ask partners of heterosexual couples and same-sex couples when partners were in front of each other. For same-sex couples, the questions need to be modified slightly, but the premise is the same (love and attraction).

- **DO YOU LOVE HIM?**
- **DO YOU LOVE HER?**
- **ARE YOU IN LOVE WITH HIM?**
- **ARE YOU IN LOVE WITH HER?**
- **ARE YOU SEXUALLY ATTRACTED TO HIM?**
- **ARE YOU SEXUALLY ATTRACTED TO HER?**

Although bold, I use these assessment questions along with many others as a way of cutting through the red tape on where partners stand in terms of physical intimacy, love, and attraction.

The men are usually quite gracious and are not negative about their partner. More often than not, their biggest complaint was that they were dissatisfied with the amount of sex in their lives. The same held true for many same-sex couples. Females often blurted out their bottled up feelings!

I would ask her, *"Are you sexually attracted to him?"*

(I just asked him the same question, and he had said, *"Yes"*)

She responds,

"Well look at him, how can I be? Look at his bald head and his fat belly. No, I'm not sexually attracted to him and I haven't been for a long time."

Meanwhile, the man looks like he's sitting with a 3-headed monster in the room. There is certainly more to this story that I could

analyze with you. Bottom line—physical attraction is a key component vital to keeping the marriage alive. It is a very important layer
on top of many other layers within the relationship (values, education,
money, kids, intellectual stimulation, etc.).

When you are in a committed relationship, you cannot put yourself on automatic pilot, nor can you expect the marriage to thrive if
you put the relationship into cruise control. YOU HAVE TO PAY
ATTENTION TO YOURSELF FIRST AND THEN TO YOUR
PARTNER. What would happen if you just gave birth to a child and
then ignored it for 18 years? I'm certain that you would vehemently
argue all the important reasons for **feeding, changing, loving,
interacting, guiding, and teaching** your beautiful child. YES!
Thank goodness you feel that way. You cannot just ignore your in-
fant, toddler, or teenager and say to yourself, "Gee, I don't feel like
being a mother (or father) today, I'm really tired."

Guess what? The same holds true for your beautiful partnership/
marriage. You have to do almost all of the same things just mentioned
for your intimate partner.

Feeding—OK, maybe cook dinner, but I'm talking about feeding your partner's psyche, mind, body, heart, and spirit! The more you
focus on your own growth and learning, the more mentally stimulating you become; you ADD more to the marriage.

Changing—When you change and grow, your partner changes
and grows in your presence. It is like a domino effect. As both of you
adjust to life changes and make the necessary changes to adapt to your
life goals and life's stressors, then you wind up growing and changing
TOGETHER.

Loving—Does this need explaining? Express love through words,
thoughts, and deeds. How about loving yourself then passing that
love onto your partner. Do you like yourself? Do you love yourself?
If you don't, then why not? What do you need to change so that you
can start loving yourself? How about changing your outlook on life?
Name the one thing, the one reason, the one event, the one person, or
the one job that makes you unhappy. Then, look at that one thing and
see it from a different perspective. See it from the perspective that you

have no control over others but you do have control over HOW you choose to view it. Can you look at this as a challenge for your own growth? What positives do you gain from this situation? What are the learnings? Have you learned something about yourself as a result of this thing, person, or event that has resulted in your unhappiness? Check yourself out. Think about it.

Interacting—This is not just texting throughout the day, but real time face-to-face (even if you have 4 kids and only spend 15 minutes at night looking at each other before you go to bed). Talk, feel, explain, hug, kiss, laugh, problem-solve. Interact in real time with each other. This is your life partner! Talk about how appreciative you are to have a good father for a husband. Tell your beautiful wife that although you don't say much, you love her and you thank her for having dinner ready on the nights that you can't help her make dinner. Talk.

Guiding—Your partner is not a mind reader (thank goodness). Guide your partner as to how you like to be treated (sexually, date night, vacations, jewelry, etc.). At first, you might have to ask for what you need, but after a while, you might only have to spend time thanking her or him sincerely for making the effort in anticipating your needs (see how well you guided him/her?).

Teaching—This is different from guiding, but similar. How about sharing information between the two of you? Share what you learn and offer that information to your spouse. Perhaps, it might mean learning something together as a couple that you share together. Mix it up anyway you want—it's called development, growth, and change. Sometimes, it might mean that if one of you is taking classes, it's about sharing and including your partner in discussion at school or work. If you do this, then as you receive information for your own growth and professional development, you also give your partner a chance to grow with you by sharing how this information is changing you or adding to **your** repertoire of skill sets.

Your relationship can NOT remain stagnant! If that happens, there could be negative ramifications. These include a lack of talk, interest, excitement, shared activities, vacations together, sex, and laughter in the marriage. What a loss! What sadness. Please begin now in some small way to reach out to each other. If you are reading this sentence together right now, stop reading and look at each other, smile, and speak.

I had one client tell me in a calm but inward-speaking voice (as if she was disconnected to the actual thought as she told her story), that if she found out today that her husband was in a car accident, she would go to the hospital emergency room. "I would care that he is OK, but you know, I wouldn't really care. I mean I don't love him; I don't feel connected to him. I would just go through the motions of being the wife by his side. God forbid if anything happened to him, but it's not like my life would be devastated without him."

I share that because, I hope that is not you. Unfortunately, her story is not uncommon. People often exist side-by-side, play the part, and look the part, BUT THEY ARE NOT CONNECTED at the heart level. It does not have to be that way. You deserve to be happy. I challenge you to dig deep within yourself to take care of yourself and to start acting for yourself. When you figure it out—reach out to your partner. Reach out to your spouse and tell him/her what you have found out about yourself. Make the connection. Start today. Please don't let years go by without living and loving and sharing. Stop the suffering and the numbness. LIVE.

INTENTION

For healthy, high-functioning couples (no domestic violence, no substance abuse, or major issues), it is important to remember intention. We forget sometimes that our partner probably 9-times-out-of-10 has good intentions. A question I frequently ask of each partner is:

"Do you think he is mal-intended toward you (plays a mind game, deliberately tries to hurt you, demeans you etc.)?" For most of us, when we see our partners acting out in a negative way—yelling, or being frustrated—it is easy to assume that they are trying to hurt us or make us feel badly. Remind yourself that your partner has good intentions and that they are just frustrated, anxious—whatever. If you can have compassion for your partner in their time of need, and not react personally, then it helps to avoid an argument or the escalation of one. I am NOT advocating that one partner should consistently be the "verbal punching bag" for the spouse who has temper flare-ups all the time!

Who knows? Maybe your spouse didn't have his second cup of coffee this morning. Or maybe he just received a text from work that a deal fell through and he has to go to work early. If you can be grounded in that moment, then you can be the one who helps stop the cycle of negativity. As a behaviorist, you being the grounded one (today) means that you are role modeling for your partner today; and the next time you are stressed out, he can be there for you in the same manner.

We are all going to have arguments, frustrations, and hurts in our relationships. I am specifically talking about manufacturing hurt toward your partner on purpose! That is a GAME! THAT IS NOT OK! I used to tell my couples if there is a game being played here, either own it and let's talk about it, stop it, or go find another therapist. It is a waste of time and energy. Certainly, it is a waste of my time.

FORGIVENESS

As part of his first session, a husband once started to tell his part of the couple's dance by apologizing to his wife and explaining what he had done wrong—basically "owning his stuff." I breathed a sigh of relief. What a great beginning! As I listened, I realized I didn't have to work through resistance or denial about how his behavior hurt his partner. With a client who so quickly admits his part in the marriage, therapy can advance quickly; in the first few minutes, this highly functional man was talking out loud, owning his behavior, and telling his partner that he was sorry for her pain! Couples often just need a little fine tuning. My job is to support them and help facilitate any misunderstandings that might result in an argument or fight. They were very productive in communicating with each other, healing past hurts and pains; they were in a safe place to explore those hurts.

One piece of advice I give my clients is that when one partner apologizes with, "I'm sorry" the receiving partner should say, "I accept your apology," instead of "It's OK." It is not OK. You deserve to hear the apology and the person who is apologizing needs to say it. Don't dismiss it! ACKNOWLEDGE IT! It can be very freeing and very healing. "Thank you for your apology, I accept it, and I also apologize to you for my role in hurting you. I am very sorry."

When your partner has been hurt by your behavior, it is important to always acknowledge that hurt. Because you don't wake up in the morning and say to yourself, "I'm going to hurt her today," it is vital that you hear your partner's hurt—even though it was not your intention.

Your job is to listen to your partner. The key is to let your partner know you are listening and that you hear them loud and clear. Your partner's job is to listen; your partner's job is to let you know that they hear you loud and clear. It sounds hokey and slow-moving, but believe me, you will find ways to streamline the conversation so that it moves along without screaming or tense silence.

So, you could say, "I am so sorry we argued earlier, and I understand that you were hurt by my behavior. I am sorry that I hurt you, that was not my intention. I would never want to hurt you. What is it you need to tell me right now?" Just because your partner says you are the "bad guy" (negative label—do not label your partner), you don't necessarily have to apologize for being the "bad guy." YOU apologize for how his or her perception of you as the "bad guy" is hurting him.

"I am so sorry that you have been stressed out because I did not tell you about my work-related trip in November. I want you to know that I will make a huge effort to communicate better with you in the future. All I was trying to do was get more information from my boss before I told you. I didn't mean to hide anything from you. I am so glad that we are talking now. How would you like me to handle it the next time?"

Forgiveness is a gift to Self and to your partner. The act of forgiveness is powerful and healing. Real forgiveness means letting go of resentments and bad energy. If it is not about winning the argument, it is about forgiving. Guess what? When you actually reach out to another person and forgive them, you reclaim your own individual power and integrate it into your own Self (being).

That is true healing! That healing is life-lasting (not temporary).

UNFORGIVENESS

Are you aware of thoughts and feelings that prevent you from having positive, loving feelings for your partner? Can you name them now? It is easier to cope with pain by remaining steadfast to anger and frustration. Negative feelings (hatred, anger, guilt, shame, fear), build a wall around your heart and prevent you from letting anything in or out. Negative feelings for another person fool us into believing that they are suffering as a result of our negative feelings. When you harbor negative thoughts and feelings, you are the one who suffers the most! After all, it is your head that hits the pillow every night.

It is imperative that you find peace within yourself first. Once you do that, love for yourself will flow through you and around you and ultimately to others. I have met many people over the years who REFUSED to do this. They openly refused to forgive their partner, themselves, their boss, or their parent. They sat on my couch and said that they would never do that. As a counselor I can only advocate healthy choices and explain the benefits. I cannot force or manipulate someone to do anything. What I can do is ask them to look at how they've handled their specific situation over time and how it feels to hold on to that unforgiving part of themselves. I give them tools to very slowly begin the process of taking one step at a time—closer and closer to the possibility of forgiveness at some point in the future (no timeline, just a process of steps). At the end of the day, it is the biggest gift you can give back to yourself. Of course, you don't forgive others to receive the gift, but when you do forgive, you immediately get back so much more.

Example: Even if it never entered your mind to forgive the other person, why don't you try it on for size? Find a quiet spot, in your backyard, or at a park, or in your bedroom and silently replay the scenario with the person you are thinking about forgiving. Do it in your mind—silently—visualizing the situation. Now, I want you to take it one step further, and visualize the situation that led to the upset, argument, or hurt. I would like you to re-engineer the scene so that you CHANGE IT. You could replay the scene differently. You could imagine that you went somewhere else that day and you never engaged with your partner or that person and the hurt or upset never happened. Or, you could replay it the way it happened but have the other person take ownership of their behavior and tell you right on the spot that they are sorry for hurting you. Each of you could talk sincerely about how bad it felt and then hug and make up. Now, you feel closer to that person. You look directly in their eyes and say, "I forgive you," and the other person tells you, "I forgive you too." Or you could replay it to where something really joyous and fun happened and there wasn't anything negative to feel bad about. How do you feel, right now? Think for a minute about how that feels and get in touch with that feeling. Let go of the hurt and rage. Let it go. Forgive and move on. Forgive and move on.

Lack of forgiveness can be a real stumbling block to growth. The more you can reclaim your own power back by letting go of the stored-up hurts and resentments, the more empowered you will be in life. You will become a happier person and you will most likely have fewer conflicts in life—a smoother sailing in the future. The choice is yours. You decide. It is your future.

FORGIVENESS FORMULA

This is a Forgiveness exercise:

STEP (A) You can do this exercise for one particular person in your life—your spouse, your mother, your best friend, or whoever you know you need to forgive. Or, you can write down a complete list of people past and present, deceased or alive, people you knew in the 3rd grade and haven't spoken to since, or people you met this morning. They could be family, friends, neighbors, co-workers, and so on. Write down a complete single-spaced list of ALL of these people in your life.

STEP (B) *THIS IS IMPORTANT.* What are the negative feelings that you know you have always displayed in your relationships throughout your life?

Example: Shame, guilt, anger, rage, anxiety, low self-esteem, depression, fear, insecurity, being overweight, co-dependency, feeling stupid, alcoholism, etc. Throughout your life, what is the common theme in your relationships that keeps surfacing (your inner thoughts, conclusions, or general feeling that emerges from your relationships)?

STEP (C) Take a large piece of paper and write the following instructions:

#1—Please choose a time when you are completely alone in the house to perform this exercise.

#2—In your mind's eye, imagine seeing a person standing in front of you, someone who you want to forgive for some past event that resulted in negative feelings. See yourself standing tall in front of that person—face-to-face.

Say these statements out loud to the person you imagine in front of you:

- *Say to that person, "I forgive you."*
- *Say to that person, "I am sorry for my dynamic, in how I chose to respond to you consistently in our relationship (behaviors, thoughts, and feelings).*
- *Say to that person, "I love you _____ (name that person).*
- *Say to that person, "I love myself and I forgive myself for bringing my feelings of _____, _____, and _____ into our relationship."*

Fill in the blanks above with at least two or three themes in your life that dominate your relationships and behavior (Step B). You know what those themes are.

- *Then say out loud (to The Creator, to God, to The Universe) "Right now, from this moment forward, I release _____, _____, and _____. I am free and I am whole. Thank you. Thank you. Thank you."*

Example: Now I am going to repeat the entire exercise, but I will fill in the blanks for you in one complete paragraph so that I can pull it all together for you without any of the explanation.

Let's say I need to forgive my mother. So for me, I am focusing on one person only and in my mind's eye. She is the person I see standing in front of me face-to-face, when I visualize during this exercise.

I say out loud to my mother, "I forgive you. I am sorry for my dynamic, in how I chose to respond to you consistently in our relationship. I love you mother. I love myself and I forgive myself for bringing my feelings of shame, guilt, and fear into our relationship. Universe, right now, from this moment forward, I release shame, guilt and fear. I am free and I am whole. Thank you. Thank you. Thank you."

This is a powerful exercise, so be prepared to be alone when you do it (not with people sitting watching TV in the next room). Also, if you choose not to focus on one person, but to do the list of everyone you've known, then, the exercise requires you to list the name of every individual that you have had a relationship with in the past or present. In my example, I brought shame, guilt, and fear into those relationships, or in your case, your own themes of negative feelings or behavior into your relationships— please name those themes. When you do this exercise with a list of names—say Uncle Charlie's name is at the top of the list and he has been deceased for several years—you would start by inserting Uncle Charlie's name in the sentence format and continue speaking the forgiveness formula until you get to the end of the paragraph. Then, cross Uncle Charlie's name off of the list and repeat the entire exercise inserting the second person's name on the list. Cross off that person's name and continue. Say the entire exercise out loud. Do not rush through it, just say it, cross off the name, then repeat the exercise for the next name on the list. Please note, you do not have to stop and think about Uncle Charlie and remember the specific event or events that resulted in shame, guilt, or fear (or your own themes). The fact that you know the themes in all of your relationships including Uncle Charlie is sufficient. So don't stop to explain a scenario, just stick to the formula and don't stop until you've crossed off everyone in your list.

When I did the exercise, it took about 40 minutes (my list was long); all I can say is that it was very powerful and cathartic (releasing). It really helped shift my energy. It is like cleaning out your own psyche with cobwebs that have been there for months, years—decades. Great Exercise! Release and Let GO!

FIGHTING TIME-OUTS DURING TIMES OF CONFLICT

A time-out is when both parties agree that if either partner says, "I need a time-out," then the conversation immediately stops. There are no words to get the last point across. Also, a time-out does not mean you never go back to talking about the issue. It does mean that each partner commits to honoring a time-out; time is allowed for both parties to calm down; a commitment is understood. An appointment to continue the discussion during calm is made out loud. The time-out can be as short or as long as agreed upon ahead of time in consideration of your respective styles of conflict and not when you are arguing. Perhaps, one partner says that he usually only needs 25 minutes to calm down in the back bedroom. Or, the other partner says that she usually will stew on it for a couple of hours and would prefer to continue the discussion the next day. This should be discussed ahead of time. Some collaborative pre-agreement needs to be reached as to when to resume the discussion. NOT WHEN YOU ARE IN THE MIDDLE OF ARGUING!

Although much has been written about conflict resolution and different conflict styles of interaction, the important thing for you to know is that each of you has two jobs at the beginning of conflict.

#1— The first is to pay attention to yourself.

#2—The second job you have is to pay attention to your partner.

How do you know you are starting to argue?

What is your first indicator that you are starting to have an argument with your mate? What is the physical feeling you have in your body? Do you get heat waves? Does your throat tighten? Does your chest feel heavy? Does your forehead feel pressured? The first physical symptoms can be a red flag that your body is reacting to the increase in emotions taking place during a potential argument. Next question: What are you feeling emotionally (happiness, sadness, frustration, anger, hurt, etc.)? Then, what are you saying to yourself in your head when all of this is happening? What is your mental chatter? This is very important. We know that there is a HUGE connection between thoughts, feelings, and behavior. Finally, what are you doing? Are you yelling? Are you pointing your finger at your mate? Are you walking away in silent rage? What behaviors do you display when you are frustrated?

NAME THAT TUNE — OBSERVATION

Even if you think you know what your partner thinks and feels, you do not. Please do not mind read! However, you CAN OBSERVE your partner. Is her face getting red? Is he slamming kitchen cupboards? Does she have a look in her eye that she gets just before you both start arguing? Is he repeating himself? What is happening?

Now when you notice the first indicator that you are starting to stress out, that would be a great time to look at your mate and say something like, "Are we starting to have an argument? I don't want to argue with you," or "I am feeling really tight in my stomach, I know this is really important to you and you want to talk about it, but I need a TIME-OUT so that I can calm down first. This is vital because IT DOES NOT MATTER WHO SAYS IT FIRST, AS SOON AS ONE OF YOU IDENTIFIES THAT YOU THINK THE ARGUMENT IS STARTING, YOU CAN SPEAK OUT. You can say what you are feeling or that you've noticed your physical symptoms and it "feels like" an argument. This is NOT about making an excuse to get out of talking. On the contrary, this is about being grounded so that you can continue the dialogue without arguing.

Couples often return to my office and tell me, "Wow! That really works! We were starting to get heated but he said that he did not want to argue, and I didn't even realize I was raising my voice. We took a step back, calmed down, and decided that we could continue talking calmly—and we did. We were successful! And, we actually resolved a big issue of ours!"

The magic between couples is amazing. One glance, one word—it means so much. The power of a couple working together moving forward in the same direction, setting goals as a family, and supporting each other's differences while loving the other is the balance of power! It is like a fine dance. Not to discount my services, but my premise has always been that once on track, some of the greatest couple's therapy sessions have taken place at home on their living room couch—without me in the room.

HOW DO YOU BEGIN?

Even if you think you both communicate without verbal explanation, I would stop you right there. You cannot speak for what your partner is thinking or feeling. NO! This book is about communicating.

#1—**Communicating with Self is the first step.**

#2—**Communicating with your partner is the second part of that process**.

You do not have control over how your partner responds, but the good news is that you did your part. You contributed in a healthy, positive manner. You took the first positive step toward loving Self and loving your partner.

NEEDS AND WANTS—MISSED EXPECTATIONS

In a counseling session, my job is to facilitate the efforts of the couple as they seek new tools on how to listen, acknowledge, and reflect back to each other. It is wonderful to see how high-functioning, motivated individuals come together in therapy as a couple and then really maximize the return on their investment in every session! They do the work and the work changes them as a couple and as individuals. It starts with "What I REALLY need from you is to do less of this or that (or Stop doing this or that) and I need more of this. Are you willing to do that for me?" It is my version of contractual agreements. Every couple has their own style. Depending how badly they really want a chance for positive change—they put down the boxing gloves, implement my code of rules, and ask for what they need. Lo and behold, it works! Then, they can begin the real work, which is to peel back the layers from their core. It is like peeling back the layers of an onion. Once the conflict stops, the games stop, the disengaged non-communication stops, they diligently work to get to what is really not working in the marriage. Unless they were completely toxic, combative, or play major games, I am honored to work with many hundreds of couples willing to work for a healthy outcome. They are successful! It is my joy to know them and to work with them. I always say, "You do the work, I get to watch!"

A professor once told me the BIGGEST SOURCE OF STRESS IN A MARRIAGE IS EXPECTATIONS or MISSED EXPECTATIONS—either conscious or subconscious—either overt (spoken) or covert (unspoken). You ever see a couple and think to yourself, "She's keeping score." OOPs! "There he goes again, she's not going to let him off the hook on that one." Well, that scenario is the result of a missed expectation that is either conscious or subconscious. For example, let's say you know what you want. You expect something from your partner. You have identified it consciously (you are aware of it). But, let's say you don't tell your partner what your expectations are. That is a conscious but unspoken (covert) expectation. Perhaps this manifests in you being frustrated a lot or keeping score in your mind. IF you are not aware of any expectations (subconscious) but you continually feel disappointed, it turns out that you can't communicate why but things are just not the way you thought they'd turn out. Or, something just does not click for you but you can't put your finger on it. This is subconscious and unspoken. Understandably, the HEALTHIEST manner is to be aware of your expectations and to speak them out loud (conscious and overt)! Thus, the conversation you want to have is the "needs and wants" between each other. I once had a client who counted the number of diapers she changed versus her husband! YIKES! Talk about keeping score! Needless to say, they were locked in a cycle.

REBUILDING TRUST AFTER THE AFFAIR

I use words like "perpetrator" to describe the person who conducted the affair. I use the term "victim" to describe the one who was cheated upon. I use the word "affair" whether it is a one-night stand or a long-term relationship with feelings of love.

This is such a huge wound in the marriage/partnership. It is the absolute betrayal to bring a third person into your intimate partnership. This is big! This is huge! This is major! This could be a deal breaker for your marriage. One of you may decide not to work on the marriage. Your marriage may remain "together" but not really healed, as you both hobble along as a couple, but never really move past the affair. Or, you might still be married but the perpetrator misspoke about their commitment to rebuilding trust. In the end they have another affair or continue with the same one.

This is a three-part approach:

NO TRUST BEFORE THE AFFAIR

My first concern is your track record as a couple. In other words, was there trust prior to the affair between the two of you? Either answer points to the two of you in decidedly different directions based upon your answer, which I will not explore here. However, if there has never been real trust between the two of you since the inception of your marriage, this is a deep-seated underlying theme that needs to be rectified before you can move forward. A common example: both partners cheat on their prior spouses, divorce and leave the spouse and kids for their current spouse (each other). So their present marriage is built on an affair (lots of core issues centering around mistrust). This could very well be a case for long-term couple's therapy. A safe environment needs to offer both of you a place (with a skilled facilitator), to explore your inner doubts and concerns regarding the trust of your commitment together when the guilt of how your relationship began weighs so heavily upon you today.

HEALTHY TRUST BEFORE THE AFFAIR

If your track record indicates that there was healthy trust prior to the affair, then what happened to cause the affair? The purpose of this question is not to assign blame but to identify when the breakdown started to happen between you. How do you know that there was the beginning of a breakdown? When did you start to go on automatic pilot and start drifting apart? Was it a month ago or was it 3 years ago? If you can both point the finger at when, then the next question is, what efforts did you make (or not make) to regain traction in the marriage when you saw it slipping away? Why was there no action by one or both of you? Can you describe that to each other?

Regardless of the event, a standard approach for any therapy is to determine the prior level of functioning to the actual crisis. A good track record of trust between you is a positive, healthy indicator that you have a good chance of returning to a healthy level of trust again. Now, I do not guarantee it. It is not necessarily a slam dunk either. If the two of you have shared space and time together on this planet with mutual trust at some point in your relationship, then you have experienced something special and unique to both of you as a couple. This is good. It's kind of like a doctor who wonders prior to the diagnosis, were you healthy with good cardiovascular capabilities? You see what I mean?

DO EACH OF YOU HONESTLY WANT TO REBUILD TRUST NOW? THINK ABOUT IT

No matter how long the affair lasted, my third concern is to determine if EACH OF YOU really wants to rebuild the trust in this marriage, right now. I often ask this question and the perpetrator immediately says, "Yes." However, the victim says, "I don't know." This is typical.

Remember, just because you have arrived at this conclusion soon after the affair, you may not remain constant in this decision. This is really a vital question. It really goes to both sides when I say, "Don't say you want to rebuild this relationship when you really don't want to!" This holds true especially for the perpetrator. Please do not say that you want to work on the marriage when you are not really convinced. The last thing you want to do is lead your partner down a trail of healing if you have begun the journey with another deception.

STEPS TOWARD REBUILDING TRUST: PERPETRATOR

If you are the perpetrator, then life as you know it is over— probably for a long time. If you really want to rebuild the trust between you because you love your spouse and want it to work— good. I wish you well and now you have to deal with your partner's reaction to the affair. Remember, just because you have decided that you want "IN," does not mean you get to stay in the marriage. Your partner might have different ideas about that. However, if you have both sincerely committed to making the effort toward genuine healing, then you NEED to follow these steps without variation or exception:

#1—You must CUT OFF all communication with your lover immediately. Also, you need to cut off the relationship with your lover with your spouse next to you on the speaker phone so that your spouse can hear everything being said. You need to tell your lover that you have decided to make your marriage work, that your spouse is listening, and that you are cutting off all communication, e-mail contact, cell phone contact, and so on. Tell your extramarital partner to **STOP ALL CONTACT FOR GOOD!**

#2—If you receive ANY contact at all from your extramarital partner—do the following: You need to hang up immediately if you get a call at work; if you get a voice mail at work (you need to save it to v/m); if you get a voice mail on your cell (you need to save it to v/m), and then you need to call your spouse immediately and tell them what just happened. Let your spouse listen to the voice mail on both your work voice mail and cell voice mail as soon as you get home! If you receive an e-mail (which you shouldn't if you've blocked e-mails), then, do not respond and read it together with your spouse. **YOUR SPOUSE NEEDS TO BE INCLUDED IN EVERY-THING! Whatever you do, do NOT respond to the contact from your extramarital partner.**

#3—If STEP #2 happens, you need to seriously consider chang-ing e-mail addresses and cell phone numbers—immediately. You need to also give your spouse complete access to any codes or log-on information!

#4—If your extramarital partner is someone from work, then you need to decide if you love your job more than your mar-riage. If the answer is WORK, well, there you go. Tell your spouse that you love your job more than your marriage to him or her. If that really is the answer—no reason to keep reading the rest of these steps.

However, if you decide that you love your marriage more than your work, this might be the deal breaker. From my perspective, if you were in therapy in my office, I would definitely ask many questions about work (Are you in different departments? Different buildings? Different field offices? Are you the boss and your lover your subor-dinate?). Best answer, you need to change employment. You cannot continue a non-affair relationship with the person you had the affair with—even if you've known him or her since childhood or they are your father's best friend! It is not an option.

#5—You need to over-communicate with your spouse/partner. That means that when you are going to be 15 minutes late because of traffic or an office meeting, then you need to be on the phone, talking to your spouse about your lateness. Believe me, your spouse is fantasizing and worrying about every minute you are at work and out the door. I encourage you to have multiple "check-ins" throughout the day to calm and steady nerves.

#6—You need to expect a lot of questions from your spouse and you need to honor those questions. There will be a lot of questions about, "Was this true? Did you lie to me at that time when you told me…?" It is very important that you answer the questions in full and do not dismiss, deny, or minimize ANYTHING!

#7—DO NOT GET ANGRY OR DEFENSIVE—if you do— game over! You are not allowed to be upset or defensive. Why are you upset? If you are over the affair, you're sorry, you've apologized (or so you believe), and you believe it is behind you, well guess what? Your spouse is just getting warmed up. So you need to get back in the saddle and sit up straight and do what you said you were committing to do—REBUILD THE TRUST!

#8—DO NOT LIE! If you tell small lies, or big lies, then you will get found out eventually. Your spouse is second-guessing EVERYTHING and will get to the bottom of the TRUTH! Listen carefully, you cannot make this marriage work if you continue to lie, cheat, or deceive your spouse. You cannot have your cake and eat it too. IT WILL NOT WORK!

#9—Do NOT immediately try to have sex with your spouse unless your spouse has expressed desire or you know that your spouse is ready.

#10—It is important that you explain what happened and answer all questions. One word answers—"yes/no" and getting upset because the questions seem endless, is tough. It is an indicator that either you are lying, or that your spouse is not getting at the core of what he or she needs to hear from you. It could be that you think that by acting as if nothing happened that things will go back to normal. WRONG ANSWER! Let me tell you again, that will not work. I heard that a lot. She was sobbing and screaming hysterically on my couch saying that her husband doesn't tell her anything and he was sitting there saying, "I just want it to be over and let's just move forward the way it was before. I want it to be normal again." Sorry—dismissing your spouse's questions as unimportant or that you've already answered that same question three times is not the approach that is helpful right now. I realize that you are hurting too, but your spouse is hurting more and you have to go through this to get out to the other side where some day it will be "normal again"—not just immediately.

It is vital that you tell your spouse—all of it. What happened? Where did you meet your lover? What time of day was it? Was it in a group setting or were you alone? Who spoke to each other first? What were you thinking and feeling when you talked to the other person you had an affair with? In therapy, I offer graphic details if needed about the actual sexual liaison. Many therapists do not do this—but you'd be amazed how quickly you can move forward once all of the dirty details are out in the open. What color was his or her underwear? What sexual position did you use? Did you go to a hotel? What was the first thing that was said after the act (did your lover say something first or did you?)? What was your first thought after you had sex? When did you first think of your spouse? Was it during the act, after the act, on the way home—when? Did you ever feel guilty? I am relentless. However, as unorthodox as my approach might be, it quickly allows all of the fantasies attached to the affair to disappear, because EVERYTHING IS OUT IN THE OPEN.

#11—How have you expressed sincere remorse? I realize as a therapist that it has to be awkward for a couple discussing this huge secret in front of a stranger, but some partners say, "I'm sorry" with a smirk. Others would refuse to say it. "She knows, I've already told her." THIS IS NOT OK!

You must really dig down deep and show genuine concern for your beautiful spouse. Have compassion and empathy for the pain that you caused them and the marriage!

#12—Be patient, be consistent, and demonstrate loyalty by giving attention to your spouse! Really connect with your spouse.

#13—Unfortunately, you can't exhibit all of the right behaviors and then 3 weeks after the affair, go back to the way you used to behave. This might take weeks, months, a year—who knows? It will never really go away. It is a wound. However, what I do know is that the more you consistently try your best effort to be your honest, loving communicative Self, the more your spouse will feel that, know it, and TRUST IT over time and therefore, TRUST YOU.

#14—Demonstrating responsibility and showing that you can be relied upon for remembering things that need to be done or helping around without being asked—goes a long way. Why? Doing the extra things helps to avoid arguments about small things that are really about larger unresolved issues. Small task completion helps your spouse feel supported during this time of crisis.

#15—Whatever you do—stop obsessing over your affair partner. When things get tight between you and your spouse, DO NOT start thinking that you were better off with the other person. Do not start personifying that person with positive attributes and compare them to your spouse. DO NOT!

#16—Forgive your spouse for acting out during this time of crisis and forgive yourself for having the affair. Then, keep doing what you are doing. You know in your heart that you love your spouse. So don't stop doing all the good things you have been doing over the past several months. Hang in there.

#17—When the crisis is over and things are smoother between you and your spouse—plan something really special (like a trip). Get someone to watch the kids long-term (4 days to a week) and go to Europe, go to Hawaii, go to Las Vegas, go for a weekend to New York City. Go SOMEWHERE together to celebrate your first 6-month or 1-year, post-affair anniversary.

#18—Whatever you do, if you come from a space and place of love and respect both for yourself and your spouse—you will be a better person because of it.

#19—What was the cause of the infidelity? Were you needing more attention from your partner? More sex? More diversity? Did you need more fun? What? Whatever was missing from your marriage, try every day in some small way to incorporate some more of it in the present.

#20—At some point down the path, when you've taken the trip, you'll feel the closeness between the two of you—you've passed the anniversary of your affair. You have achieved all the good things you wanted in your present marriage. **Give yourself a hug.** You dedicated yourself to doing your part to make your marriage better and stronger after the wound of the affair. Good for you.

VICTIM

If you have both committed to making the effort toward sincere and genuine healing, then you NEED to follow these steps without variation or exception:

#1—Whatever you are thinking and feeling, it is a natural reaction (as long as you are not a danger to Self or others). So if you can't seem to stop crying, it is understandable. If you feel that you need to talk to someone, then go to a counselor to talk, but do not use that as a substitute for talking to your mate (the perpetrator).

#2—Even if your spouse did every one of the 20 steps just mentioned, you will have your own journey to go through. It is natural to question your partner. One question leads to the next and can result in more unanswered questions. Once you move through the immediate shock, anger, screaming, and tears, I encourage you to gather your thoughts and make an appointment to really talk together. Inform your spouse that you are still missing some key information and you've tried to think of questions that will answer what you need to know. In other words, do not dribble questions every half hour throughout the day as you think of them. You need to get your ducks in a row and gather as many questions as you can so that you can be assured of clear answers.

In my sessions with couples who present with affairs, I often find that it is the victim who does not feel that his or her questions have been answered and the perpetrator thinks that they have been asked and answered many times. So whatever you believe to be the key answer you are missing, think about it, write it down, then ask it.

#3—There is one word of caution here. If you have productive questions answered and you bring up the "other" person in an argument or screaming match and use it as ammunition—this is NOT OK! What was given to you in full disclosure by your mate was given openly to help you both move forward. There comes a time called Return on Your Investment (ROI). So, at some point, you have to stop screaming, yelling, blaming, and questioning. It is a natural reaction in the early stages of discovery, but if you pursue it over weeks and months, then it means you are stuck in hurt and anger (you might consider individual counseling to help you move through those feelings).

After ALL of the cards are out on the table and all questions have been answered to the victim's satisfaction (if you can call it that), then I let both partners know that there is a cutoff time (approximately 4-to-5 weeks post-affair) where ALL questions about the affair have to be stopped. Bringing up the affair in every other sentence is a No No! If you continue to browbeat your partner, you will be successful in driving that person out the door. **So decide, what is it that you want? Do you want to start rebuilding Trust? Or do you want to drive your partner out the door?**

#4—This step is very important. If you have the information based upon all the answered questions, but now you have flashes of seeing your mate visually (in your mind) with the other person, it is natural to get upset. Do you start cognitively comparing yourself to the "other person?"—this too is a natural initial reaction.

You need to STOP it if you intend to move forward in this marriage! If the stop sign does not help you (see cognitive section), then you might need to see a cognitive behavioral therapist so that you can refresh the tools you need to stop re-injuring yourself mentally and emotionally by visualizing your spouse with someone else. This is a visualization that results in negative feelings and negative thoughts. This is the step where you have to take care of yourself. This is where you do your part to take care of Self. If you don't, you will continue to feel negatively and probably continue to punish your spouse for your pain and your anger. Time to Stop!

#5—If you still believe your spouse is lying. Perhaps you need to say so for your spouse to convince or prove you wrong. It is completely natural to not believe too much after a shocker like this. However, at some point you have to decide to move forward in this marriage (or not). To stay stuck in mistrust will only poison your marriage if you decide to move forward.

#6—Do not have sex with your spouse unless you want to. Tell your partner how you feel about having or not having sex. Ask your partner for what you need—more time, better relationship (feeling more connected), or space. However, also know that the longer you avoid sex, the more awkward it can become.

#7—Can you forgive your spouse for having an affair? Can you forgive yourself for subconsciously allowing your spouse to have an affair? Did you kind of know? Were there clues or suspicions that you ignored? Does this make it your fault? NO! It means that both of you drifted apart and your spouse "acted out" by having an affair.

#8—Can you identify any of your negative behaviors that might have contributed to your spouse straying from the marriage? Do you drink alcohol excessively? Can you see the signs of when the marriage broke down? When was that? What was your thinking back then?

#9—If you continue to be depressed and feel stuck, it might be helpful for you to consult with your doctor to see if there are any low-dosage antidepressants that would help you during this difficult time. It will help take the edge off, balance your emotional ups and downs, help you feel stronger on the inside as you continue to gather information, and help you make necessary decisions.

#10—Ask yourself this: "If my spouse is honest, communicative, and remorseful, do I want to move past this point into the future to a better place together?" If the answer is, "YES!" then, do everything you can to take care of yourself, but at some point you must acknowledge, appreciate, communicate, and express your thoughts and feelings to your spouse about the past, about the present, and about the future. If you do not do this, you might not regain the intimacy you want so badly. OK?

#11—Visualize (in your mind's eye) the two of you holding hands and feeling closer together and forgiving each other. If you want you can share that vision with your partner or not, what is important is that you can actually see it in your mind and feel it in your heart. I wish you well.

#12—If YOU DO ALL THIS AND BOTH OF YOU STILL FEEL STUCK, THEN YOU NEED TO SEE A COUPLE'S THERAPIST IF YOU ARE STILL WILLING TO WORK ON THE RELATIONSHIP. If not, then perhaps an individual counselor can help you make some personal strides toward your own well-being.

WHAT CAN YOU LOOK FORWARD TO POST-AFFAIR?

My heart goes out to both partners who come for counseling post-affair (usually within 1 week of the revelation). Each suffers. However, my goal as facilitator is to inform, guide, and steer each partner through the crisis so that they can achieve rebuilding their trust together. Allowing each partner to experience their pain, act out their anger, and move along the journey with their eye on the brass ring is a fine dance. This back and forth process of advocating for one, and then the other, empathizing with one and then the other, is all done to produce a final outcome— TRUTH, HEALING, and TRUST. Of course, the reintegration of their love is a huge part of the process also.

I remember one female who came for individual counseling; she was the one who had the 1-year affair—her husband found out and so did her lover's spouse. The problem was that her lover was her boss. She lost her high-paying job and things unraveled from there. Because she had an inactive sex life with her husband for more than a decade, she considered divorce. Every night was filled with horror as her husband kept calling her shameful names and demanding answers! However, what happened was miraculous (that's why I try not to give up on couples—they can always surprise me)! As she told me the story, her husband went to individual therapy (something he said he would never do), then she went to individual therapy, and finally they both went to couple's therapy (post-affair). They had three separate therapists. It did not look hopeful for several weeks. As soon as her husband turned the corner and started to forgive her and stopped shaming her for having the affair, they were immediately catapulted into a loving bubble of understanding, love, forgiveness, and healing. They FELL BACK IN LOVE WITH EACH OTHER, more than they had prior to the affair! Everything was renewed, reborn, and recharged! These two distant roommates began discussing everything! They talked and talked and talked! They spent time together. They dated each other. They even went on an international trip without the kids and they never stopped talking. They felt a deeper love, a more earnest desire, and a stronger connection than they had ever felt previously! THEY DISCOVERED THAT THEY REALLY LOVED EACH OTHER! I still get excited when I remember that story.

Many couples successfully migrate from one end of the dark tunnel into the light. They emerge stronger and even more committed. They emerge cleansed from the depths of despair. This applies to the majority of clients who come post-affair—as a couple. I believe that the reason they show up for therapy is because they have already made the commitment to work together and rebuild their trust. I congratulate them for their hard work and I congratulate you if you are reading this book and you decide to fight for your marriage. Blessings.

RESISTANCE TO CHANGE

In the world of therapy, I cringe when I think about clients who are resistant to change. I go through some kind of automatic mental check list, almost blathering to myself about how typical it is for a therapist to "blame the client" for not making any progress! Talk about projection! Now, for the record, you do realize that there are people who come to therapy and are resistant? Of course! However, getting back to my internal dialogue, I question my own intentions first. I start "checking myself out first" to figure out if the resistance is mine or my client's. In other words, there could be another reason beside the fact that they are simply resistant. Yes, it could be me! I could be the wrong therapist; I could be pushing too hard (my pacing is off and so my timing of interventions is not working); I could be in a bad space or a foul mood and not neutral and clean in my own "stuff" to be totally present in the room with the client, the list goes on and on.

On the other hand, it could be the client who is digging their heels in the sand and giving me signals that he or she isn't buying what I am selling. So what to do? I simply announce that I feel stuck. I calmly tell the couple (or the person) that I feel there is no movement in therapy and I ask for their help. Do they feel the same? I explain that my job is not to injure or push or make anyone do anything that they are not ready to do, and I would never want to hurt them. I even announce that maybe my style isn't the right style for them and that I am the wrong therapist. Couples often don't even let me get as far as the words I have typed in this paragraph. They emphatically start moving their heads up and down or sideways depending upon my question (I feel stuck, do you feel stuck?). Then, it comes pouring out—either one partner or the other has felt stuck in therapy. Their TRUTH is always a mind blower to me because I always feel it before I can name it. But, by naming it out loud, it allows all of us to put the cards on the table and tell it like it is.

Perhaps, I did not deliver the goods in a timely manner. I may have already seen them much longer than my typical couple (15 sessions instead of 10 sessions). Their TRUTH is revealed. In expressing my frustrations about feeling stuck, I am actually role modeling for them about how to bring up awkward conversations when things are not working—instead of silence or ignoring the problem. It is a powerful moment for me. It is a powerful moment for all of us. After that, a few decisions need to be made on-the-spot by the couple and me. They agree (collaboratively with me) that perhaps they need to take a break from therapy (since nothing is changing). Perhaps one or both might need to go to individual therapy for a while until there is more clarity. They can return to couple's therapy with me or with someone else. Just as often, the actual "check-in moment" spurs them on to continue with me and to work harder. It always amazes me how that works! Anyway, the point here is that resistance can be a two-way street, so be sure to cross the street and check out the view from the other side. No hard feelings— just each person taking care of him or herself. I'd feel relief either way—if they stayed or if they left. The reason being, is that I could not work with them the way it was going and to NOT mention it would be to replicate the dysfunctional behaviors displayed in the marriage where nothing was talked about, issues were ignored and too much was left unsaid.

HOW DO YOU BEGIN TALKING TO EACH OTHER IF YOU HAVEN'T TALKED TO EACH OTHER IN YEARS?

I once counseled a beautiful female client in her late 30s. She had been unhappily married for 15 years. She recalled never having really been "in love" with her husband. What a sad story. She married while in college and stayed in a loveless, non-communicative, non-sexual marriage. I hear stories like this from clients every day. Sad stories.

Unfortunately, these are your stories—your lives. I'm just a witness to the pain that people subject themselves to. It is such a waste of life and love and pleasure and dreams.

This is one of those important moments where I keep repeating myself and remind you that you deserve to be happy. I might be wrong, but my take on it is that we are not put on this earth to be miserable, self-sacrificing, or unhappy for our entire lives. It is all out there available to us equally. We all deserve abundance, prosperity, and happiness. There's enough for everyone to go around and then some. So, why, why, why would you give up all of that to be miserable? As a therapist I can give you many answers and you probably have a few of your own. At the end of the day, what matters is that you realize you have options.

In the example just described, the client went to see a couple's therapist with her husband. Unfortunately, the communication skills learned inside therapy did not continue outside therapy. Conversations were brief and clipped. They talked about schedules but did not really talk intimately about thoughts and feelings—to each other and about each other. She froze whenever we discussed couple's therapy; my focus was to help her speak her truth.

She was obviously fear-driven and paralyzed. Either talk and rediscover each other in a new way (she claimed that was not possible as there was nothing to reclaim), or tell the truth and set each other free. Granted, I did not meet or know her husband. I could not know what his experience was like in that marriage. However, at the end of the day, I heard there was a lot of silence and disconnection. How could he claim happiness?

From what I've witnessed over the years, people become used to not getting what they need or want and after a while they no longer try to reach out and strive for that connection. It takes too much effort. After a period of time, it becomes strange and awkward to make the effort. So they just hobble along, unhappy and alone in a marriage in which they are not satisfied.

After years of not talking, how do you begin to talk? There are several techniques. I find that talking about the relationship rather than pointing the finger at your mate goes a long way in generating conversation.

#1—Talk in the bathroom mirror alone when no one is in the house, or sit in your car in the garage and practice repeatedly the conversation that you intend to have with your spouse. Say it out loud to help you hear yourself say it. Listen to what you are saying. Keep practicing.

#2—Make an appointment to talk at home with your spouse, where you will not be interrupted.

#3—Talk about the marriage as a relationship rather than your partner's actions. This makes it less confronting. "It seems like we don't talk too much or spend time together, what do you think?"

#4—Talk about the marriage, your concerns, and your thoughts. "I need to talk to you and this is really hard for me, but I have something I want to say to you and ask you. I'm really unhappy and I have been for a long time. I look at you and you do not seem happy. Are you happy?" Or, "I want to talk, but I don't want to fight with you."

#5—Then, stop talking for a minute and allow your partner to talk. **The biggest challenge is stopping yourself from doing all of the talking—trying to compensate for all of the silence throughout the years.** Then, the conversation is over and you walk away and you realize you don't have any new information from your partner about what is going on between you.

#6—Even if your partner is the silent type, you MUST allow him or her to talk. Sit in the silence and whatever they say, repeat it back and ask them to say more. "You say to me you are confused. Can you tell me more? What do you mean exactly?" Or, "You say to me you don't know. What is it you don't know?" THEN BE SILENT.

#7—If your partner has not read this book alone or with you, and if your partner gets irritated, it is important for you to NOT GET DEFENSIVE. I realize I am asking you to be a partner while simultaneously being observant of the process. Yet, this is key.

#8—If you get defensive and your partner is already irritable, this is a sure-fire way of having a blow-up. This will go nowhere fast. ONE OF YOU HAS TO maintain control of emotions.

#9—If there is too much silence and your partner won't budge, try a different approach and say something that encourages your partner to talk to you. If he or she asks you to go first, then by all means, say what you want, be honest, and couch it in love. Talk to your partner as a best friend bearing bad news. Be kind and respectful as you talk to each other. It will help de-escalate the pain, fear, and the anxiety attached to the situation.

#10—Whatever the outcome, do not give up. If it is a small successful step toward communicating, then at the end of the meeting, make a mutual commitment to do it again, in 2 days or on your days off—together. Don't put it too far off. Mark it on the calendar.

Do something that formalizes the next conversation. Thank each other for the conversation.

I probably could write 20 more steps and you could probably re-write my first 10 steps. What is important is that you decide to either work on the problem together (by talking), or decide to acknowledge that the relationship is NOT working (by talking). Either way, to end the relationship, you have to talk and to re-start the relationship you have to talk. Yes, you could do nothing. Then, I would ask: "Why are you reading this book?"

THE VICTIM / EMPOWERMENT CYCLE OF BEHAVIOR

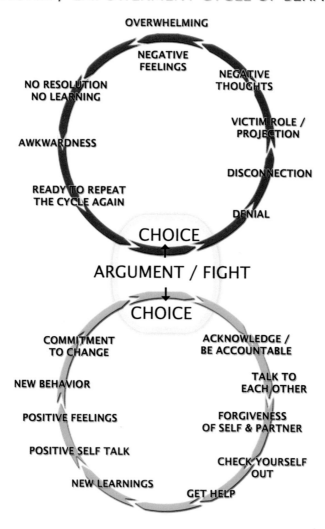

OVERWHELMING

NEGATIVE FEELINGS

NEGATIVE THOUGHTS

NO RESOLUTION NO LEARNING

VICTIM ROLE / PROJECTION

AWKWARDNESS

DISCONNECTION

READY TO REPEAT THE CYCLE AGAIN

DENIAL

CHOICE

ARGUMENT / FIGHT

CHOICE

COMMITMENT TO CHANGE

ACKNOWLEDGE / BE ACCOUNTABLE

NEW BEHAVIOR

TALK TO EACH OTHER

POSITIVE FEELINGS

FORGIVENESS OF SELF & PARTNER

POSITIVE SELF TALK

CHECK YOURSELF OUT

NEW LEARNINGS

GET HELP

THE VICTIM / EMPOWERMENT CYCLE OF BEHAVIOR

At the end of an argument, fight, or negative event, each person can choose a path to follow. When an argument happens between you and your partner, you have a choice right afterward as to how you will cope with that event. You can choose to be a VICTIM and blame your partner, or you can choose to be EMPOWERED having learned from the situation as you move forward in your growth—individually and as a couple.

You can choose a less functional way of behaving (The Victim Cycle), or, a healthy functional way of behaving (The Empowerment Cycle).

The first circle on top depicts the Victim Cycle or "The Blame Game." There are eight separate segments or phases that each individual partner may experience in reaction to a negative event or argument/fight. **After a negative event like an argument with your partner, you have a CHOICE to continue to be a victim or to choose a different path.**

Please note that each cycle represents a **guideline** as to phases that each person experiences within either of the two groupings— remaining a victim or breaking free into an empowered cycle of new behavior. Each step of each cycle (Victim vs. Empowerment) is not mandatory or sequential! You may not experience all of the steps. It is just a directional guideline for each dynamic set of behaviors.

THE VICTIM CYCLE

• **Denial**
  "I can't believe it!"
  "What just happened?"
  "I'm shocked and confused!"

The argument/fight happens and although it is over, you are still in DENIAL. You say things like, "I can't believe (s)he treats me like that!" By commenting on your partner's behavior, you are in denial about your own role in this cycle. This is a stage in which you may be mentally numb. It probably feels like you are stuck with a paper bag over your head and you can't figure it out because you keep focusing on the other person's behavior.

- **Disconnection**
  —isolation
  —quiet
  —feeling distant from each other

Then, you isolate. Perhaps you are not talking to each other. You're kind of numb, you aren't really thinking—just DISCONNECTED.

Neither of you is arguing. You are quiet. The quietness is not a stillness but a silence after the harsh words have been spoken. These words cannot be taken back—they are still hanging silently in the air between the two of you. There is a large canyon of silence between you. You feel very disconnected and alone in your marriage. This is a really uncomfortable feeling for all of us, especially for those of us who have underlying issues of abandonment.

- **Victim Role/Projection onto Partner**
  "You did this...."
  "You did that...."
  "You are such a jerk!"
  "You're a LOSER!"
  "You...You...You..."
  (finger-pointing)

You start playing the VICTIM and you blame your partner. You point the finger at him or her with accusations. You might tell your best friend; or, it might be that you say these accusations silently to yourself. At this point, you are still stuck in looking outside yourself for the reason or cause for the fight. From your perspective, it is ALL about the other person. They started it. They keep doing the same old thing that makes you angry. Whatever you choose to focus upon, you have concluded that it all begins with your partner (not you). At this moment, you might encounter your mate and you both continue your verbal tirade with more finger pointing (this is secondary to the original argument—Round 2).

- **Negative Thoughts**

  "This relationship won't work."

  "I can't do this anymore."

  "I'm so done in this relationship!"

  "I am so trapped...."

Time passes and you have more and more NEGATIVE THOUGHTS, such as: "I'm done with this relationship!"; "I am so trapped!" You stew in your juice (ruminate, brood, obsess, etc.). You probably focus on how different you are from each other. Whatever you think about, the result is negative. I call it going down the spiral staircase of negativity. You might go deeper into really negative scenarios from a while ago, and keep repeating to yourself "She is like this and I am like that...." or, "He keeps doing that and I am more like this." You compare, you keep mental score on past failures and mistakes, and you itemize what is not working in the relationship. You continue from one negative thought to another.

- **Overwhelming Negative Feelings**

  Anger/Rage

  Hurt/Devastation

  Sadness/Pain

  Guilt/Shame

  Fear/Anxiety

As a direct result of those negative thoughts, you begin to feel OVERWHELMED with negative feelings. You are hurt, you are sad, and you are angry. It's not possible to think negative and not feel negative as a result! Guess what? Now you feel terrible. You just finished stewing in negative thoughts for the past 2 hours and now you feel really down. You feel hopeless. You are really scared that this might be the end of the relationship. Or, you might have worked yourself into such a negative spiral of thoughts that now you are very angry and resentful. Your heart is hardened. You are in a dark mood. You are not in a space of forgiveness or openness to change. Rather, you feel completely overwhelmed like there is no hope for change. At this point, you feel the emotional equivalent of those words you kept saying to yourself over and over, "I am so trapped!" Now, you feel trapped. You feel like you are in a box and you are paralyzed by the hugeness of the negative emotion that surrounds you at this moment.

- **No Resolution/No Learning**
  —no commitment toward positive change
  —no ownership of my own behavior

As a result, there is NO LEARNING and you continue to be other-focused instead of self-focused. Because you do not own your part of the cyclical dance between you and your partner, you choose to look outside yourself for the answers. **You are still looking at your partner's behavior instead of your own.** This is another crucial step in the being stuck. In other words, by focusing on your mate's actions and words, you avoid looking at how you contributed to this dilemma.

No learning automatically results in a guaranteed repetition of the cycle. This is usually where most people get stuck in expecting their partner to do something to change first. They resent having to look inside themselves, so they conclude, "Well, I'll just wait for him to take the first step toward change." Believe me when I say that you are just as stuck as he is for multiple reasons. #1—He doesn't know that you expect him to change. #2—IF you have told him to do so and he chooses not to change, then you are still the one who is stuck waiting. #3—By refusing to act on your own behalf and on behalf of the partnership, then you also are just as accountable as your partner for not moving forward positively. Instead of waiting for him or her to do it first, ask yourself this, "What can I do differently right now that would be more positive than waiting for him or her to do something that (s)he doesn't even know that I'm waiting for?"

- **Awkwardness**
  —acting like nothing happened
  —ignoring each other
  —refusing to talk, avoidance

Then, there is a final AWKWARDNESS where you walk on egg-shells. There is no dialogue. There is no discussion. There is a lot of silence with one-word answers as you both move through your routines in the house. If you have children or other distractions, excuses for being busy could keep this stage prolonged indefinitely unless you make an appointment to talk about what is happening between you. You negatively anticipate tension, "What if it happens again?" This stage can last a few hours or even days (or even years for many couples). Then, finally some event happens and you prepare yourself for round two of the same ole,' same ole' fight the two of you keep having. NOTHING CHANGES.

- **Ready to Repeat the Cycle AGAIN!**
  So it goes, over and over and sometimes for decades!

THE EMPOWERMENT CYCLE OF BEHAVIOR

The second circle on the bottom of the page 294 depicts The Empowerment Cycle of Behavior. There are 10 separate segments or phases that each individual partner may experience in reaction to a negative event or argument or fight. **After a negative event (argument) you have a CHOICE to continue to be a victim or to choose a different path.** In this case, if you choose a different path other than the same old Victim Cycle, then you choose to be successful and make positive changes. Those cyclical phases can look like this:

- **Acknowledge What Happened/Be Accountable**
  (instead of silence)
  "I'm sorry we argued."
  "I'm sorry I yelled at you."

Own your behavior (you know what you did)
"I started the argument when I assumed..."

The argument/fight happened and although it is over, you decide to do something about it. You make a choice because not to do anything differently only means you will face the same pain again and again. The first thing you do is you ACKNOWLEDGE WHAT HAPPENED.

Identify what happened and acknowledge it first to yourself and then to your partner. Say something to your partner about what just happened. The last thing you want to do is act like nothing happened or ignore what just occurred.

This may not be 5 minutes after the argument; you might still be emotionally involved in your own stuff at that moment. However, as soon as you can get centered and calm yourself down, then approach your partner and say something sincere about your role in the argument or about your relationship together. Don't delay and wait hours or days to speak. Do NOT speak about your partner's behavior! For example: "I really blew it, I do not want to argue with you. Can we talk?"; "I need to talk to you about what just happened. Can we start over?"; "I am so sorry we argued, what can I do to help stop this cycle we are in?"

Then, you are ACCOUNTABLE for your own behavior—in other words, you own your stuff. You realize exactly what your role was in the argument. You know your behavior, you know your own cycle of thoughts, feelings, and behaviors. At first, this is an internal process where you say to yourself, "I did... to her/him." I call this "Owning Your Own Stuff." If you can own it first, then anything your partner says afterward has already been stated, acknowledged, and allows you to be less defensive. Also, after you own your own behavior and actions mentally (silently), you are in a state of readiness to say it out loud to your mate.

• TALK TO EACH OTHER
"I want to talk to you calmly. Is this a good time to talk? "
"I really want to hear what you have to say."

"I want to talk and call a time-out if needed, OK?"

As soon as you have calmed down and sorted through your thoughts, acknowledging and owning your role in the argument, when you talk to each other you have a HUGE opportunity to make it a different conversation. You share with your partner all of what you have been thinking; the next time there is an argument, it will either end quicker or be less intense. The effort you are making to do it differently today opens the door to a series of other opportunities such as asking for forgiveness, seeking outside help, and learning more about what you bring to the table in this partnership. Ultimately, the goal is to talk and open the lines of communication at all levels!

- **Forgiveness of Self and Your Partner**
  "I am so sorry I was angry." (say to partner)
  "Thank you for your apology." (say to partner)
  "I forgive myself for how I contributed to this argument and I forgive.... for his or her behavior." (say to Self silently)
  "I feel better that we talked. I want to move forward in this marriage." (say to partner)

You migrate toward FORGIVENESS of yourself and your partner. Through your realization of your participation in this argument, you decide to forgive yourself for all of the past arguments and your role in them. Then, you forgive your partner. You can say this silently to yourself. Even by coming to this realization silently, your entire being and presence will change and through your silent forgiveness of Self and partner, your partner will feel the change. It might not be a conscious thought on your partner's part, but he or she will subconsciously feel the difference in your vibe. This alone could be enough to open the doors to sincere communication. Next, this "change of heart" can allow you to state your forgiveness out loud.

Obviously, you don't walk up to your partner and say "I forgive you for what you did." What if your partner has not acknowledged to themselves their part of the dance? They will become defensive and throw that statement right back at you. However, by being open to forgiveness and the feeling of forgiveness when you talk to your spouse and your spouse says, "I'm sorry," then that is your opportunity to say, "I accept your apology and I am sorry too." This heartfelt exchange can be very healing as you both move forward in the relationship.

- **Check Yourself Out**
  "Is this becoming a pattern for me?"
  "It seems like we have the same old arguments."
  "Deep down, what's really bothering me?"

  Next, you identify how your behavior is a pattern in your arguments with your mate (and probably others also). Call it processing, evaluating, analyzing, or assessing. It does not matter. What matters is that you take the time introspectively to check yourself out silently. This is your chance to conduct what they call in 12-step programs "a moral inventory" to figure out what you have done repeatedly that has resulted in this negative cycle you are in with your partner. The focus needs to be ON YOUR ROLE.

- **Get Help from Outside Resources**
  (if you are unable to see how to change)
  You might decide to get professional help, if needed, to help you break this cycle. If the cycle you are in together has been going on for months or years, you are probably locked into a pattern that is very difficult to break. Otherwise, you would have done it by yourself, right? I do believe in the power of a couple to dig deep, work hard, get real, be honest, have good intentions, and to speak functionally (no put downs) and express their desire to move from their place of being stuck. Can you do it on your living room couch? Probably, but if you can't, don't rule out psychotherapy. Treat it like any other disorder. Ask trusted friends or call your insurance company and make calls to many therapists. Determine which one might work best based upon your needs. Then make the appointment as soon as possible. Do not wait! You have been waiting for years. Make the appointment and then go to the appointment. Go

to your couple's sessions at least 4 times to see if you can utilize the help of the therapist to get you unhooked from your cycle of pain. Find another therapist if you need to. Do not give up on your relationship. It took you years to get where you are now, so at least give it more than one session to see what it takes to get out of your current negative loop.

- **New Learnings**

  What have you learned from this situation? Now you are REDIS-COVERING YOU! You notice that by changing your thoughts, processing, analyzing, and concluding a different outcome, you see how your attitudes (thoughts and feelings) change; you become more open to the possibilities of change. This gives you hope in your heart for your own well-being and for that of your mate. As you start to uncover and discover who you are in this relationship, you can begin to identify what you need and want in this relationship. This is a good thing. Remember, this is about focusing totally on yourself first. By focusing on what you have learned and what can do differently—that automatically benefits the partnership in a positive way!

- **Positive Self-Talk**

  "I CAN do this."

  "I AM READY to be a better person and partner."

  You advance to having more POSITIVE SELF-TALK. Try to be your own best friend. Say something a good friend would say in being supportive and kind. "Every day, I love myself more and more. Starting today, I am taking positive steps toward taking care of myself and contributing more positively to my marriage. I am a good person and I deserve to be happy. Starting today, I will start taking healthy steps to take better care of myself. I am going to walk for 25 minutes every day and choose lower carbohydrates when I eat. I want to get my body in shape—this will make me happier and also make me more affectionate in our marriage." Or, "Right now, I am going to the doctor for a physical exam and to ask for help. I want to be less angry. I am focusing on my own anger-management."

- **Positive Feelings for Self and Partner**
Confidence
Hope
Compassion
Love

You start to have POSITIVE FEELINGS that give you more hope in this relationship. After you focus on your role in the marriage and what you need to change, then focus on what you need from your partner. Communicate this need to your partner. With supportive comments from your partner in return, you begin to see the possibilities of hope. Regardless of how your partner responds to your revelations of Self and commitment toward change, remember the focus is on you to do your part. This in turn can have a positive domino effect on the relationship.

- **NEW Behavior**
(Instead of doing it that old way, change
and try a different approach)

You are ready to identify a NEW BEHAVIOR to incorporate into your relationship. Maybe with your partner's help you both have identified one small behavior that helps you in a really powerful way. For example, you decide that when you start to get angry you tell her, "I am starting to get angry and I don't want to argue with you." Then, your partner agrees that when you say that, she calls a time-out and agrees to give you space without having to have the last word, or do something that escalates you into full-blown anger (like follow you into the back bedroom). This is a collaborative agreement for change.

- **Commitment to Change**
Tell your partner "I commit to STOP doing...."
"I commit to START doing more of...."

Once you have evaluated your own role then you are in a better position to make a COMMITMENT TO CHANGE. First, you can make this promise silently to yourself. After you have identified your own negative behavior that contributes to the arguments and unhappiness in the marriage, then you can decide what small but important behavior you are willing to change or stop. Afterward, you can verbally communicate what you think to your partner. By doing this, you ensure that what you think you need to change is what your partner needs you to change.

For example, "I commit to you to stop doing X." Then ask: "Is that what you need from me?" Your learning will expand. You will feel more empowered and confident both as an individual and as a partner. As a result, your relationship can take positive shifts away from the ingrained argument that ended in the same ole' way. You did it! You have chosen change vs. being stuck. Congratulations!

WHAT IS THE 72-HOUR RULE?

Basically, the 72-Hour Rule is a two-part concept. It consists of time, both literal time (an exact 72-hour time frame) and it consists of time as it is used in language when referring to the past.

When couples sit on my office couch, part of the Communication 101 tools that I give them is the "72-Hour Rule." I have them write down three words in large letters:

HERE AND NOW
The 72-Hour Time Frame:
I inform them that, from this moment forward, they are only allowed to talk about the upsetting behavior or situation if it had happened in the past 72 hours! So take a minute and think about what time it is right now and backtrack 72 hours from this point in time.

If you are reading this book together, you can discuss what day/time that would be for the both of you. If you have an issue that you are starting to stew on about something your spouse did in the past

72 hours, then this time limit forces you to discuss it within the 72-hour time frame, when you say, "Ya' know, I have to tell you that last Saturday night, when you did …, I was irritated and I'm still irritated." Otherwise, if you brood on the issue and don't talk about it, as you approach the 72-hour mark, you have to let it go. It is in the PAST!

Using the Past in Your Choice of Words:
One client remarked, "Well, what she just said right now, ticks me off right now but there she goes, she did it now and she did it 19,000 other times!" I said to him that it doesn't matter how many 19,000 times her behavior "reminds" him of what ticks him off, the important thing is for him to turn to her (on my office couch) and say, "I am really angry right now. It irritates me now that you said this or did this/that." Have you heard of the power of now? You got it! The power of now is in this very moment. When you can identify what you are feeling and thinking right now, then explain that to your mate.

When a male client turns to his wife and says, "I've told you this 100 times and I'll tell you again…" or, "If I've told you once, I've told you before, but you never listen…."

WRONG! Please stop this.

Please do not preface your statements with a condescending scolding statement that infers that she is stupid, or she "never" listens because you have to keep telling her (like she is 3 years old). This is parental and abusive. It sounds like lecturing; I am better and smarter than you, so listen up because I'm only going to tell you one more time.

STOP IT! You have to start listening to yourself as you speak. If you really want it to get better between you, then YOU have to do your part. So start by cleaning up your act and changing your tone, changing your choice of words, changing your parental style, and start by asking directly for what you need. Do you see how in the above example the person using a parental, admonishing tone is actually using tone and language from the PAST? If that person is you, pay attention! By restating, "I've told you this before…" you are referring to the past before you even deliver the information you are trying to express. At the very least it can be a BIG turn off! If you said that to me, I can tell you I would probably stop listening to you right on the spot, because I'm thinking, "Here we go again, another lecture." So in essence both the speaker (sender of the message) and the listener (receiver of the message) are both positioned to remain stuck in this cyclical argument. You probably know the words by heart. STOP! Perhaps if you can find a nicer way of asking or discussing, you might be shocked at how much easier it is for the two of you to communicate.

Start with:
"I think…"
"I feel…"
"I need…"
"I want…"
"My hope is…"
"My fear is…"
"I wonder…"

It is important that you **don't embed the "you" within the statement. Truly make it an "I" statement.** Do you know the difference? Do not think about your partner or keep reminding yourself about THEIR BEHAVIOR. Instead, come from a gentle place that focuses ONLY ON YOUR OWN EXPERIENCE of this partnership. The focus is on your own feelings, your own needs/wants, your own perspective—not what your partner says or does.

First Example: "What I really want is to be with you all day today. I just need to share some pleasant time with you, even if we run errands all day and go out to lunch. I just want to have a mellow day with you." In this example, I am expressing my wants and desires. I am directly stating what I need to my partner. I realize you might find it confusing because there are several "You's" in the example, but if you read it again, examine how the focus is on me, not you. "What I really need is…" I just want to have…" In this particular example, I am using "you" as the object of my intention.

Second Example: "I really need time to study for this exam and I was hoping that I could have that time alone. Then, after you run the errands with the kids, when you come back we could go out together later—just the two of us. What do you think? If you need me, I am all yours to run some errands, I just need about 3 solid hours to concentrate on this study material at some point this weekend."

Yes, I am negotiating, but I am clearly putting it out there as to what I need and want. Regardless of how my partner comes back at me, with his or her own needs and wants, I have clearly stated my intentions to date my partner and to help out with errands, if absolutely necessary. My thoughts about my partner running the errands with the kids kills two birds with one stone (the errands get run, the kids get out, and I get silence to study), then I promise adult time tonight when we date. I also promise that, "I'm all yours," except I need 3 hours sometime this weekend alone to study and concentrate. I'm doing my best here to get what I need and still give back collaboratively to my partner.

Bad examples:
"I feel like **you** want me to argue with **you**."
"I want **you** to start picking up the slack around this house."
"You are the one who makes me mad."
"I start out being in a good mood, but **you** make me mad."

Do you see the difference? Here I am blaming, pointing the finger at my partner. I judge (you are not doing your share around the house); I even use the old tried and true "YOU MAKE ME MAD," like it's your fault that I feel the way I feel!—THAT IS IRRATIONAL! We only feel what we feel because of how we choose to think, believe, and feel. This has a totally different vibe to it. Do you agree?

Forget the Past:

The answer lies in the moment. Forget the past and your conclusion as to what negative impression you have about how your partner keeps doing that same behavior. Make today a new and fresh day—free of agendas—just this conversation at this moment. Try it as an experiment. The goal is to focus right on what you are thinking and feeling now. When your partner starts talking to you (and you are both facing each other not doing something else with your back to each other), tell your partner what you heard, how you feel, and what you need, RIGHT NOW!

You have nothing to lose except perhaps a large and looming past that always comes between you every time you sit down and talk. What would it be like if you were kind to each other and talking became fun and easy? What if talking made you feel close to each other (the way it used to be)? You deserve to have a healthy, happy relationship. We all do. **You can only be responsible for your part. Are you doing your part?**

Usually, when couples come in to see me, I listen and pick up quite rapidly if they tend to use the past in their arguments. Either they use that premise in their sentence structure when they speak to each other, or I see it first hand when they start an argument. If they start out being extra polite to each other during the session, I inquire about their fighting style and ask them how the past is used in their arguments. One partner might say, "Oh, yeah, she's always bringing up something that happened 8 months ago." Or, the other partner might say, "Yes we do! And, we keep having the same argument over and over again about something that happened 6 years ago!"

When couples start mastering the 72-Hour Rule which is easy to do, you'd be amazed at how fast the relationship can move forward down the road of communication:

#1—**They've stopped blaming each other about the past** (months and years ago when such and such happened….).

#2—**They are able to trust the moment. They trust** that what they are talking about is real and in the present, rather than some old stored-up feeling or perception about the past that is being communicated now. Addressing the present moment feels doable, rather than dealing with a series of past events piled up on top of each other—that seems overwhelming!

#3—Staying grounded in the now eliminates surprises in the conversation by not seeing a new or "another" topic being thrown into the mix while things are getting heated. It contains the arena around the topic of discussion and can help simplify it.

#4—This often results in a powerful feeling of staying connected to what you are saying to each other, listening to each other, and moving step-by-step through the conversation. It creates a sense of balance and equality. It positively reinforces each partner to keep focused and abide by the rule of "no past."

#5—You can literally feel the shift of energy as you are able to complete the conversation! It does NOT mean you have to agree, you can absolutely disagree, but you remain focused, non-blaming, and connected throughout the entire process. Thus, you end the conversation with success (even without agreement)!

#6—This attained success makes each partner more willing to practice having more mini-conversations that can emerge into deeper issues that require trust from each other.

#7—After more success, the couple will come to therapy and say, "We have abided by the 72-Hour Rule and it works! But, what if we have some issues that have been around a long time and they extend beyond the 72-Hour Rule?" That is when I know they are ready to go back into the past and clean house, so-to-speak. They have the ground rules for paying attention in the moment to each other and to themselves as they engineer the conversation to more painful and "older" hot-button topics. What a huge and powerful journey for a couple to reach this moment of reckoning! In this case, whether they are in a therapist's office or they have come to the point that they want to do it on the living room couch, then they are probably ready to do it. They have mentally and emotionally prepared themselves to launch into the deeper issues.

My heart goes out to every couple who wants to make their marriage work. My heart also goes out to those couples who have tried and failed, or who waited and stopped trying, and to those who waited too long and in their hearts and minds feel there is nothing left to salvage; they choose to leave the partnership.

All I ask is that you use the tools. The tools within this book will either help you uncover and discover your buried deep love for each other and help re-ignite your love together. Or, the tools will give you what you need to discover that the relationship is over. Either way, it is a journey you need to take. First, for yourself and second, for your partner. Next, to those who angrily say: "What's the point? It's over…I'm out of here." I would respond with complete confidence, "Actually, you owe it yourself and your partner to end this marriage in civility and Functional Communication. This is your chance to express yourselves honestly and openly. Couch your pain and frustrations in love without blame since you both contributed to this situation. By "working through" the process of REALLY TALKING TO EACH OTHER right now, you will have grown and evolved. By practicing new skills of communication with your partner that you've chosen to leave, you are actually preparing yourself for your next relationship. **THIS IS ESSENTIAL SO THAT YOU DO NOT LEAVE THIS MARRIAGE AND GO REPEAT THE SAME MISTAKES WITH YOUR NEXT PARTNER!"**

DATE NIGHT

My favorite topic is date night. Oh my goodness, if I kept statistics of what percentage of my couple's DID NOT DATE AND HAD NOT DATED IN YEARS! Wow! It had to be at least 80-to-95 percent. If you have children and have not dated in a long time, I know I am spending your money for you, but you have to start interviewing for a babysitter, a live-in sitter, or switch off with another couple who has a child the same age as yours. You can rotate childcare so each couple can go out alone. Just because you have in-laws and family close by—it does not automatically mean they are the automatic choice for childcare—you have to start thinking outside the box. If you don't do anything differently 9 months after you have read this book you'll be saying to yourself, "Oh yeah, we never did go out on any dates, did we?" I have met many couples whose families were thousands of miles away. It is tough. But you have to start putting the word out, tell your fellow church members, join a mother's group or mother's circle—I don't know—just do it. I tell my couples who have not dated in years that I do not expect them to make a date and find a babysitter by the next session. However, I do expect something dramatic for a big night out within the next 2 months (8 weeks). So they have 8 weeks to begin the research and find some support. Once they do that, I expect them to find a second person as a back up in case the first sitter got busy or did not work out. How much more clear can I make it? **DATE NIGHT IS ESSENTIAL TO YOUR COUPLENESS!**

I have had some couples tell me that they do not know what to talk about.

So I say (even though this can be negative), read something in the newspaper or on the Internet. Read something political, related to the economy, or some human-interest article, and discuss it at dinner. Talk about something other than the children or each other's hurts. Go talk about anything and start dating each other again!

Depending on the age of your child, and if your child is somewhat older—4 years or more—or if you have no children—you just both work too hard and have not dated in a long time—then I have a different suggestion (please understand that I am NOT saying you must wait until you have a 4-year-old). If you can afford it, please have a night in a fancy hotel, bring your nicest clothes, go out to dinner in a place with a white tablecloth, and go dancing. Or just go to the hotel and get room service. Do something together that is romantic and fun and different. To be honest, the most success I have had with couples was after they started making time for themselves. When they started dating, lots of the negative energy started shifting rapidly.

If you resent the fact that your partner seems to be always going out somewhere with friends and you are at home with the kids, guess what happens when balance happens in your marriage? When your husband starts balancing his time between others and you, and you get time for yourself, then you start feeling a little better. You encourage him to have time for himself; he feels better and wants to spend more time with you. All of a sudden life is better! You don't have to resent his time away from you because you know you both have a big date set up for this Saturday night at a nice restaurant and you can't wait! You also know that on Saturday morning you are devoting time to yourself alone—just for you! Every relationship needs attention. We need to give ourselves attention, we need to give our partner attention, and we need to find the balance. It is magical, I am a witness to the fact that it really does work!

BOUNDARIES

What is a boundary? Well, it's almost like a line you draw in the sand. However, it is invisible. Yet, it is extremely important in defining "The Couple." You may have extended family over several generations, but "The Couple" is the most integral part of the nuclear family (the family you chose, by marrying and having children). It clearly indicates that your relationship as a couple (with or without children of your own) has a hierarchical position in the family unit. The couple is a unit. It is imperative for the couple unit to have an invisible but appropriate boundary around your partnership. WHAT DOES THIS MEAN? It means that it is NOT OK to gang up with your mother or siblings (your family of origin) against your spouse. You cannot take sides. NO! It means that it is NOT OK for your wife to align herself with your child against you. This is unhealthy.

Example: Your wife verbally puts you down in front of your child or behind your back. Or, you tell your child they cannot go somewhere, and when you are gone on a business trip, your wife lets your child do the exact opposite.

When communication breaks down in the couple, one spouse might call a friend or an in-law and pour their heart out to discuss how terrible their mate is for this or that reason. Excluding domestic violence/abuse, it is unhealthy to include some third-party into your domestic woes. It is natural to do so because it takes the pressure off of the stress between the couple. However, the whole idea is for the couple to work through the pressure and resolve it together (this can be done in a therapeutic setting). Imagine telling all of your relatives what a jerk your husband is and then you continue to stay in the marriage and at every family gathering he is embarrassed because they know all of your little dirty secrets. NO!

NO OUTSIDE INFLUENCES

Maintaining and nurturing a relationship is difficult enough these days without the unneeded "help" of negative comments or outside influence from family or friends.

Things you can do to enhance that healthy boundary around both of you:

- Compromise when holidays become tense and stress-inducing. Holidays can divide you rather than unite you; holiday events can create friction between you, your mate, and both of your families.

- Whether you have children or not, you should get away for a long weekend once a month—just the two of you.

- Be firm with your family and tell them your relationship is off-limits to their negative input!

- Don't allow your friends or family members to take sides in your relationship.

- Don't take sides with your family/friends against your spouse. Do not use your spouse as the brunt of a joke in front of your friends (it is a put down and the same thing as taking sides against your mate)!

- Don't listen to in-laws or friends who dictate advice that you or your mate "should" do such and such. When they do that, change the subject.

- Don't spend all your available time with your mate accompanied with family/friends. Allow some private moments for you and your mate ALONE!

INTIMACY

This is one basic technique that is very effective. Tell it like it is! Speak out loud what you see, what you feel, and what you hear. This is what is known as reflection back to your partner. Of course, I am saying this out of context. I tell my couples that when I am talking about intimacy, it is not sexual relations. Intimacy is **THOUGHTS, FEEL-INGS AND BEHAVIORS**. Do you know what intimacy might sound like between you and your partner?

Example: Both of you are in the bedroom on a Sunday night; it is 11:15 (work night). Your spouse is animated and fired up, wanting to talk about an issue before you both go to bed. You are exhausted and all you want to do is go to sleep. Practicing the skills you have learned in this book or in couple's therapy, you decide to reflect to your partner. So you say,

> *"I can see this is really important to you and I know you want to talk right now. And I want you to know that I do want to talk about this issue. And, I will talk to you right now if you want, but I need you to know that I'm really exhausted and my fear is that if we talk right now, it might derail into an argument. I don't want to argue with you sweetie. Let me ask you this, how about we talk on Saturday morning? I'll get my mom or Patty to watch the kids for a few hours and I'll make you hash browns and sausage and we'll sit at the kitchen table and talk this out. We'll both be refreshed after a good sleep. What do you think? But, just to let you know, if you really insist on talking right now, we can."*

Highlights: What did you basically say? You said that you didn't want to talk right now. However, you did not turn your back in silence and walk out of the room. You did not snap and say, "I don't want to talk right now!" Instead, you let your partner know that either way you would be there for him or her. You talked about being tired; you said you feared that it would lead to an argument; you said you'd even have someone watch the kids and promised to make an appointment to talk. Then, you said you would talk right now if that was not agreeable! Of course, this is said with good intentions and calmness (no sarcasm). This is my version of intimacy because you described your physical being (tired), your emotional being (fear of arguing) and your mental being (commitment to talk—either now or later). That's pretty cool. You did not make demands and you did not control the outcome. You gave your mate the choice.

I get a lot of questions about intimacy. I had one couple who had three children under the age of six. When I described intimacy, they looked at each other and then back at me a few times and then she said, "I don't think we have EVER been intimate in the way that you are describing—even back in college when we first met." Needless to say, they were smiling at the end of their first hour of intimacy. When couples got on a roll, I have them sit on the couch facing each other and talk. They pick their topic as long as they reflect back and forth; they "check in" with each other to maintain the accuracy of their perception. This results in couples going deeper very quickly to the core underlying issues of their partnership and to their deeper feelings. Even though my behavioral approach is formatted in a reflective back and forth, upon each successful reflection, it works. When they trust the process and themselves as they communicate more of their inner thoughts and feelings, they are reinforced.

The process:

"I heard you say this…, is that what you said?"

The spouse replies, "Yes, that's accurate. How do you feel about what I said?"

"It feels good to hear you say it and I have a positive feeling inside while I listen to you."

Each partner switches from speaker to listener and from listener back to speaker.

That is intimacy! This person is explaining and describing thoughts, feelings, and behavior. This person could be feeling really down and irritable but instead of snapping and pointing the finger, "You make me so mad and I'm tired of it—leave me alone," reflection and check-in alleviates the problem.

I once saw a recently engaged couple. They both came from a high-functioning family-of-origin. They each had loving parents who

were still married. They both had siblings who were highly accomplished professionals. Each partner benefited from a loving, supportive
extended family. Usually, therapists don't often get the privilege to
witness that kind of family. It was interesting to see how this young
couple really matched each other in values, family ideals, education,
and in love for each other. I remember she wanted me to give her a
guarantee that her fiancé (sitting right next to her) was the RIGHT
ONE to marry. I told her that there are no guarantees in life. Then in
the same breath, I contradicted my answer by telling her that I could
give her one tried and true guarantee that would last her the rest of
her life! They both looked at me as I began to tell them the answer to
her question.

"It's real simple," I explained. It's the kind of simple when the
doctor tells you to give up salt. That's easy—it's only one ingredient.
Then, you look at packages, boxes, and ingredients—EVERYTHING
HAS SALT IN IT! Wow! So, yes my answer was simple but sometimes simple requires attentiveness. You can't just blindly say you're
going to give up salt and just because you stopped using it at the dinner table—you've cut back on salt! No, it's not that easy!

So back to my beautiful young couple who were totally in love. I
told them both that thoughts, feelings and behaviors—are everything
in life. When you talk to each other you are explaining your thoughts
and your feelings and you are expressing those through your behaviors to your partner. Your partner who is listening and loves you very
much is responding to you, telling you what he thinks and feels; he
expresses those feelings to you in his behavior. That moment is a moment of intimacy—a moment of connection! This is the moment that
takes your relationship one step at a time to the next deeper level of
connection—to the heart level and then to the soul level. That is the
most perfect connection! As long as you talk and share and respect
each other and surround each other in love, you will be able to read
every expression and notice every nuance. In life, we all have thoughts,
conclusions, and beliefs constantly running through our minds while
we process what we smell, taste, hear, see, and feel (all the senses). This
bombardment of stimuli can certainly affect our impressions of Self
and others. Our mood can shift. The power of your connection to

each other is to "check in" with each other and maintain the line of open communication (just like a phone line).

Once the connection is lost, and there might be times where you become disconnected, then the challenge is to notice the disconnection and act on it ASAP. Don't wait months and years to say "I feel disconnected." Rather, after a few days or perhaps after 3 weeks, say, "Ya' know, I've been feeling really off lately and I sense a kind of disconnection from you the last few weeks. Are you OK? Are we OK?" This is the key to checking in and reconnecting with your partner. As long as you remain connected, you will be guaranteed to feel each other and know that you are joined at all levels. It's like eating healthy. Healthy eating tastes better and is better for you than unhealthy eating. You will know immediately if you veer off track and start down a negative unhealthy path. THAT IS YOUR GUARANTEE! Needless to say, the young couple married and they have been together and happy ever since. I meant what I said and I live by what I say—every day in my own life, in my own marriage.

SEXUAL INTIMACY

Sex is the most intimate form of communication between two people. It is symbolic of the love coupled with the physical needs and desires of each person. Just like every other category in this book where I have stressed the importance of communication, this section is no different. It is very important to communicate with your mate even when it comes to sex.

Questions:

1. Do you talk to your mate about sex? (you should)

2. Do you tell your mate what you like vs. dislike sexually, in other words, what turns you on? Where to touch you?

3. Are your sex roles always the same, does one person always pursue the other? (why not switch roles?)

4. Do you play with your mate sexually in a fun way (tickle, wrestle, massage)? (you should)

5. Do you mutually masturbate together?

6. Do you have sex the same way every time? If so, maybe you should try changing positions or settings.

7. Do you share your fantasies with your mate? (even though it might be embarrassing it could stimulate some interesting conversation and perhaps lead to other stimulating activities!)

8. Do you have adequate foreplay? If not, ask to slow it down and play ahead of time.

9. Do you both give and receive when you are sexually intimate?

10. If you are open to watching erotic films or using erotic toys, have you ever talked about it as a couple? Have you done it together?

In my master's degree program, I remember one of the core requirements was a sexual education class. I forget the actual title. Anyway, the professor told me (in front of the class), "Sex is an appetite just like anything else." The professor said, "Think of it like this. Your partner says, 'Honey, I'm going downstairs for cookies and milk, do you want some?'" The professor went on to say that either you have a yen or desire for cookies and milk, or not. You might say, "No thanks," simply because you do not feel like it. Sex is like that, he said. You must have an appetite for it. You and your partner must be on the same page at the same time, wanting the same thing. Timing is everything.

Is your partner still stressed out from different events of the day?

Did you just finish having an argument? Do you go to bed angry? If you do, you should try to resolve the issues before going to bed.

HEALTHY COMMUNICATION

In summary, healthy communication consists of the following:

1. Do you both understand the basics in communicating such as listening to each other and negotiating your differences? When one speaks, is the other always defensive? How can you stop that cycle?

2. Do you respect each other's opinions and contributions to the marriage? In other words, do you value your partner's viewpoint?

3. Is there a balance of power in your relationship? Or, does one of you dominate the other?

4. Is there financial parity between you?

5. Do you make your spouse a priority? Does your spouse make you a priority? How do you know?

6. Do you have emotional intimacy? Do you trust your partner enough to reveal your inner feelings and thoughts?

7. Do you have physical intimacy? If not, have you recently talked to each other about how it feels for each of you to not have sex?

A NON-VIOLENT RELATIONSHIP

Although the statistics are not promising for men who have been identified as domestic violent abusers, for the small percentage of men that do change, it is important to know what that behavior looks like. It is very different from the behavior previously mentioned in the Cycle of Violence. The following indicates positive and healthy attitudes and behaviors that men achieve when transitioning from violent to non-violent and healthy.

Just because someone stops drinking or using substances does not necessarily mean they are in recovery. They can be clean and sober with all of the same unhealthy outlooks and negative emotions that they had previously. They are just not using substances. There has been no core cleansing or complete healing from the issues that kick-started their drug and substance abuse. The same holds true for the man (or woman) who stops the violence but does not get therapy or does not attend a domestic violence abuser group or an anger-management group/therapy. Just because an individual does not hit you anymore does not eliminate negative angry blow-ups, attitudes, projections, or punishing emotional behavior. A lot has to change to make it truly a non-violent environment. As you see, "The Equality Wheel" depicts the changes needed to heal from within and in the marriage.

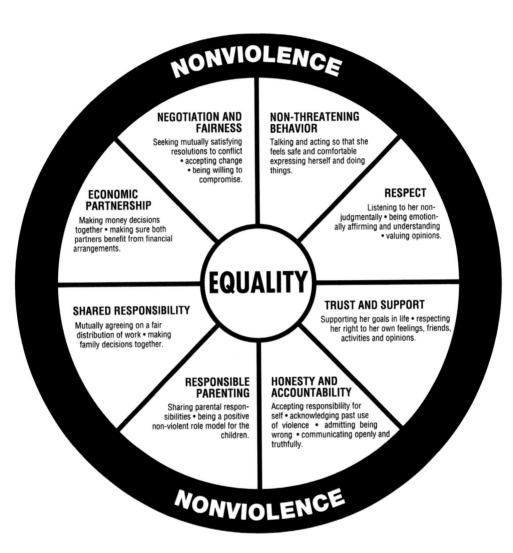

The Equality Wheel

THE EQUALITY WHEEL

By The Domestic Abuse Intervention Project, Duluth, MN

This Equality Wheel was developed by battered women who had been abused by their male partners. The Duluth women's shelter conducted educational groups that fostered the inception of both The Power and Control Wheel in addition to the Equality Wheel, created by the women participants attending the educational group.

The Equality Wheel is an important tool used in men's educational groups or domestic abuser classes. The Equality Wheel is a composite of the healthy behaviors men in Domestic Violence Recovery strive to demonstrate.

Non-Threatening Behavior

Using words and acting in a collaborative safe environment so that the female partner is comfortable and willing to express herself without threat or harm.

Respect

Honoring your partner's opinion. Giving value to her opinions. Being non-judgmental.

Trust and Support

Allowing her to have a social life, supporting her interests and activities, and encouraging her to set her own goals in life. Emotionally supporting her in her efforts to discover her own strengths.

Honesty and Accountability

The male abuser OWNS his behavior as abusive. He acknowledges, identifies and is accountable for his past behaviors. He openly admits being wrong. He engages in dialogue and honestly talks about accepting responsibility for his past actions, rather than a one-word response, "Yes."

Responsible Parenting

He provides a healthy role model for the children by being non-violent or non-abusive. He actively participates in the children's day-to-day needs without harm or negativity. He is a positive factor in the developmental growth of his children.

Shared Responsibility

Having a collaborative discussion means that both partners decide who does what, or who would like to do what, from the dishes, to the yard work, to paying the bills, to doing the laundry, to attending the children's activities, and so on.

Economic Partnership

Having a collaborative discussion means that both partners make money decisions and both partners share in the mutual benefit of those decisions.

Negotiation and Fairness

Having healthy conflict resolution skills means being able to make adjustments in life when stressors arise. Being fair and able to give-and-take in all negotiations for the best possible outcome. Compromising while stating individual needs and wants.

MAKING ADJUSTMENTS IN LIFE

There is a diagnosis called "Adjustment Disorder" (DSM-5). DSM-5 criteria state that an event (stressor) or stimuli occurs and within 3 months of the onset of the stressor you either demonstrate "marked distress that is out of proportion to the severity or intensity of the stressor" or "significant impairment in social or occupational (academic) functioning."

Making adjustments is the answer to what we all need to do every day of our lives. Right? Absolutely. Life is just making one adjustment after another—when you move in with your significant other, marry or partner with your soul-mate, or move from one location to another. It all adds up to making adjustments in response to a stressor or stimulus in life. As time passes, life can get more complicated with more added to the mix—school graduation, job changes, birth of a child, death of a parent, purchase of a first home, promotions, and lay offs. Shall I go on? If I could bottle the formula to help every one make adjustments needed for a smooth life—I promise you I would give it to you and to everyone else for free! I think it is your right to be able to have the formula that guarantees smooth sailing in life. Well, it was a nice thought.

Aging

Aging is something we don't think about until we see the gray hair on our own heads, the wrinkled eyes staring back in the mirror, or have a parent who is old and frail die. Aging is another phase of life and, most certainly, a phase in your life as a couple.

I have seen older couples go through early struggles financially, sacrifice for their children's education, gain prosperity in their prime, become loving grandparents, only to suffer within their own marriage at a time when everyone else thinks they have it made. As a therapist, it always makes me wonder if their foundation had faltered years ago and now the cracks cannot withstand the stressor of aging and mortality. Or, could it be that their foundation was strong and aging placed undue pressure upon the marriage? Aging, as we know, covers a multitude of opportunities for more stress in the marriage (physical health, extended family members, personal looks, retirement, finances, mental health, etc.). It does not simply come down to a one-word category of "aging." Rather, it is an intra-connected unfolding, long-term change that takes place within each partner at the same time! This results in an inter-connected unfolding long-term change that is taking place in the marriage or partnership at the same time! WHAT? Yes, think of it. You are changing in multiple areas of your life; simultaneously, your partner is changing across multiple areas within his or her life; the marriage or partnership is also evolving simultaneously!

That is a lot to take on. As therapists, we automatically assess whether or not the client has multiple stressors. Well, aging fits the bill doesn't it? This is a fascinating topic that could be an entire book.

What tools can I offer you regarding this specific topic? I encourage you to utilize what we have been talking about since Page 1. Take care of yourself first. Choose both small and big ways to take care of yourself and what you need. This does NOT mean that you go out and do something impulsive and foolish just because you have always wanted to do it, without regard for your partner. Rather, it means take a day out for yourself—perhaps a weekend without your partner or a 6-week class that interests you and benefits you! This will re-energize YOU! Your emotional and mental capacity to be a better partner to your aging mate will be reinvigorated. You can bring all of that vibrancy to your marriage! Then, perhaps you can do something together as a couple—an outing for the day (beach, lunch, wine-tasting, etc.) or a long weekend or vacation. Either way, it is about infusing your relationship with renewed energy. No matter how many years you have been together—you still have to work on it.

Basically, the formula we have been talking about is the same regardless of which life stressor is hitting you now. You must pay attention to yourself first and your thoughts and your feelings. By doing something for yourself, in turn, you automatically become a more attentive and giving partner; your own needs have been satisfied; you feel fulfilled. You are more joyous and want to share that joy with your beautiful partner!

Health Problems (Physical)

Specifically, I am talking about your own physical illness or that of your partner. This is a clear stressor, whether it is a short-term physical crisis that takes place before a normal recovery or a long-term chronic condition that changes your lives forever. Such stressors reach out to other aspects of survival such as job security, financial status (income, assets, career options, medical bills, etc.), permanent/short-term disability, self-esteem, dependency issues (ability to care for self), social isolation, and so on. At a minimum, the health condition has an impact on both of you across the board—mentally, emotionally, physically, financially, and spiritually. If they are short-term or long-term physical issues, all members of the family ramp up to face the challenges.

This intense rising to the occasion reaches a peak whether it is just you and your partner or you and younger children, or you and your parents and adult siblings. Then, there is a falling off of activity as life continues and other family members return to their day-to-day routines. At the end of the day, it is you and your partner who must cope. This can be the biggest challenge of all.

After the dust settles and reality sets in (even if it was a crisis that after rehab returns to normalcy), it can be a real wake-up call. How well did your partner compassionately and lovingly provide support for you in your time of need? How well were you at accepting that support? How did it feel for the primary caregiver to be put in that position? Are you usually the one on the receiving end? How did it feel for you to see your strong mate be so dependent upon you? What are your thoughts? What did you conclude about it? Is the crisis over? Have you talked about your thoughts and feelings to each other privately? What if your partner is permanently incapacitated? How do you take care of your partner and yourself? Who do you turn to in your time of need? Do you have someone who is objectively there for you? Should you go to your pastor/minister; counselor/therapist; or neighbor/friend? Sometimes it helps to be able to talk to an outsider in order to help sort through your thoughts and feelings.

Hormonal Imbalance in Both Men and Women

Symptoms of hormonal imbalance can include the following:

- Hot flashes or night sweats; fatigue; weight gain; loss of sexual desire;
- Insomnia or sleep disruption; anxiety; depression; irritability;
- Increased dryness in mouth, eyes & genitalia; joint pain; heart palpitations; urinary dysfunction; hair loss; irregular periods; fibroids.

Hormones affect every aspect of quality of life including mood, cognitions, bodily functions, sleep, sex, appetite, and so on. It is imperative that you educate yourself about the impact a hormonal imbalance can have on your overall sense of well-being. In my private practice, I see many young and older females who were either misdiagnosed or not treated. It is horrific to watch hair fall out or relationships crumble; they wonder why they do not feel like themselves. They describe feeling "off" and are shamed by the physical symptoms they experience. Please do not take this lightly. Hormonal imbalances can be very insidious, go unnoticed, or assumed to be "mystery" problems. If you go to an endocrinologist you might be surprised to find the answers for which you have been searching.

Although every organ system secretes and responds to hormones (including the brain, lungs, heart, intestine, skin, and the kidney), the clinical specialty of endocrinology focuses primarily on the *endocrine organs*, meaning the organs whose primary function is hormone secretion. These organs include the pituitary, thyroid, adrenals, ovaries, testes, and pancreas. An *endocrinologist* is a doctor who specializes in treating disorders of the endocrine system, such as diabetes, hyperthyroidism, and many others (see list of diseases next). There are many endocrine glands in the body with the main ones being the pituitary gland, thyroid, thymus, adrenal glands, and the pancreas. Both men and women produce hormones in the same areas with one exception, the sexual organs. Additional male hormones are produced in the testes while women's are produced in the ovaries. (Retrieved from Wikipedia on August 4, 2014).

Facing Death Together

Over the years, I have seen many couples with one partner still in his or her prime and the other suffering from a debilitating illness. Therapy focuses on helping the couple face the death of one partner together. You don't need a therapist who sugar coats the realities of the situation ("Everything will be alright," etc.). It always challenges me to honor both the dying partner who is facing their final weeks/months of life as well as the spouse's emotional and mental reaction to losing a partner. I have to be real, otherwise, it will not work. Couples come to therapy for real feedback. This stage of grief is called "anticipatory grief." This couple is advancing through the stages of grief pre-death.

Everyone reacts to grief differently. I don't believe in right or wrong. I try to focus on healthy rather than unhealthy. I counseled one couple who absolutely cherished EVERY SINGLE MOMENT TOGETHER! They came to therapy so that I could do hypnosis to help with the husband's negative reaction to chemotherapy. You could feel the love in the room. What a beautiful couple. Their love just grew stronger as they faced his death together. They went on a couple of short international trips before his rapid physical decline.

I counseled another younger couple after his cancer came back after years of remission. Each partner demonstrated very different behaviors in their efforts to cope with his cancer diagnosis. He wanted to travel and reach out to alternative and holistic programs to help with his illness. His partner was overly focused on herself. She reacted angrily; he didn't help do the dishes; he was traveling the world. Of course, all relationships are a two-way street. Perhaps one might say that he was taking advantage of the situation. HOWEVER, let me remind you that the situation that he was supposedly taking advantage of was his own death! He had few months left to live. His female partner nagged, complained, and whined about what he was not doing for her. Granted, I am not an analytical therapist; some might say that she was experiencing anticipatory grief (grief stages prior to the actual loss or death). But one could say that she was experiencing another kind of loss because her husband's personality had changed; he was carefree and loose as he flew around the world without her. On the other hand, he clearly expressed that he loved her dearly and he wanted her to be with him in his final days—but without the nagging. In the end, he was steadfast in his choice to take care of himself and went in search of his own answers.

This very decision to spend his final months of life separated from his partner was a direct statement to her and to the world. This was his time and he was using it the way he wanted to use it. As a therapist, I can't help but think that if she had nagged a little less and had opened up more to his perspective, she could see and hear that, while she complained, he was verbally trying to comfort her. However, she remained stuck in her panic; he refused to be victimized by her enduring selfishness (as he saw it). Perhaps, there could have been more commonality in their partnership in those final days. She kept screaming that she was facing reality by doing the dishes! He kept repeating that he was the one facing reality—his own death! After some time, she was able to be more compassionate to him (slightly) and the nagging stopped. However, he was determined to experience any alternative therapies he could find in New Zealand, Oregon or elsewhere. I could go on and analyze this with you. However, you get the idea. Physical illnesses are demanding and can be a deal breaker in your marriage—literally.

Having a Baby

The entire dynamic changes once there are three of you. This stage of life is dramatic and all-encompassing. Feelings, biochemical reactions and physical changes, thinking, behaviors, logistics and space, finances, extended family expectations, cultural expectations, educational expectations, religious/spiritual expectations, goals/purpose in life, parenting styles/beliefs and couple balance are all affected. It can be the most exciting of times and the most challenging of times. Your life as you know it will never be the same. Your entire worldview changes. Of course, you need to talk about it before you do it! Even before you have a surprise birth, dialogue should focus on the "What if…?" and "How will you…?" If you do that then really there are NO surprises! Or, the fact that you both have contemplated possible future outcomes will help you to be more grounded and prepared for the unexpected together.

Behavioral Health

Although you have previously read this topic in more detail in prior chapters, I summarize by stating that mental well-being is no less challenging than physical illness. Mental illness diagnoses can be missed completely and professionals can misdiagnose symptoms. At the very least, one partner might suspect something problematic but be in denial. Either way, both partners suffer without the aid of community or mental health resources.

A woman from the east coast called me about a year ago. She had seen me several years earlier with her boyfriend. She had my business card and called the number.

Luckily, I remembered her after some prompting. The conversation lasted 15 minutes. Evidently, she was distressed because she was sitting in her father-in-law's house; her spouse was in bed and had been there for more than 10 days; he refused to eat. Her husband was very weak and kept saying that he wanted to die. She called me to ask what to do! Once I gathered a few details— and determined that there was a major crisis happening—I asked to speak to her father-in-law. He said that his son refused to have them call 911 or get an ambulance to take him to the hospital! I raised my voice but firmly stated that it did not matter what his son wanted or did not want. I explained that his son was a clear danger to himself. I clearly stated that his son was more than likely clinically depressed and not thinking clearly as a result of the depression and nutritional deficits. I asked the father if he was prepared to have his son die in the bed because he did not want to hurt his feelings or go against the wishes of his very ill son? They called 911. I'll never forget that. Here I was in California and a previous client from 8 years ago called me from the east coast for help.

Why do I share these stories with you? To point out that denial can be very subtle or very blatant depending on how you want to look at it. Do you realize that denial had immobilized them as a family unit into accepting the debilitating illness of the young man in bed as normal? They wanted to respect his wishes, including him laying in bed until he migrated into unconsciousness. I get that people can become frozen in fear or choose to not decide rather than face the possibility that things are out of balance. Please remember that mental illness is exactly that—an illness. It can be properly diagnosed, treated medically (pharmaceutically) and psychotherapeutically (counseling). Books, magazines, and the Internet have very good information. There are clinics, hospitals, doctors, therapists in private practice, and group therapy programs—even 911. Please face it. Acknowledge it. Work through it. Do not deny it. Do something rather than nothing.

Joblessness

Although joblessness has decreased statistically to 6.3 percent as of June 6, 2014, many families and single heads of households are still suffering. No matter how you justify the data and economic theory (depression, recession, inflation, etc.), joblessness can be a major disruption to the dynamic of families. Joblessness affects multiple aspects of life, ranging from role disruption (no longer breadwinner for the family), to decreased standard of living (financial stressors), to psychological (mental and emotional) impact upon each individual family member. The outcome can be lowered self-esteem, depression, anxiety, stress, irritability, guilt, and shame.

According to The Huffington Post,

> *"Four out of 5 U.S. adults struggle with joblessness, near-poverty or reliance on welfare for at least parts of their lives, a sign of deteriorating economic security and an elusive American dream."*

So, regardless of how you define joblessness (underemployment, loss of employment, unemployed with benefits, unemployed without benefits, people working three part-time jobs), unemployment can be a huge stressor.

The impact that joblessness has on the individual, the couple and the family is far-reaching. Not only does the income stream dry up, but the individual who has worked successfully for decades as the primary or secondary earner finds himself in limbo without an identity. This major disruption (loss of job) can derail the individual's career path toward higher income potential and have a negative impact on self-esteem.

I am certain that there are numerous examples in your neighborhood, in your family, or for you, which describes kids being forced to reconsider college plans, or smaller children being forced out of private lessons for music, art or athletic camps. This is a revolution of our societal values and living standards, not to mention our national economy! We more than likely face years of what I call "Fortune Reversal." This can have an impact on family units and couples with a relentless demand upon value shifting. If the money is not there—then the money is not there. How do you cope? Have you figured out how you feel as an individual about your dilemma? Have you spoken to your partner about your perceptions and feelings? What do you tell your 9-year-old daughter about the extracurricular ballet program—that your salary has always paid for—about leaving her friends and the activity she loves the most? What if you are blessed to have a large savings account but it gets depleted monthly? How do you move forward as an individual and as a couple when facing these huge challenges? Joblessness is not just a word. It is a reality tied to strong financial and emotional ramifications. This is just one more example of another stressor that we face in our modern-day society. You know you are not alone, yet, it does not remove the pain or make the pain any less.

As a couple, this situation challenges you both to talk, be real, and to take the high road in being really supportive of each other during this time of crisis. This can be a time one partner is catapulted to the primary wage earner role. For even the strongest of couples, it can be a time of adjustment to acknowledge how different this feels or how insecure and afraid you feel. Perhaps, it is a period of time in your marriage that inspires more confidence in both of you because of the adjustments. It is vital that you be best friends and non-blaming during this time of strife. Pull together and become a team. Strengthen your resolve and your love for each other. Don't give up! Take one day at a time with a long-term strategy. Take care of yourselves mentally by being kind to yourselves instead of cycling downward into a negative spiral. I should add this one important comment. If you find that you are spiraling downward emotionally, it is natural. It is OK. It means you are probably depressed. Please reach out to a medical professional (psychotherapist, medical doctor) and get help to support yourself during this difficult time. Remember, by taking care of yourself in this matter you are ultimately taking care of your marriage and family too! Do it. Taking prescribed antidepressants or seeing a counselor can be effective tools in helping you feel better.

THE 72-HOUR RULE COMPLETED

As stated earlier, when couples master the "72-Hour Rule," the natural next step for them is to express a readiness to bring up the OLD and unresolved issues (spoken or unspoken from the past). They choose the topic and I watch and listen (only intervening if needed). Sometimes, the couple continues a discussion they had in the car on the way over to therapy (they started therapy without me!). Or, they talk about the following: a refinance they did on a house they owned prior to their current home, buried resentment about past finances, abandonment issues, dependency issues, how disconnected they feel, lack of sex, sexual imbalances, or unhappiness in the past 2-to-3 years. This list goes on. Once couples learn the technique of staying in the present while talking about the past, then they can talk about anything with a successful outcome. Staying grounded in the present means being able to talk about a past hurt or unresolved problem but describe what you think and feel right now. What are you feeling right now (*disappointed*)? Where do you feel that disappointment (*in my heart*)? How do you feel right now, while listening to your partner's perception of what happened in the past? "I feel good, I finally understand his experience during that time in our marriage. Now I feel closer to him." And so it continues. Remember success is not agreement!

Successful Outcome Using the 72-Hour Rule
Success is:

#1—Staying in the now.

#2—Expressing your own needs/wants clearly without blame.

#3—Paying attention and monitoring Self as to your own thoughts and feelings during the information exchange.

#4—Communicating those thoughts and feelings directly and non-threateningly to your partner.

#5—If you feel tense, agree to take a break (20 minutes), and agree to come back to finish the conversation. Just stay in this moment. Do not let your thoughts stray. Think of the NOW as an anchor to the moment.

#6—Communicating acknowledgment, not necessarily agreement.

#7—Finishing the discussion successfully (without misinterpreting, making false assumptions, speaking with raised voices, and having full-blown arguments/fights that cycle to nowhere except more pain).

#8—Thanking each other for a successful conversation without upset. Talk about how it feels right now to be successful in finishing a potentially huge topic without argument! What an achievement! Congratulations! YOU DID IT! YOU BOTH DID IT!

My hope for you is that you will start this process and stick with it. For sure it will feel awkward at first; you are outside your comfort zone. The more you do it the more it will become part of your comfort zone. Over time, you will do it automatically and it will work! Then this mastery you have in communication will spread positively to all areas of your life. Finally, your healthy communication style will have a positive impact on the lives of other people and so it goes—on and on.

THE BASICS—JUST LIKE IN THE NFL

The basics, that's what we are talking about! The basics. Think of the sporting analogy. The best NFL teams are the teams that are talented, disciplined and well coached. Why? It means they go out there on the field with passion for their game, executing plays to win and they do so with few or little penalties. No interceptions, good blocking, no fumbles, no holding, and so on. They play hard and they play well. They are grounded in the basics and they have perfected their role on the team as they cohesively work as one unit. In football, one person cannot play all of the positions to make the play. They have to rhythmically support each other to accomplish their goal of moving the football down the field to score a touchdown! In your relationship it is the same thing! The basics is a foundation of good communication skills (being executed on the field), with lots of passion, good teamwork (give and take), good support between the two of you and no penalties (this means covering the basics of talking, caring, "checking in," demonstrating love (not just thinking about it) and moving down the field of life together (time shared). You share lots of goals together. You work well together. Individually, you are the only one who can run down to make the play (one football player can not lift and carry his teammate while running for the winning touchdown). Rather, you have to do your part and your partner has to do his or her part. You have responsibilities in this relationship! **I remember seeing a famous NFL coach on the sidelines; he screamed at the players on the bench, "Go out there and do your job!" That's right, each of you have to do your job!** What I am trying to point out is that the job isn't really a job. At this point, it might seem like a big job. However, the more you get the basics down, the easier it will become for you. After a while, you'll remember the little things automatically and it will no longer take effort. I'm simply asking you to do it. I'm asking you to make it happen. You deserve to feel that closeness you haven't felt in a long time.

LEAVE YOUR BAG OF BURDENS IN THE PAST

Let the past go, leave it behind you. Choose to take what you have learned from the past and move forward into the future. If you keep judgments and resentments frozen in your heart, they will weigh you down, no matter where you go, or who your partner is; you will be frozen inside. Leave the past behind, focus on today, this morning, this moment and allow yourself to thaw from the pain, the anger, and the fear in your heart. Just let it go. Say out loud to yourself, "I am letting the past go now!" Aren't you tired of carrying your burden of resentments with you (think of it as a huge sack of potatoes)? Isn't it time to stop carrying your **bag of burdens** every place you go with whomever you meet? Find the courage to take your first step forward into the future without the past clinging to you. Take that first step for you! In that first step, you have broken through the frozen barrier that has blocked your heart from feeling and healing. You can heal yourself by letting it go. Can you feel the numbness leave you as you take your second step for both you and your partner? Now, you are free. Keep walking, taking one step, then another step. In doing so, you will find new ways to love yourself and find so many more ways to **love** your spouse, lover, partner, soul-mate, and best friend. Life is awaiting you. Love is ready to heal you. Reach out to life and love. Reach out to loving yourself and your partner. Say "Yes" to loving yourself and all of the rest will flow to you with ease. I wish you well.

References

Abraham, J. (2008). Divorce mediation—limiting the profession to family/matrimonial lawyers. *Conflict Resolution,* 10(1), 241-268. Retrieved on June 29, 2014, from: http://cojcr.org/vol10no1/241-268.pdf

Balsam, K.F., Beauchaine, T.P., Rothblum, E.D., & Solomon, S.E. (2008). Three year follow-up of same-sex couples who had civil unions in Vermont, same-sex couples not in civil unions, and heterosexual married couples. *Developmental Psychology,* 44(1), 102-116. Retrieved on June 29, 2014, from APA online journals.

Bancroft, L. (2002). *Why does he do that? Inside the minds of angry and controlling men.* NY: A Berkley Book.

Basile, K.C. (2002). Prevalence of wife rape and other intimate partner sexual coercion in a nationally representative sample of women. *Violence and Victims* 17(511). Retrieved online June 29, 2014, from: http://www.americanbar.org/groups/domestic_violence/resources/statistics.html

Beck, A., Emery, G., with Greenberg, R.L. (1985). *Anxiety disorders and phobias: A cognitive perspective.* NY: Basic Books.

Bell, L.G., Bell, D.C. & Nakata, Y. (2001). Triangulation and adolescent development in the U.S. and Japan. *Family Process,* 40 (2), 173-186. Retrieved from: http://online library.wiley.com

Bookwala, J. (2005). The role of marital quality in physical health during the mature years. *Journal of Aging and Health*, 17, 85–104.

Bridges, W. (2004). *Transitions*. Cambridge: DaCapo Press.

Catalano, Shannan. Intimate Partner Violence. (1993–2010). Bureau of Justice Statistics website, revised November 27, 2012; NCJ239203.

Catalino, S.; Smith, E.; Snyder, H.; Rand, M. (2009). Female Victims of Violence: Selected Findings, NCJ228356, Bureau of Justice Statistics. Retrieved on August 4, 2014, from: http://www.bjs.gov/content/pub/ascii/fvv.txt.

Chemaly, Soraya. (2012, November 30). "50 facts about domestic violence." Huffington Post Blog. Retrieved on June 29, 2014, from: http://www.huffingtonpost.com/soraya-chemaly/50-actual-facts-about-dom_b_2193904.html

Diagnostic and statistical manual of mental disorders (5th ed.). (2013). Arlington, VA: American Psychiatric Association.

Ehrensaft, M.K., Cohen, P., Brown, J., Smailes, E., Chen, H., & Johnson, J.G. (2003). Intergenerational transmission of partner violence: A 20-year prospective study. *Journal of Consulting and Clinical Psychology*, 71(4), 741–573. Retrieved on June 1, 2014, from: http://www.ncbi.nim.nih.gov/pubmed 12924679

Ellis, A. (1997). *A guide to rational living* (3rd ed.). CA: Melvin Powers.

Engle, E.K. (2008). The body-image behavioral inventory-3: Development and validation of the body-image compulsive actions and body-image avoidance scales. (Dissertation Completed May 2008). *Body Image and Dissertation Abstracts Summaries*. The Virginia Consortium Program in Clinical Psychology. Virginia Beach, VA. Retrieved on June 29, 2014, from: www.bodyimagedissertationandabstracts

Erectile dysfunction: Overview. (1995–2014). Retrieved June 1, 2014, from: The Cleveland Clinic Foundation database. http://my.clevelandclinic.org/disorders/Erectile_Disorder_impotence/hic_Erectile_Dysfunction_Overview.aspx

Erectile dysfunction: Overview. (2008, August 14). Retrieved June 8, 2014, from: *US News World Report: Health* database. http://health.usnews.com/health-conditions/sexual-health/erectile-dysfunction/overview

Erectile dysfunction: Symptoms. (Mayo Clinic staff; 1998-2010). Retrieved June 29, 2014, from Mayo Foundation for Medical Education and Research. http://www.mayoclinic.com/health/erectile-dysfunction/DS00162/DSECTION=symptoms

Evans, P. (1996). *The verbally abusive relationship: How to recognize it and how to respond.* (2nd ed.). MA: Adams Media Corporation.

Friel, J.C., & Friel, L.D. (1990). *An adult child's guide as to what is 'normal.'* FL: Health Communications, Inc.

Gawain, S. (1998). *Living in the light.* Novato: New World Library.

Goldstein, I. (1998, May 12). The truth about impotence. Retrieved on June 29, 2014, from: Public Broadcast System online transcript. http://www.pbs.org/wgbh/nova/impotence/causes/

Grant, I., Atkinson, J.H., Mattison, A., & Coates, T.J. (2010). Report to the legislature and governor of the state of California presenting findings pursuant to SB847 which created the CMCR and provided state funding. The Center for Medicinal Cannabis Research. University of California San Diego, Health Sciences Web site. Retrieved on June 29, 2014, from: www.cmcr.ucsd.edu

Hemphill, S.A., Smith, R., Toumbourou, J.W., Herrenkohl, T.I., Catalano, R.F., McMorris, B.J., & Romaniuk, H. (2009). Modifiable determinants of youth violence in Australia and the United States: A longitudinal study. *Australian and New Zealand Journal of Criminology*, 42(3), 289-309. Retrieved from Australian Academic Press on June 29, 2014, from: http://www.atypon-link.com/AAP/doi/abs/10.1375/acri.42.3.289

Hess, J.A., Fannin, A.D., & Pollom, L.H. (2007). Creating closeness: Discerning and measuring strategies for fostering closer relationships. *Personal Relationships*, 14: 25-44. Retrieved on June 29, 2014, from Wiley Online Library from: http://onlinelibrary.wileycom/doi/10.1111/j.1475-6811.2006.00140.x/full

Hill, E.W. (2010). Discovering forgiveness through empathy: Implications for couple and family therapy. *Journal of Family Therapy*, 32: 169-185. Retrieved on June 29, 2014, from Wiley Online Library from: http://onlinelibrary.wiley.com/doi/10.1111/j.1467-6427.2010.00492.x/abstract http://www.apa.org/pubs/journals/releases/dev-441102.pdf

Kielpikowski, M.M., & Pryor, J.E. (2008). Silent parental conflict: Parent's perspective. *Journal of Family Studies: Innovative Approaches to Family Violence*, 14(2-3), 217-227. Retrieved from Journal of Family Studies database on June 29, 2014, from: http://www.atypon-link.com/EMP/doi/abs/10.5172/jfs.327.14.2-3.217

Levinger, G. (1966). Sources of marital dissatisfaction among applicants for divorce. *American Journal of Orthopsychiatry*, 36: 803–807. Retrieved on June 29, 2014, from the Wiley Online Library from: http://onlinelibrary.wiley.com/doi/10.1111/j.1939-0025.1966.tb02407.xabstract

Lewis, L. (unpublished). Forgiveness formula. (2005). Quantum Source Healing.

Maloney, L. (2008). Editorial family violence: What's in a name? *Journal of Family Studies* (14), 157-159. Retrieved on June 29, 2014, from: http://www.eContentmanagementptyltd.journalofamilystudies

McIntosh, J.E. (2003). Children living with domestic violence: Research foundations for early intervention. *Journal of Family Studies* (9)2, 219-234. Retrieved on June 29, 2014, from: http://jfs.e-contentmanagement.com/archives/vol/9/issue/2/article/84/children-living-with-domestic-violence

McLoyd, V.C. (1998). Socioeconomic disadvantage and child development. *American Psychologist* 53(2), 185-204. Retrieved on June 29, 2014, from: http://psycnet.apa.org

Northrup, C. (1995). *Women's Bodies, Women's Wisdom.* NY: Bantam Books.

Padesky, C., & Greenberger, D. (1995*). Mind over mood.* NY: The Guilford Press.

Rampage, C. (1994). Power, gender, and marital intimacy. *Journal of Family Therapy*, 16, 125-137. Retrieved on June 29, 2014, from Wiley Online Library from: http://onlinelibrary.wiley.com/doi/10.1111/j.1467-6427.1994.00783.x/pdf

Rennison, C.M. (2003). Intimate partner violence, 1993-2001. U.S. Department of Justice, NCJ 197838, Bureau of Justice Statistics Crime Data Brief. (1) Retrieved on June 1, 2014, from: The American Bar Association database. http://www.ojp.usdoj.gov/bjs/pub/pdf/ipv01.pdf http://new.abanet.org/domesticviolence/Pages/Statistics.aspx

Roberts, L.J. (2000), Fire and ice in marital communication: Hostile and distancing behaviors as predictors of marital distress. *Journal of Marriage and Family*, 62: 693-707. Retrieved on June 1, 2014, from Wiley Online Library from: http://onlinelibrary.wiley.com/doi/10.1111/j.1741-3737.20000.00693.x/abstract

Rolsman, G.I., Balsam, K.F., & Rothblum, E.D. (2008, January). New research finds equal level of commitment and relationship among same-sex and heterosexual couples. APA Press release retrieved on June 1, 2014, from: http://www.apa.org/news/press/releases/2008/01/satisfaction.aspx

Seth, H. (2014, January 1). Infidelity statistics. Associated Press, *Journal of Marital and Family Therapy*. Retrieved on June 29, 2014, from: http://www.statisticbrain.com/infidelity-statistics

Sheinfeld, R. (2006*). Busting loose from the money game.* Hoboken: John Wiley & Sons, Inc.

Statistics. (2010, reviewed). U.S. Department of Health and Human Services. Retrieved from National Institute of Mental Health Web site on June 29, 2014, from: http://www.nimh.nih.gov/statistics/index.shtml

Sternberg, R.J. (1988). *The triangle of love: Intimacy, passion, commitment.* NY: Basic Books.

Straussner, S.L.A. (1994). The impact of alcohol and other drug abuse on the American family. *Drug and Alcohol Review*, 13: 393-399. Retrieved from Wiley Online Library on June 29, 2014, from: http://onlinelibrary.wileycom/doi/10.1080/095952394001185521 abstract

"The Duluth Model, Wheel Gallery." Retrieved on December 3, 2010, from: http://www.theduluthmodel.org/wheelgallery.php

Tjaden, P. & Thoennes, N. (2000). Extent, Nature, and Consequences of Intimate Partner Violence, at U.S. Department of Justice. NCJ 181867 National Institute of Justice: Research, Development, Education. Retrieved on June 29, 2014, from: http://www.ojp.usdoj.gov/nij/pubs-sum/181867.htm Retrieved June 1, 2014, from: http://new.abanet.org/domesticviolence/Pages/Statistics.aspx

Tjaden, P. & Thoennes, N. (2000). Full Report of the Prevalence, Incidence, and Consequences of Intimate Partner Violence Against Women at U.S. Department of Justice, NCJ 183781. Findings from: The National Violence Against Women Survey. Retrieved on June 29, 2014, from: http://www.ojp.usdoj.gov/nij/pubs-sum/183781.htm http://new.abanet.org/domesticviolence/Pages/Statistics.aspx

Twenty-two legal medical marijuana states and DC: Laws, fees, and possession limits. (2014, June 3). Retrieved on June 8, 2014, from: ProCon.org from: http://medicalmarijuana.procon.org/view.resource.php?

U.S. adds 217,000 jobs in May, unemployment rate remains at 6.3%. (2014, June 6). Retrieved on June 29, 2014, from: http://www.huffingtonpost.com/2014/06/06/may-jobs-report-unemployment-rate_n_5454893.htmlresourceID=000881

Van der Kolk, B.A. (1989). The compulsion to repeat the trauma re-enactment, revictimization, and masochism. *Psychiatric Clinics of*

North America, 12(2), 389-411. Retrieved on June 29, 2014, from: The Circumcision Reference Library: http://www.cirp.org/library/psych/vanderkolk/

What are the symptoms of bipolar disorder? (2012). U.S. Department of Health and Human Services, NIH Publication: No. 12-3679. Retrieved from: National Institute of Mental Health Web site on June 1, 2014. From: http://www.nimh.nig.gov/health/publications/bipolar-disorder

Whisman, M.A., Uebelacker, L.A. ,& Weinstock, L.M. (2004). Psychopathology and marital satisfaction: Importance of evaluating both partners. *Journal of Consulting and Clinical Psychology*, 72(5), 830-838. Retrieved on June 29, 2014, from: APA Online Published Journals, from: http://www.apa.org/pubs/journals/releases/ccp-725830.pdf

Yen, H. (2013, June 28). 80 percent of U.S. adults face near-poverty, unemployment: Survey. Retrieved on June 29, 2014, from: http://www.huffingtonpost.com/2013/07/28/poverty-unemployment-rates_n_3666594.html

Yodanis, C. & Lauer, S. (2007). Managing money in marriage: Multilevel and cross-national effects of the breadwinner role. *Journal of Marriage and Family*, 69(5), 1307-1325. Retrieved on June 29, 2014, from Wiley Online Library from: http://onlinelibrary.wiley.com/doi/10.1111/j.1741-3737.2007.00449.x/abstract

Image Credits